T0271134

Late Neoclassical Economics

Several contemporary economic theories revolve around different concepts: market failures, institutions, transaction costs, information asymmetries, motivational diversity, cognitive limitations, strategic behaviors, and evolutionary stability. In recent years, many economists have argued that the increase in circulation and mobilization of these new and heterogeneous concepts and their associated methodologies (e.g., experiments, evolutionary modeling, simulations) signify the death of neoclassical economics.

Late Neoclassical Economics: the restoration of theoretical humanism in contemporary economic theory draws on the work of Louis Althusser, Michel Foucault, and the Amherst School, and reconstructs the concept of a self-transparent and self-conscious human subject (Homo economicus) as the theoretical humanist core of the neoclassical tradition. Instead of identifying the emergent heterogeneity as a break from neoclassicism, this book offers a careful genealogy of many of the new concepts and approaches—including evolutionary game theory, experimental economics, and behavioral economics—and reads their elaboration as part of the restoration of the theoretical humanist core of the tradition in response to its drift towards structuralism.

This book is suitable for those who study political economy, history of economic thought, and philosophy of economics. The arguments put forward in this text will also resonate with anyone who is interested in the fate of the neoclassical tradition and the future of economic theory.

Yahya M. Madra teaches Economics at Boğaziçi University, Istanbul, Turkey. He has published and co-authored articles on various issues in political economy in both edited book volumes and journals.

New Political Economy
Richard McIntyre, General Editor

Late Neoclassical Economics

The restoration of theoretical humanism in contemporary economic theory

Yahya M. Madra

Routledge
Taylor & Francis Group

LONDON AND NEW YORK

First published 2017
by Routledge
2 Park Square, Milton Park, Abingdon, Oxon OX14 4RN

and by Routledge
711 Third Avenue, New York, NY 10017

Routledge is an imprint of the Taylor & Francis Group, an informa business

British Library Cataloguing in Publication Data
A catalogue record for this book is available from the British Library

Library of Congress Cataloging in Publication Data
Names: Madra, Yahya M., author.
Title: Late neoclassical economics: the restoration of theoretical humanism
in contemporary economic theory/Yahya M. Madra.
Description: Abingdon, Oxon; New York, NY: Routledge, 2016.
Identifiers: LCCN 2016002712
Subjects: LCSH: Neoclassical school of economics.
Classification: LCC HB98.2.M33 2016 | DDC 330.15/7--dc23
LC record available at http://lccn.loc.gov/2016002712

ISBN: 978-0-415-73850-7 (hbk)
ISBN: 978-1-315-81725-5 (ebk)

Typeset in Times New Roman
by Deanta Global Publishing Services, Chennai, India

In memory of Stephen A. Resnick, 1938–2013

Contents

Illustrations

.

Figure

Tables

Acknowledgments

This volume you are holding in your hand (or reading on your screen) is a specimen of that difficult genre, a dissertation turned into a book. I apologize in advance for the shortcomings of the format.

The dissertation that this book is based on has benefited immensely from the comments and criticisms of my committee, Richard D. Wolff, the late Stephen A. Resnick, Donald Katzner, and the late Julie Graham. Rick and Don kept me in touch with the truth of the Marxian and the Walrasian traditions, respectively. Without the support of Julie Graham, I would not have survived graduate school. Steve Resnick was also instrumental, together with his successor as the editor of the series, Richard McIntyre, in encouraging me to turn the original document into a book manuscript.

My two mentors, Fikret Adaman and Jack Amariglio, made it possible for me to bring together my interests in the recent developments in modern microeconomic theory and in critical and post-structuralist thinking, respectively. Fikret also did the crucial final read of the book manuscript and made several key suggestions. I tried to incorporate them to the best of my ability. Jack, on the other hand, together with Christina Hatgis, provided the warmth I needed to finalize my dissertation during the winter of 2007.

My dear friends and colleagues Ceren Özselçuk, Kenan Erçel, Phil Kozel, Erik Olsen, Stephen Healy, Maliha Safri, and Joseph Rebello provided the intellectual support and the benefit of close reading and engaged commentary at the different stages of this document. (If you are looking for juicier comments, see the acknowledgments section of the dissertation.) The very early versions of the ideas that ended up in this book were formed during the early 2000s at 1 Graves Ave., Northampton, MA, when I was living with Erik, Stephen, and Rose Heyer, and were fleshed out while I was traveling back and forth between Noho and Saratoga Springs, NY, from 2003 to 2006. During that period, Mehmet Odekon and Mary Crone Odekon provided many of the crucial conditions of existence of the graduate student/adjunct faculty hybrid that I was. I finished the first draft of the dissertation in the loving presence of Ryvka Barnard, in the communal home that we formed together in, of all places, Saratoga Springs, during the academic year of 2005–2006.

Later on, in Istanbul, the molding of the document into a book format benefited from the comments and discussions of the participants of our semi-regular annual methodology group in Istanbul: Fikret, Ayşe Mumcu, Emrah Aydınonat, Serhat Koloğlugil, and Ozan İşler. I presented versions and parts of the manuscript in faculty seminars at Gettysburg College, Boğaziçi University, and Middle East Technical University, as well as at the international conferences of the Association of Economics and Social Analysis, the International Confederation of the Associations for Pluralism in Economics, and the European Society of History of Economic Thought. I benefited immensely from the various reactions and comments I received in those platforms.

My family, my sweet grandmother Kamuran Kefeli, my dear mother Beral Madra, my humorous father Teoman Madra, and my lovely sister Tulya Madra, have always been very supportive and patient with my academic journey. I cannot thank them enough for their support.

And, if it hadn't been for my beautiful and courageous wife Lara Fresko's encouragement and support, and crucial help with the index, I could never have completed this book.

Needless to say, the usual caveat applies.

Part I

Introduction

1 Introduction

Making sense of an emergent heterogeneity

Today, the mainstream of contemporary economic theory is comprised of an arguably heterogeneous set of approaches that include, among others, new institutional economics, new information economics, social choice theory, behavioral economics, evolutionary game theory, and experimental economics.[1] Moreover, this heterogeneity cuts across different fields of inquiry, from public sector to environment, and from development to industrial organization.[2] A number of commentators have interpreted this proliferation of diverse theoretical approaches and their associated concepts as a sign of the "death of neoclassical economics" (Colander 2000) and found a clear break (i.e., rupture, paradigm shift) between neoclassical economics (as practiced up to the 1970s) and the number of contemporary mainstream approaches listed above. This monograph, while recognizing and accounting for the very reality of an emergent heterogeneity, will argue that these diverse approaches actually constitute a unified discursive formation articulated around a theoretical problematic that they share not only with one another but also with neoclassical economics. For this reason, in order to underscore the philosophico-theoretical as well as the historico-genealogical continuity between neoclassical economics (up to the 1970s) and the contemporary mainstream economic approaches listed above, the latter will collectively be referred to as *late neoclassical economics.*[3]

These predominant narratives of *break from the neoclassical tradition* and *the plurality of approaches in contemporary mainstream economics* need to be problematized, as they tend to occlude the existence of other, non-mainstream and self-consciously heterodox perspectives that carefully distinguish themselves from the neoclassical tradition. Within this other field, also characterized by a significant degree of heterogeneity with respect to ontology, methodology, and epistemology, one can mention the Marxian tradition, with its own internal diversity ranging from classical determinist to postmodern non-determinist versions (Resnick and Wolff 2013); the "old" institutionalism, which carefully distinguishes its holistic and sociologistic perspective from the individualist and economistic perspective of new institutionalism (Rutherford 1994); the post-Keynesian tradition, built upon the concept of fundamental uncertainty in close alliance with the Sraffian mark-up pricing firm-level analyses (Davidson 1991; Lee 1998); the Austrian School, with its trademark characterization of competition as a rivalrous knowledge discovery process among purposeful individuals (Caldwell 2004); and the feminist economics perspective that questions the male-centric view of the economy found not only in mainstream neoclassicism but also in many heterodox approaches (Ferber and Nelson 1993). The list can be extended, but the point must be clear. The emergent heterogeneity in the mainstream of economic theory that is correctly identified by some commentators is only the tip of an iceberg. The field of economics is much wider, and the delimited nature of the heterogeneity that characterizes the late neoclassical condition in mainstream economics must be acknowledged. Otherwise, we would risk accepting uncritically the recurrent presentations of the emergent heterogeneity as a genuine alternative to the neo-classical tradition and occluding the enduring presence of a truly diverse and rich range of other (heterodox) approaches to economics.

The aim of this book is to make sense of the extent as well as the limits of this emergent heterogeneity of approaches within the contemporary mainstream. By identifying their shared theoretical problematic, both the continuity with the neoclassical tradition and the common thread that cuts across the range of approaches will hopefully become discernible for the reader. In this manner, not only will the truncatedness of the late neoclassical diversity be highlighted, but also the historical and theoretical sources of this diversity will be analyzed through conceptual genealogies. The book problematizes the emergent heteroge-neity in contemporary mainstream economic theory along two axes: the axis of continuity/discontinuity with the neoclassical tradition, by theorizing the late neo-classical condition as a variety of responses to the perceived crisis of Walrasian general equilibrium theory, *and* the axis of sameness/difference, by theorizing the diversity as an outcome of the overdetermined variety of responses to a common theoretical problematic. Put differently, we have an underlying *continuity* that appears to be discontinuous because the late neoclassical condition is a *response* to the perceived crisis of post-war neoclassicism; and we also have an underlying *unity* that silently structures an apparent *dispersion* and *diversity* because each late neoclassical approach is a different take on a shared theoretical problematic.

*   *   *

What, then, is this shared theoretical problematic? There are two presuppositions of the neoclassical problematic that, when taken together, distinguish the tradi-tion (and its derivatives and correlates) from other, non-mainstream or heterodox traditions in economics. On the one hand, all neoclassical approaches aim to specify the conditions of existence of a harmonious and contradiction-free socio-economic order. Neoclassical economists call such socio-economic states *states of equilibrium*. On the other hand, in positing a teleological vision of a harmo-nious economic order, each approach, explicitly or implicitly, refers back to a notion of the human subject as an autonomous, self-transparent, and rational self-consciousness, who knows (who is conscious of) or can eventually know (can come to the consciousness of) what her true needs (preferences) are and what is good for her (i.e., what improves her welfare), who can translate these true and essentially transparent preferences into her choices, and who recognizes herself as (and is recognized by others as) an intentional and autonomous subject who is responsible for her choices (as is presupposed, for instance, in the contract law). Certainly, the neoclassical tradition is not the only school of economic thought that systematically deploys the equilibrium construct or refers back to an intentional, autonomous, and rational conception of the human subject. For instance, modern structuralist macroeconomic or Sraffian approaches, while making use of an equilibrium construct in setting up their relational models of the economy, do not refer back to any notion of a self-transparent human subject as described above; and the proponents of the Austrian School, while subscribing to a strictly individualist methodology, vehemently reject static notions of equilibrium.[4] What defines the neoclassical tradition is the unique conjoining of these two presuppositions: the pre-destined vision of a harmonious socio-economic order is one that should be chosen by, and hence that would best accommodate the needs of, self-transparent, unified, rational, autonomous, and self-conscious human subjects.[5]

In short, the constitutive theoretical problematic of the neoclassical tradition is to address the various facets of the following question: what are the conditions of existence of a harmonious and contradiction-free socio-economic order (ranging from an efficient and stable state of equilibrium to a vision of social order that would facilitate economic growth) that would best accommodate the needs of human subjects as they are postulated in theory (according to the standard neoclassical axioms of rationality)? Or, to put it as *economically* as possible, the neoclassical tradition is structured around the theoretical problematic of reconciling the individual and the aggregate (collective, social, market) rationality.[6]

These concerns of harmonious reconciliation belong to *theoretical humanism*, a decidedly post-Enlightenment philosophical orientation that establishes a vision of social harmony premised upon a notion of a human subject who is self-conscious, self-transparent, rational, and autonomous. Theoretical humanism, as a philosophical orientation, cuts across numerous schools of thought within the discipline of economics, including even, for instance, some skeins of Marxian economics (e.g., Analytical Marxism) as well as other disciplines of social theory.[7] In fact, the ideological grip of theoretical humanism on social theory in general and the discipline of economics in particular has been so strong that, despite the fact that it has been challenged on numerous occasions and from various angles, it continues to remain as the dominant philosophical orientation that informs not only late neoclassicism but also many of its alternatives (an ontologically, methodologically, and epistemologically diverse set usually gathered together under the term *heterodox economic approaches*).

In reconstructing the history of theoretical humanism in the field of economics, we are confronted with a persistent challenge from theoretical structuralism as a rival philosophical orientation that repeatedly destabilizes and displaces the solidity of the theoretical humanist presuppositions of the neoclassical tradition. These challenges of structuralism, however, did not materialize in the form of attacks on the tradition that were issued from outside, from the heterodox detractors of neoclassicism. Such attacks are rarely effective, and on most occasions they tend to cause further consolidation of the research program around its constitutive presuppositions. Much more destabilizing and dislocating are the structuralist challenges that emerge through theoretical developments that occur endogenously, among the practitioners of the discipline itself. "Structuralist moments" might be a better term to describe such challenges, as they emerge either due to a certain cross-disciplinary exchange of methods, metaphors, or models, or as a result of a *bricolage* activity on the part of innovative and resourceful economic theorists to address a theoretical challenge or controversy. For instance, consider the intro-duction of mathematical formalism, which came, along with a strong structuralist accent, to post-war (Walrasian) general equilibrium theory—the core model of the neoclassical tradition in the period. Or consider the less acknowledged case of the Chicago-style selectionism: certain inter-war controversies in and chal-lenges to neoclassical marginalism compelled a number of neoclassical econo-mists (mainly holding positions in the Economics Department of the University of Chicago) to borrow metaphors from evolutionary theory and conceptualize com-petitive market dynamics as a selection process—whereby the structuralism of the market rationality supplanted the humanism of individual rationality. Such drifts towards structuralism are rarely self-conscious, and mostly reflect a certain lack of interest in dealing systematically and thoroughly with concerns of philosophy of science and questions of methodological consistency. Precisely for this reason, the evolution of the tradition can be read as a dialectic of oscillation between the emergence of structuralist moments and their subsequent containment through theoretical humanist restoration.

Indeed, the late neoclassical heterogeneity of contemporary mainstream eco-nomics can be best understood as a series of responses to the structuralist drift of neoclassical general equilibrium theory and its perceived damaging implications for the theoretical humanist project of the neoclassical tradition. Alternatively, the late neoclassical condition can be best characterized as a patchwork of attempts at restoring, rehabilitating, and reconstituting the theoretical humanist *presupposi-tions* of neoclassical economics.[8] Yet, it is important to emphasize that these are all *attempts*, as late neoclassical economics itself is not immune to its own new and unexpected structuralist moments.

In the late neoclassical context, neither the essentialist notions of the human subject that involve self-transparency, autonomy, rationality, and intentional agency nor the ontologies of concordance, harmony, order, and equilibrium are thoroughly scrutinized. On the contrary, the late neoclassical context is character-ized by a concerted and multi-pronged effort to extend the scope of application of these notions and ontologies, either by way of broadening and enriching their meanings or by way of introducing newer concepts that formulate the problem in slightly different ways (e.g., static versus dynamic, general versus partial, price adjustment versus market adjustment, cooperative versus non-cooperative) that would not necessarily address, but would essentially sidestep, the prob-lems that troubled the earlier formulations. In fact, in this sense, contemporary mainstream economics is nothing but the shape that neoclassical economics has taken as a mature and developed theoretical tradition. For this reason, in oppo-sition to those who identify in the apparent heterogeneity of the contemporary economic approaches a break with the neoclassical tradition, this book, tracking the development of economic discourses, insists that *no* clear break separating the contemporary mainstream approaches from the earlier neoclassical approaches can be discerned.

This introductory chapter will address two matters. First, it will motivate the project and situate it in the context of contemporary methodological debates on the "pluralism" of mainstream economics and the difference between the disciplinary mainstream and heterodoxy. Second, it will provide a brief sketch of the transition from post-WWII neoclassicism to the contemporary late neoclassical condition. A detailed philosophical discussion of this historical trajectory of the neoclassical tradition is the subject matter of the subsequent chapters.

1.1 Is neoclassical economics dead?

An important fault line traverses the discipline of economics, dividing the field into two internally heterogeneous yet discernible sectors: mainstream and heterodox.[9] Heterodox economists are defined by their criticisms of mainstream economic theories and policies and their desire to develop alternative frameworks. Yet, in return, these heterodox dissenters are themselves usually criticized for misrepresenting the mainstream as a unified and monolithic discourse (Garnett 2005: 2). In the lexicon of the heterodox literature that "succumbs" to this tendency, the term "mainstream economics" refers to those approaches that explain all economic (and social) phenomena as states of equilibrium that should be systematically "microfounded" in the rational choices and actions of utility-maximizing individual economic agents (i.e., *homo economicus*). Moreover, these heterodox critics tend to argue that the mainstream economics amounts to nothing more than an elaborate apologetics (usually with the theological connotations of the word intended) for the existing state of affairs (i.e., the global hegemony of the neoliberal ideology and the multinational capitalism).[10]

It should come as no surprise, then, that those who find contemporary mainstream approaches to be substantially different from post-war neoclassicism are the most vocal critics of such heterodox representations that see no essential difference between neoclassical economics circa 1950 and the mainstream economics at the turn of the twenty-first century.[11] According to these critics of "heterodox reductionism," the representation of contemporary mainstream economics as a cohesive and unified discourse and the claim that it is not much different from post-war neoclassical economics paper over important differences among the aforementioned new mainstream approaches and thereby prevent the heterodox economists from recognizing and acknowledging the "emerging pluralism" in contemporary mainstream economic thinking.

Indeed, a new narrative regarding the emergence of a mainstream pluralism is swiftly gaining currency in economics among the proponents of contemporary mainstream approaches as well as those who write on the contemporary state of mainstream economics. According to this narrative, by the 1970s, with the full development of the Walras–Arrow–Debreu general equilibrium model, the results of Sonnenschein–Mantel–Debreu, and the politically charged controversies surrounding the auctioneer fiction at the center of the general equilibrium model, the neoclassical project of formalizing the invisible hand theorem had fallen into a crisis (Davis 2003: 82). In the aftermath of "the death of neoclassical economics" (Colander 2000), mainstream economic thinking began to move away "from a strict adherence to the holy trinity—rationality, selfishness, and equilibrium—to a more *eclectic* position of purposeful behavior, enlightened self-interest and sustainability" (Colander et al. 2004: 485; emphasis added), and in fact, it is claimed, the mid-century Walrasian neoclassicism was an unnecessary detour that delayed the development of "analytical models of *incomplete contracts* and *broader models of human behavior*" (Bowles and Gintis 2000: 1429; emphasis added)— namely, the development of the hallmark themes of what this book designates as late neoclassical economics.

It is important to note, however, that those who find "pluralism" in the contemporary mainstream do not only see a *clear break* between contemporary mainstream and post-war neoclassicism, but also argue that it is inappropriate to brand the contemporary mainstream as the new "orthodoxy" (as the "other" of heterodox economics). For, it is argued, there are a number of approaches within the contemporary mainstream that are quite different from and critical of the standard neoclassical model (Colander et al. 2004: 490–3). Nevertheless, curiously enough, none of the self-identified heterodox economic approaches are cited among those that constitute this "pluralist turn" in economics. For instance, David Colander (2000), when defining "New Millennium Economics," mentions only three approaches: evolutionary game theory, experimental economics, and complexity theory. In an expanded version, John B. Davis (2006) lists game theory, experimental economics, behavioral economics, evolutionary economics, and complexity theory (see also Colander et al. 2004: 496). Samuel Bowles and Herbert Gintis (2000) identify Ronald Coase, Friedrich von Hayek, Duncan Luce and Howard Riaffa, and Herbert Simon as the predecessors of contemporary "multidisciplinary" economics, which emerged as the "younger generation of economists" realized that "the Walrasian economic model should be taken with a grain of salt" (2000: 1431).[12] Going through a quick checklist of which schools of thought are included and which are excluded in these lists renders it clear that we are not dealing with a comprehensive "pluralism" here (for a similar critique, see Davis, 2006; 2008). In fact, we can speak of two different understandings of pluralism: mainstream and heterodox. While the "new" mainstream understanding of pluralism recognizes only the emergent pluralism in the mainstream, the heterodox notion recognizes the heterogeneity that characterizes both the mainstream and the heterodox sides of the fault line that traverses the discipline of economics. As a neologism, late neoclassical economics is coined to designate precisely the emergent pluralism that characterizes the "new" mainstream.

*   *   *

This book recasts the terms of this debate between those who find sameness across the past and the present of mainstream economics and those who find difference between the past and the present and within the present of mainstream economics. In contrast, the book finds *both* sameness *and* difference, *both* unity *and* diversity within both neoclassical and late neoclassical economics. Without doubt, a lot has changed in the neoclassical tradition since the 1950s. Nevertheless, these changes do not add up to a paradigm shift in, or a radical break from, the tradition. Both post-war neoclassicism and the "new" mainstream (i.e., late neoclassical economics) are structured around the same theoretical humanist problematic. They may formulate the theoretical problematic in different ways, using different concepts, and they may even derive different inferences and policy conclusions, but they are still structured around the problem of how to reconcile the individual rationality with that of the collective.

Let me try to unpack the three aspects of the position from which this book is written. First, the neoclassical tradition has always been internally differentiated: diversity, debate, and difference are not new to the tradition. It is, perhaps, now well known that the genealogy of the neoclassical tradition can be traced back to at least two (if not three) sources: the Lausanne School of Léon Walras and Vilfredo Pareto, and the British utilitarian skein of Stanley Jevons and Alfred Marshall (Ingrao and Israel 1990).[13] Perhaps more recently established is the division of the tradition into two main camps in the post-WWII North American context. This post-war division roughly maps onto the two sources of neoclassicism: the rationalist mathematical structuralism of the Walrasian general equilibrium approach at the Cowles Commission versus the empiricist pragmatism of the Marshallian applied microeconomics of the Chicago School (Novshek and Sonnenschein 1987; Hands and Mirowski 1998; Mirowski and Hands 1998; Mirowski 2002; De Vroey 2003).[14] Moreover, these tendencies diverge not only with respect to their methodological commitments (the abstract, axiomatic models and "equilibrium proofmaking" versus the industry-level applied econometric studies) and ontological orientations (general equilibrium analysis with individual agents versus partial equilibrium analysis with representative agents) but also with respect to their policy orientation. On the latter aspect, contrast the pro-government (and in some cases, "market socialist") general equilibrium analysts at the Cowles Commission,[15] who likened themselves to social engineers with the presumed responsibility to demonstrate and remedy the deficiencies of the price mechanism (Ingrao and Israel 1990: 245–88; Mirowski 2002: 232–308), with the decidedly pro-market economists at the Economics Department of the University of Chicago,[16] who were eager to highlight government failures by conducting cost–benefit analyses of public regulatory policies that tend to conclude that regulation does not benefit consumers (Breit and Spencer 1995: 109).[17]

It is, however, very important to underscore that this conflictual coexistence of divergent tendencies within neoclassical economics did not necessarily undermine the tradition. On the contrary, to the extent that neoclassical economics established itself as a "public sphere" inhabited by a multiplicity of methodologies, ontological orientations, and political agendas—to the extent that neoclassical economics became synonymous with economics—the tradition reinforced its disciplinary hegemony.

Which brings us to the second point regarding the importance of the perceived "shortcomings" of the Arrow–Debreu (A-D) model. For those who believe that the Sonnenschein–Debreu–Mantel results regarding the arbitrariness of aggregate excess demands or the controversy around the meaning of "the auctioneer" caused a paradigm crisis in neoclassical economics, it is necessary to remind them that the tradition always, even at the very moment of its inception, struggled with numerous controversies. Neoclassical economists have repeatedly found themselves responding to a number of potentially damaging criticisms and struggling with (and, more often than not, failing to resolve) equally serious theoretical as well as empirical controversies pertaining to the theoretical humanist presuppositions of the tradition: the controversy around the "psychologism" of the assumption of utility maximization (Lewin 1996); the marginalist controversy pertaining to the decision-making criteria of the real-world firms (Lavoie 1990; Vromen 1995); the controversy around the theory of revealed preferences (Wong 1978); the Cambridge capital controversy (Harcourt 1972; Cullenberg and Dasgupta 2001); the controversies around the empirical verification of the neoclassical theories of demand (Mirowski and Hands 1998); and the socialist calculation controversy and Hayek's critique of the epistemological presuppositions of Walrasian neoclassicism (Caldwell 1988; Burczak 1994). And, this is only a partial list. Given this long list of controversies pertaining to foundational issues, it would be an exaggeration to single out the impact of the post-war developments.[18] It is indeed true that late neoclassical economists do situate their theories and models in relation and as a response to the controversies surrounding the post-war general equilibrium theory. Nonetheless, it would be a categorical mistake to deduce "the death of neoclassical economics" from the loss of the disciplinary hegemony of general equilibrium theory, if only because the general equilibrium theory has always been only one skein of neoclassical economics. At best, one can speak of the death of Walrasian general equilibrium theory, but even that would be incorrect, given the vibrancy of the tradition in a research program such as computable general equilibrium modeling. Moreover, it would be epistemologically essentialist to claim that the general equilibrium theory has lost its disciplinary predominance due to its "shortcomings," if only because no universal criteria exist by which the scientific community can judge the success or failure of a particular theory.[19]

And finally, the third point. The approaches that constitute the contemporary mainstream are articulated around the theoretical problematic of neoclassical humanism (i.e., the problem of the reconciliation of the individual and the collective rationality). In this sense, despite its claimed eclecticism, pluralism, and multidisciplinarity, late neoclassical economics continues to operate within the neoclassical problematic. To put it differently, late neoclassical economics is the shape of neoclassical economics at the turn of the twenty-first century, when the tradition had splintered into multiple sub-approaches and branched out into applied fields, and as the themes explored and the research methodologies deployed became diversified. In fact, the heterogeneous state of the tradition goes to show that neoclassical economics was never united around an object of analysis (e.g., the markets), or a core model (e.g., the A-D model), or even a research methodology (e.g., a particular style of mathematical modeling), but rather, around a theoretical problematic.

Therefore, steering away from both the temptation to disavow the presence of "difference" within the neoclassical tradition *and* the temptation to narrate the history of mainstream economics as a progressive movement from "neoclassical dominance to mainstream pluralism," the book offers a novel conceptualization of the transition from the neoclassical to the late neoclassical configuration of mainstream economics: one that simultaneously acknowledges the presence of difference, heterogeneity, and fragmentation as well as sameness, homogeneity, and continuity between post-war neoclassicism and the late neoclassical condition that defines the field today. The sameness, homogeneity, and continuity are due to the fact that all neoclassical approaches aim to address the same theoretical problematic; the difference, heterogeneity, and fragmentation, on the other hand, arise from the fact that each approach formulates and addresses the very same theoretical problematic in different ways, with different policy implications, normative accents, and social visions. The particular way in which the question of the reconciliation of the individual and the collective rationality is formulated and addressed by particular (late) neoclassical approaches depends on the political/normative commitments and the thematic orientations of, as well as the diverse methodologies (usually borrowed from disciplines such as physics, mathematics, biology, engineering, and psychology) deployed by, that particular approach.

* * *

The project of reading the recent history of neoclassical tradition as one of both sameness and difference, the project of making sense of the unity and the diversity of mainstream economics, is, admittedly, strategically motivated. There is indeed a diversity, a plurality, of approaches and research programs within the mainstream, yet there are very strict limits to this pluralism. Any approach that abandons or even questions the theoretical humanist presuppositions (i.e., pertaining to the notion of a self-conscious, rational, autonomous subject and its corollary, the equilibrium state of reconciliation) of neoclassical economics is pushed to the margins of the discipline. In this sense, notwithstanding the trope of the "pluralist turn" in mainstream economics and its supposed "break" from the neoclassical orthodoxy, the discipline continues to be a highly exclusive club. In a rather revealing passage, Colander, Holt and Rosser define "the edge of economics" as "that part of mainstream economics that is critical of orthodoxy, and that part of heterodox economics that is taken seriously by the elite of the profession" (2004: 492). They continue:

> Our argument is that modern mainstream economics is open to new approaches, as long as they are done with a careful understanding of the strengths of the recent orthodox approach and with a modeling methodology acceptable to the mainstream. (Colander et al. 2004: 492)

By claiming that anyone who uses "a modeling methodology acceptable to the mainstream" can be a part of the mainstream, Colander et al. reduce the problem to a matter of being up to date with the recent mathematical fashions of the day. But what if those modeling methodologies acceptable to the mainstream are the ones that are underpinned by the theoretical humanist presuppositions of neoclassical economics? And what if there are those who reject using these "acceptable" modeling methodologies precisely because of the philosophical presuppositions that underpin them?

Perhaps more insidiously (and insultingly), the "death of neoclassical economics" narrative implies that neoclassical economics, the object of critique of many heterodox traditions of economics, is a matter of the past, that no one really does neoclassical economics anymore, that the heterodox critics of mainstream economics are out of touch with what goes on in the contemporary mainstream, that they lack "a careful understanding of the strengths of the recent orthodox approach" (Colander et al. 2004: 492). Moreover, it further implies that there is indeed an appropriate way of criticizing neoclassical economics, and it is accomplished only by the usual protagonists of the pluralist turn in (mainstream) economics and not by those self-identified heterodox traditions that never get a "mention."

Therefore, because this emerging narrative of a "pluralist turn" has implications for how we differentiate the heterodoxy from the mainstream, and because contemporary mainstream economic approaches are pushing the heterodox ones to the margins of the discipline by trying to shape what constitutes a legitimate criticism of neoclassical economics, it is necessary for heterodox economists to develop a clear, rigorous, and consistent position with respect to the "pluralist turn" narrative. Unless heterodox economists are willing to go along with Colander et al.'s thesis that the contemporary mainstream is not "orthodox" (their terminology) anymore and that the only thing that is common to all contemporary mainstream economic approaches is that each uses "a modeling methodology acceptable to the mainstream," it is necessary to offer a "heterodox" *demonstration* of how these seemingly disparate research agendas and approaches, not despite but precisely because of their undeniable diversity, continue to remain committed to the theoretical humanist presuppositions (i.e., the centered, self-conscious, and autonomous subject and its corollary teleological vision of social reconciliation) and the constitutive theoretical problematic (i.e., how to reconcile the individual and the collective rationality) of neoclassicism. That is precisely the objective of this book.

1.2 From neoclassical to late neoclassical economics

Although it is not a historical study, the book inevitably offers a narrative of the history of neoclassical economics primarily in the twentieth century. According to this narrative, the genealogy of neoclassical tradition can be traced back to two distinct geo-philosophical origins. On the one hand, there is the tradition of the utility calculus, which originated in Britain and was constituted by the Scottish

Enlightenment and Humean empiricism, but also by the utilitarianism of Jeremy Bentham. On the other hand, there is the general equilibrium tradition, which originated in Lausanne and was marked by French rationalism, Cartesian philosophy of science, and the tradition of elite engineering colleges. Starting with the work of Jevons in Manchester and, later, Marshall and Edgeworth in Cambridge, UK, the British orientation was focused on the analysis of individual exchange, and the utilitarian influences were evinced by the idea that an exchange can occur when the price ratio is equal to the ratio of the marginal utility of the two goods exchanged. For Walras in Lausanne, on the other hand, the central problem of economic analysis was defined as "the problem of how prices are established in a large number of markets at the same time" (Backhouse 2002: 170). In both traditions, it is possible to find the humanist construct of a utility-maximizing human subject (*rareté* in the case of Walras) and the teleological construct of a harmonious reconciliation (the concepts of exchange equilibrium in Jevons, market equilibrium in Marshall, and general equilibrium in Walras). In other words, both traditions share the problem of how to achieve social reconciliation of the diverse demands of self-conscious, rational and autonomous agents, the central theoretical problematic of neoclassical humanism.

The invisible hand theorem embodies the best-known and most canonical formulation of the theoretical problematic of neoclassical humanism: the competitive markets and the private ownership of economic resources will harness the independent, decentralized, and self-interested activities of economic agents, and will deliver a general, economy-wide equilibrium that maximizes the social welfare. To put it differently, the neoclassical tradition is structured around the theoretical humanist problematic of reconciling the rationality of the collective with that of the individual, and the invisible hand scenario, with its various versions, is just a particular formulation of this constitutive theoretical problematic of neoclassical humanism. While the Lausanne (or the Walrasian) skein tended to construct general equilibrium models from the ground up from individual rational agents, the British Marshallian skein (later, in the North American context, embodied in a transformed form in the Chicago approach) tended to take a partial equilibrium approach that emphasized the use of representative agents and market-level analysis.[20] In the Walrasian tradition, competitive markets are conceptualized as an auction. In this case, the invisible hand is the hand of an imaginary auctioneer (or in Walras' own terms, a *crieur*). In contrast to the static equilibrium, *ex ante* allocation, price-adjustment approach of Walrasian economics, the Marshallian Chicago School tended to formulate the theoretical problematic of neoclassical humanism in an evolutionary idiom that is dynamic only in gesture: the competition is theorized, with explicit, yet almost always undertheorized, references to biology and Darwinian theory, as an evolutionary selection process that would weed out underperforming, inefficient firms or households. In this case, the invisible hand materializes in the anthropomorphized hand of the selection mechanism.[21]

In other words, while there are many differences between the two skeins of neoclassicism, arguably the most pivotal one is the different metaphors they use to describe the invisible hand process. Metaphors that economists use to conceptualize how markets function and how prices or quantities or both adjust towards equilibrium are not without their material consequences pertaining to theoretical constructions and policy prescriptions (McCloskey 1994). In that regard, it is important to emphasize that for the neoclassical tradition, the invisible hand theorem is indeed a *theorem*—i.e., not all the proponents of neoclassical economics are advocates of *laissez faire*. On the contrary, there have always been neoclassical economists who found justification in a version of neoclassical theory for different degrees of government involvement in the economy (e.g., before the ordinalist turn, Henry Sedgwick, Alfred Marshall, A. C. Pigou; after the ordinalist turn, Abba Lerner, Oskar Lange, Jacob Marschak, Tjalling Koopmans, Kenneth Arrow). For those who believe that the reconciliation of the individual and the collective rationality *can* be realized through competitive markets and rules of property, the policy prescription has always been to institute the requisite market institutions (e.g., through the liberalization of trade and factor markets, through the privatization of public assets); for those who believe that such a reconciliation *cannot* be realized through competitive markets and rules of property, the policy prescription has always been to remedy various market failures (ranging from underprovisioning of public goods to externalities) either through direct government intervention and regulation or, if necessary, with the help of non-market and non-governmental institutions. Even though both traditions have their share of market skeptics and market advocates, the line that divides the former type of neoclassical economist from the latter type tends to overlap, at least in the postwar North American context, with the line that separates the Walrasian and the Marshallian skeins, respectively.

Despite this divergence of opinion in their policy prescriptions, both positions ascribe a privileged and constitutive role to the model of perfect competition as their ultimate point of reference. In the case of the *laissez faire* camp, the model of perfect competition (whether it is enframed in the Walrasian or the Marshallian vision) figures as an "ideal" state to be approximated as much as possible in real economies; in the case of the interventionist camp, the model serves as the standard of efficiency to be "emulated" or "approximated" with the help of second-best alternatives. In both cases, the model of perfect competition retains its status as the description of a socio-economic order that would best accommodate the postulated essence of centered, rational, and autonomous human subjects.

* * *

Beginning with the 1930s, weakened by its failure to address the worldwide depression, the neoclassical tradition began to go through its first important transition: partly in response to charges of "psychologism" by the American institutionalists and partly due to a positivist discomfort borne out of the non-measurable notion of *utils*, neoclassical economics took an *ordinalist turn* and abandoned the earlier cardinalist models that took the utility function as their description of the choice process. Even though the standard neoclassical theory of demand still remained true to its theoretical humanist presuppositions, the ordinalist turn marked a certain change of attitude in the way the economic agents are treated in the standard neoclassical models. It became preferable *to assume as little as possible* about the preferences of the actual economic agents. Lionel Robbins (1932) was one of the first neoclassical economists to publicly criticize the notion of utility as an interpersonal measure of well-being; Samuelson (1938) wanted to read the preferences directly from the revealed choices of the consumers; Arrow (1963) rendered the concept of preference indifferent to the underlying motivations of the economic agents; Debreu (1959) proved the existence and efficiency of the general equilibrium by imposing minimal restrictions on the preferences of the consumer; Becker (1962) went so far as to argue that, even if the consumers and the producers do not respond to changes in prices rationally (i.e., by responding impulsively or remaining inert), market forces (i.e., changes in opportunity sets) will tend to produce "rational" results that will systematically satisfy the basic predictions of neoclassical economic theory.[22]

Despite this accentuated and widespread tendency to refrain from assuming too much about the economic agent, let us note that all of these neoclassical approaches, when it came to making normative claims about the efficiency of the equilibrium, continued to harbor crucial and common assumptions regarding the psyche of the economic agent. Even though it became impossible with the ordinalist turn to compare the states of well-being of individuals with each other, these mid-century neoclassical models continued to assume that (i) the *choices* of the agent reflect her/his *preferences* and (ii) the *preferences* of the agent (even when s/he is not selfish), in turn, reflect the *welfare* of the agent (Sen 2002). In this sense, the mid-century "ordinalist" neoclassical economics continued to be a theoretical humanist research program that held on to a centered, unified, and autonomous conceptualization of the human subject who knows what would improve her/his welfare, who can form preferences that would reflect her/his welfare, and who would be able to make choices according to her/his preferences.

* * *

This process culminated roughly in the mid-1970s. In the late 1960s and early 1970s, when the invisible hand theorem was fully formalized in the A-D general exchange equilibrium models, a number of Walrasian economists swiftly recognized and acknowledged that there are indeed limitations to this neoclassical model of the market equilibrium and the concept of economic agent associated with it (Arrow and Hahn 1971; Hahn 1984; Arrow 1987; Kirman 1992; Katzner 1999; 2004). With the full development of the A-D model, a widespread perception emerged among neoclassical economists: if they wished to develop the idea of general equilibrium (i.e., harmonious and contradiction-free economic order) as a spontaneous and unintended outcome of the rational actions of individual economic agents, they had to give up the idea that each individual is unique, distinct, and autonomous. The Sonnenschein–Mantel–Debreu results, although more recent research has proved them to be less general than they were perceived to be at the time, demonstrated that, unless further restrictions are imposed on the types of preference that the consumers can have in an A-D exchange economy, it is impossible to obtain the proper market excess demand functions that will always guarantee full reconciliation. Imposing further restrictions, however, while providing the necessary conditions for the *uniqueness* and *global stability* of the general equilibrium, meant for many (but not all) the loss of the intended generality of a thoroughly individualist general equilibrium model.

Accompanying the matters that pertain to the uniqueness and global stability of the general equilibrium, there was the problem of conceptualizing the process of *price adjustment* (price determination). In the general equilibrium literature, the auctioneer metaphor is invoked in order to motivate the *tâtonnement* process through which suppliers and buyers modify their plans (in relation to everyone else's plans and outside of real time) until the equilibrium is finally reached.[23] Nevertheless, due to its lack of conformity with the precepts of methodological individualism, this conceptualization of the price-adjustment process was far from convincing in the eyes of many neoclassical economists. Indeed, the auctioneer and its contradictory position within the intendedly individualist framework of the Walrasian system have already been identified by a number of scholars as a *structuralist moment* of an otherwise theoretical humanist discourse (Amariglio et al. 1990; Charusheela 2004; see also Hahn 1984). Moreover, historically, the auctioneer metaphor was used by left-leaning Walrasian economists (e.g., Abba Lerner, Oskar Lange) as a euphemism for the Central Planning Board. In other words, the Walrasian skein of neoclassical economics, at the time, did not only fail to provide the promised microfoundations[24] for the general competitive equilibrium with a desired level of generality (and hence defaulted on its promise to formalize the invisible hand theorem in a convincing manner), but also promulgated in the minds of some a vision of the market economy that necessitated government intervention to undertake its most basic function—namely, the determination of the equilibrium price vector![25]

Many commentators saw in these two clusters of issues (namely, the issues that pertain to the generality of uniqueness and stability theorems and those that pertain to the absence of methodological individualism in the price-adjustment process) the necessary justification for abandoning the Walrasian program. But more importantly, in part encouraged by Debreu's claim to present the A-D model as "the root structure from which all further work in economics would eventuate" (Weintraub, 2002: 121), many late neoclassical economists tended to equate the Walrasian program with neoclassical economics as such, and began to represent the loss of the disciplinary hegemony of the former as the "death" of the latter. Without doubt, the loss of the disciplinary hegemony of the general equilibrium theory is a significant moment in the history of the neoclassical tradition. By theorizing late neoclassical economics as a response to the perceived "shortcomings" of the A-D model, I also acknowledge the importance of this moment. But, as mentioned earlier, it would be erroneous to reduce the rich internal diversity of the neoclassical tradition to its Walrasian skein. Such a conflation of a species (the Walrasian skein) with the genus (the neoclassical tradition) is precisely what prevents us from "seeing" the underlying continuities between neoclassical and late neoclassical economics. Accordingly, if one uncritically subscribes to this conflation, any critique of the A-D model and its assumptions will automatically be registered as a critique of neoclassical economics as such, and the continuity between a more broadly defined neoclassical tradition and the contemporary mainstream (i.e., late neoclassical economics) will be rendered invisible. In other words, even though these two clusters of problems, namely the restrictiveness of the assumptions necessary to prove the uniqueness and stability of the general equilibrium as well as the conceptual murkiness that taints the price-adjustment scenario, do stem from the definitive theoretical humanist presuppositions of the neoclassical tradition, the Walras–Arrow–Debreu model is just one of the many renditions of this theoretical humanist problematic of the tradition: its "demise" does not entail the demise of neoclassical humanism in general.

Therefore, in response to those who announce "the death of neoclassical economics," it is necessary to remind them that criticizing a particular rendition of the theoretical problematic of neoclassical humanism does not add up to a thoroughgoing critique of the neoclassical problematic as such. This is precisely why contemporary mainstream economic approaches fail to occasion a radical break from the neoclassical tradition. Even though they criticize the A-D model and its particular rendition of the theorem of the invisible hand, they neither criticize nor eventually abandon the project of reconciling the diverse demands of rational and autonomous individuals (and, in some cases, they don't even abandon the theorem of the invisible hand). Moreover, they criticize the A-D rendition of the theorem not because it is theoretical humanist, but rather, because it is not theoretical humanist enough, because it collapses into theoretical structuralism!

$$* \quad * \quad *$$

First and foremost, then, late neoclassical economics defines itself in relation to and, in a sense, in opposition to the concept of perfect competition as it is defined and formalized in the A-D model.[26] One of the defining themes of late neoclassical economics, therefore, is the study of the different aspects of market failures and imperfections—which are defined with reference to a concept of perfect competition. Accordingly, one typical late neoclassical operation is to relax an assumption or two of the A-D model (while, of course, leaving the presuppositions of neoclassical humanism untouched). A second is to draw upon the non-Walrasian skeins of the neoclassical tradition (e.g., the evolutionary themes of the Marshallian/ Chicago approach, the concept of transaction costs of the neighboring Coasean tradition, the Nash equilibrium concept of classical game theory).[27] Through these reconfigurations, late neoclassical economists shifted their attention to offering explanations as to why either it is impossible to obtain the conditions necessary for the invisible hand theorem to hold true or it is necessary to do something to realize the invisible hand theorem. In other words, the neoclassical theoretical problematic and its corollary policy debate (pro-intervention versus *laissez faire*) is reproduced once more in the late neoclassical context. While the details of the arguments, the sets of concepts, and the research methodologies deployed have changed in the late neoclassical context, the terrain of the debate has remained the same.

As I noted above, late neoclassical economics appears to be comprised of a fairly heterogeneous group of approaches, and it lacks a central model and a central research methodology. Ironically, in the late neoclassical context, the A-D model still serves a central role, albeit not as "the root structure" or a central model, as intended by, for instance, Debreu, but rather as a point of departure, as a benchmark. The various assumptions of the A-D model (pertaining to the commodity space, the theory of the firm, the axioms and the implicit assumptions of rationality, and the concept of equilibrium and its efficiency attributes) serve as possible points of departure for a late neoclassical economist: What if we incorporate the idea that there are transaction costs to the writing and enforcing of contracts? What if information is not perfectly available to the exchanging agents? If there are market failures, aren't there government failures as well? Why are there firms in a market economy? What if the "cooperating inputs" in a production process are inherently opportunistic? What if human beings have altruistic preferences? What if human beings have only bounded rationality? What if choice is an interdependent and strategic phenomenon? The list can easily be extended. In posing and answering such questions, late neoclassical approaches caused the models by which the various aspects of the theoretical problematic of neoclassical economics are reformulated to proliferate.

The fact that not all approaches ask all these questions simultaneously contributes to the overall heterogeneity that characterizes the late neoclassical context. Some approaches relax only one assumption; others relax a number of them. Some approaches focus only on two questions; others tackle a number of them.[28] Moreover, in order to revise and re-activate the theoretical humanist presuppositions of the neoclassical tradition, late neoclassical economists, not unlike their neoclassical predecessors who borrowed from physics (Mirowski 1989), continued to borrow modeling techniques, simulation technologies, and experimental methodologies from disciplines such as evolutionary biology (Hodgson 1993; Vromen 1995), cognitive and behavioral sciences (Davis 2003; Sent 2004; 2005), cyborg sciences (Mirowski 2002), engineering (Sent 1997), and, of course, mathematics (Weintraub 2002).

Accordingly, unless we read contemporary mainstream approaches by positioning them genealogically in relation to the A-D model, it will be difficult to render comprehensible the theoretical humanist problematic that structures the apparent dispersion characteristic of the late neoclassical context. Late neoclassical approaches are united in the way that each approach relaxes, scrutinizes, enriches, and modifies this or that assumption, opens up this or that black box, and revisits, reformulates, or re-stages the same theoretical humanist problematic that was part and parcel of the A-D model (as well as the other models of the neoclassical tradition). In this sense, to the extent that it continues to be structured around the problem of how to reconcile individual rationality with that of the collective, contemporary mainstream economics is squarely within the neoclassical tradition.

1.3 Outline of the book

Neoclassical discourse privileges consistency and order. At the heart of its understanding of the human subject, we find the postulate of consistency along with other postulates of rationality. This notion of (rationality as) consistency also underpins the concept of social order embodied in the concept of equilibrium. In the A-D model, the equilibrium is defined as a price vector that renders compatible (and hence "consistent with each other") the profit-maximizing production plans with the "utility"-maximizing consumption plans. Similarly, in the Marshallian system, the equilibrium in a particular market is reached when the exit and entry of firms ceases, when the market stabilizes. Nevertheless, as a discursive formation, the neoclassical tradition, early or late, cannot constitute itself as a consistent formation. This is not to say that neoclassical economists are not committed to constructing a consistent discourse. Indeed, for instance, the use of mathematics and symbolic logic in the mid-century neoclassical economics is, in part, motivated by this (aesthetic) concern to establish a consistent discourse. Despite this deliberate effort to achieve discursive consistency, the tradition is fraught with inconsistent and, in many cases, conflicting models, metaphors, and methodologies. As articulated earlier, the task of this volume is to delineate and render visible the thread that sutures together the various neighborhoods of this discursive sprawl.

In this sense, the task of mastering (and, in the final analysis, reading consistency into) this complex, uneven, inconsistent, and internally fractured discursive formation is an impossible one. The impossibility of this task is further aggravated by the responsibility for producing a "convincing reading" that will have consequences in the economics discipline, an intended audience of this book. This is an "impossible" responsibility, which compels one to attend to the various subtle and, no doubt, consequential differences among various, early and late, neoclassical approaches.

In an attempt to introduce some semblance of order to the proposed analysis of the internal dynamics of neoclassical tradition, the book is divided into two main parts: Chapters 3, 4, and 5 deal with neoclassical economics from the 1930s to the 1970s, and Chapters 6, 7, 8, and 9 deal with late neoclassical economics. These two parts are bookended by Chapter 2, which is a philosophical excursion into theoretical humanism that complements this introductory chapter, and Chapter 10, which concludes the argument of the book by providing a brief (and inevitably speculative) account of the state of the discipline of economics in the aftermath of the 2008 Crash and sketches the contours of a Marxian surplus alternative. Significantly, Chapters 2 and 10 are the only places in this book where the particular Marxian perspective that silently informs the rest of the book is explicitly explored.

The discussions of both neoclassical and late neoclassical economics are structured around two constitutive presuppositions of the theoretical problematic of the tradition: the concepts of *economic agent* and *equilibrium*. For instance, in Part 2, Chapter 3 traces the changes in and the variations of the neoclassical concept of economic agent from the early days of the "marginalist" revolution to the mid-century ordinalism in the context of North American academia. In contrast, the remaining two chapters of Part 2 are devoted to the Walrasian and the Marshallian concepts of equilibrium. While Chapter 4 explores the structuralist moments of the mid-century axiomatic general equilibrium models as developed by the various affiliates of the Cowles Commission, Chapter 5 provides a discussion of the "selectionist arguments" articulated in the same period by the proponents of the Chicago approaches.

Chapter 6, intended as an introduction to the second half of the book, serves the purpose of preparing the reader for the subsequent identification and analysis of late neoclassical economics. The chapter puts forward three theses regarding contemporary mainstream economics: that it is unified despite a significant degree of internal heterogeneity; that it remains within the neoclassical problematic; and that it consists of returns to and re-elaborations of the theoretical presuppositions of neoclassical humanism. Through a close reading of the writings of a number of important forerunners and figures of late neoclassical economics (Ronald Coase, Steven Cheung, Samuel Bowles, Herbert Gintis, Douglass North, and Joseph Stiglitz), the chapter establishes the constitutive (albeit negatively so) importance of the general equilibrium theory for late neoclassical economics.

Chapter 7 discusses the different and conflicting ways in which late neoclassical approaches produced the concept of *market failures* and mobilized it to understand the *economic institutions* in general and firms in particular. The chapter establishes that the transitions from the study of perfect competition to that of imperfect competition and from market exchange to economic institutions do not add up to a radical break from the neoclassical problematic. Chapter 8 focuses on the treatment of the concept of the human subject in late neoclassical economics and offers a critical evaluation of the accentuated pre-occupation of late neoclassical economists with the motivational and cognitive dimensions of the assumption of *rationality*. The chapter demonstrates that the late neoclassical turn towards a "richer" and more "subtle" concept of the human subject that incorporates bounded rationality and self-reflexivity is not only a rehabilitation of the theoretical humanist project of early neoclassicism but also a response to the impoverished concept of the human subject that was expounded by post-war neoclassicism. Finally, Chapter 9 focuses on the concepts of *equilibrium, efficiency*, and *institutions* in the game theoretic corridors of the late neoclassical condition. The chapter traces the trajectory of a transition from the concept of Nash equilibrium associated with classical game theory to the concept of evolutionary stability associated with evolutionary game theory. The chapter demonstrates how these concepts and their various refinements are developed for revitalizing, rather than abandoning, the ideal of harmonious reconciliation of the interests of autonomous and centered actors.

Notes

1 For surveys, see Bowles and Gintis (2000), Colander (2000), Mirowski (2002), Colander et al. (2004) and Davis (2006).

2 For attempts to make sense of this heterogeneity in the context of different fields of inquiry, see Madra and Adaman (2010; 2014), Adaman and Madra (2014), and Akbulut et al. (2015).

3 This term is chosen over the two other contenders: *post-neoclassical economics* and *neo-* (or new) *neoclassical economics*. The former was inappropriate because it gave the impression of an accentuated break with neoclassical economics. For instance, Bowles and Gintis (1993) used the term *post-Walrasian economics* to signal their claim to have occasioned a break with Walrasian economics. The latter, on the other hand, was simply too clumsy and risked being confused with new classical economics— a macroeconomic school of thought within broadly defined neoclassical tradition. In contrast, the designator "late neoclassical economics" connotes the idea of continuity rather clearly.

4 Note, however, that the notion of "spontaneous order," as articulated forcefully by Austrian economist and philosopher Friedrich von Hayek (1988), can indeed be construed as a concept of socio-economic order. Yet, in the case of this notion, there is indeed strong opposition from within the Austrian School, arguing that Hayek, by turning towards evolutionary theory to elaborate on the process of cultural evolution of institutions such as private property and price mechanism, has abandoned his commitment to methodological individualism. See, in particular, Vanberg (2001).

5 In his now well-known Jevons Memorial Lecture entitled "In Praise of Economic Theory," Frank Hahn specified the following as the essential features of neoclassical economics (Hahn 1985; cf. Lawson 1997: 87):

an individualistic perspective, a requirement that explanations be couched solely in terms of individuals;

an acceptance of some rationality axiom; and

a commitment to the study of equilibrium states.

All these features are captured in the working definition of the neoclassical problematic provided here. However, while the latter two remained intact throughout the history of the neoclassical tradition and continue to remain intact today, the first feature (i.e., individualism), whether it is acknowledged by neoclassical economists or not, has been repeatedly violated by "structuralist moments" throughout the history of the tradition.

6 The formulation relies on Kenneth Arrow's formulation of the different types of social choice in his *Social Choice and Individual Values* (1963: 1–3): "In a capitalist democracy there are essentially two methods by which social choices can be made: voting, typically used to make 'political' decisions, and the market mechanism, typically used to make 'economic' decisions. [...] The methods of voting and the market are methods of amalgamating the tastes of many individuals in the making of social choices. [...] Can we find other methods of aggregating individual tastes which imply rational behavior on the part of the community?" In other words, like the voting mechanism, the market mechanism is also a method for reconciling the individual and the collective (aggregate) rationality.

7 For critiques of theoretical humanism in the discipline of economics and in the Marxian tradition, see Foucault (1973[1966]), Althusser (1969; 1996; 2003), Hindess (1977), Coward and Ellis (1977), Callari (1981), Resnick and Wolff (1987), Amariglio (1988), Amariglio et al. (1990), and Ruccio and Amariglio (2003).

8 I intend to use the term "presuppositions" by distinguishing it from the "assumptions" or "postulates" of a theoretical approach. The latter can be modified depending on the requirements of a specific theoretical and applied context. In contrast, the presuppositions of a theory are its entry points or points of departure. For a definition of the notion of "entry points," see Resnick and Wolff (1987). Also, presuppositions, unlike axioms (which are explicitly acknowledged presuppositions), can be unconscious and remain unacknowledged.

9 Let us note that not everyone perceives or accepts the validity of this division. For instance, recently a colleague of mine argued that he does not accept the heterodox versus mainstream difference, and claimed that the only legitimate difference is one between "good" and "bad" economics. Needless to say, we disagreed on the criteria by which we define what is good economics. Mainstream and heterodox approaches to economics differ from each other first and foremost in the way they define what is "good" and what is "bad" economics.

10 Note that, contrary to this claim, within late neoclassical economics, there is a rather powerful pro-intervention, left liberal wing. For a survey that highlights the importance and limits of "left neoliberalism" in mainstream economic thought, see Madra and Adaman (2014).

11 This is not to say that no heterodox economists are critical of this "heterodox" tendency to represent neoclassical economics as a monolithic discourse. For instance, among others, Robert Garnett (2005), Edward Fullbrook (2001), John B. Davis (2008), and Esther Mirjam Sent (2003) have all noted their various misgivings about this heterodox tendency to reduce mainstream economics to a monolithic discourse. According to these scholars, this reductionist tendency emanates from a widely held commitment among heterodox economists to a Kuhnian vision of science as a contested field of social discourse and practice consisting of distinct and incompatible scientific paradigms (Garnett 2005: 6; see also Fullbrook 2001). Garnett (2005) reminds us that this vision of "paradigm warfare" emerged in the mid- to late 1960s, during the height of the Cold War, in reaction to mainstream microeconomists such as Gérard Debreu, who, using the language of Bourbakist mathematical structuralism, referred to the model of Walrasian equilibrium as "the root structure from which all further work in economics would eventuate" (Weintraub 2002: 121). In response to this absolutist high modernism of the mainstream, heterodox economists of various stripes were forced to embrace the vision of paradigm warfare, if only "to survive under difficult professional circumstances" (Garnett 2005: 6). According to the vision of paradigm warfare, the task of heterodox economists was not only to articulate a rigorous critique of mainstream economics but also to supplant the latter with a compelling, systematic, complete, and superior alternative framework (Garnett 2005: 7). Nonetheless, even if the representation of mainstream economics as a monolithic discourse was inevitable during the hostile environment of the Cold War era, it has become, Garnett argues, "largely anachronistic and self-defeating for heterodox economists today" (2005: 6). It is anachronistic because it is factually incorrect. (Garnett seems to concur on this account with the likes of Davis (2003; 2006), Colander (2000), Colander et al. (2004), and others.) It is self-defeating because it promotes an isolationist "bunker mentality" (Garnett 2005: 7), "encourages an all-or-nothing view of intellectual change" (Garnett 2005: 7), and "undercuts heterodox economists' commitments to pluralism" (Garnett 2005: 7).

12 The proper names that Bowles and Gintis invoke stand for, respectively, the new institutional economics, the evolutionary game theory, the Nash refinements tradition of game theory, and behavioral economics. Given their more recent work (Heinrich et al. 2004; Gintis et al. 2005), one should probably add experimental economics to their list.

13 Some histories of neoclassical economics add to these two sources a third one: the "Austrian" subjectivism of Carl Menger (e.g., Blaug 1997). On the other hand, Philip Mirowski (1989) argues that Menger did not belong to the neoclassical tradition because he did not subscribe to the "field" conceptualization that Jevons and Walras borrowed from the physics of their day in fashioning their versions of the concept of utility in reference to the concept of energy. Notably, unlike Jevons and Walras, who had a static view of competition and equilibrium, Menger viewed competition as a dynamic process and tended towards "the idea that there is a spontaneous order underlying social phenomena" (Backhouse 2002: 177).

14 To these two, Mirowski and Wade Hands (1998; Hands and Mirowski 1998) would add the "midway" operationalist revealed preference approach of Paul Samuelson at the Massachusetts Institute of Technology (MIT). Samuelson's "operationalist" program demanded that the scientificity of an economic theory (or any theory) should be assessed on the basis of its intersubjectively observable, empirical consequences. Empirically invalid or untestable portions of a given theory should be discarded. The fact that the concept of utility is unobservable led Samuelson to try to discard the introspective portions of the theory of choice through the theory of revealed preference. For further discussions, see Wong (1978), Blaug (1980: 99–103), Hausman (1992: 156–8), and Mirowski and Hands (1998: 282). See Chapter 3 for a more detailed discussion of Samuelsonian operationalism.

15 Among others, we can list Oskar Lange, Jacob Marschak, Tjalling Koopmans, Gérard Debreu, Kenneth Arrow, Frank Hahn, and Lawrence Klein. Beyond the Cowles Commission, we can refer to a Samuelsonian lineage coming from the MIT PhD program in Economics: George Akerlof, Joseph Stiglitz, Michael Rothschild, Peter A. Diamond, and Paul Krugman. Even though they were never directly affiliated with the Cowles Commission, given the trajectory of their work, these figures should be considered in the Walrasian skein of the neoclassical tradition.

16 Starting with Frank Knight, who taught at the University of Chicago in the inter-war period, we can mention Ronald Coase, Milton Friedman, Theodore Schultz, George Stigler, Harold Demsetz, Armen Alchian, Robert Fogel, Gary Becker, Steven Cheung, Deirdre N. McCloskey, and, most recently, Stephen D. Levitt among the proponents of the Chicago skein of the neoclassical tradition (Reder 1987; McCloskey 1994; Vromen 1995; Emmett 1997; Mirowski and Hands 1998; Farrant 2004; Van Horn et al. 2012).

17 In an interesting attempt to synthesize the Walrasian general equilibrium theory (as it is embodied in the Arrow–Debreu–McKenzie (henceforth, ADM) model) and the Marshallian partial equilibrium analysis, William Novshek and Hugo Sonnenschein (1987: 1281–2) identify the following five differences: (1) in the ADM model, there is a fixed number of firms, whereas in the Marshallian model, there is a pool of firms; (2) in the ADM model, convex technology implies no increasing returns to scale, whereas in the Marshallian model, a U-shaped average cost curve implies regions of increasing returns to scale; (3) the ADM theory assumes price-taking behavior, whereas the Marshallian theory assumes price-taking behavior only if the efficient scale of production is small relative to the demand; (4) the ADM theory, precisely because it is a *general* equilibrium theory, relates perfect competition to Pareto efficiency, whereas the Marshallian theory, because it is a partial equilibrium theory, fails in taking into account intermarket effects; (5) the ADM theory is static, whereby the equilibrium is reached through *price* adjustment (*tâtonnement*), whereas the Marshallian analysis of equilibria is dynamic, whereby *market* adjustment occurs through exit and entry of firms. Another way of marking this difference is to contrast the *ex ante* nature of allocation in the ADM theory with the *ex post* nature of allocation in the Marshallian vision. I thank Fikret Adaman for bringing this last point to my attention.

18 For a detailed survey of such enduring foundational issues of neoclassical choice theory, see Mandler (1999).

19 For a critique of essentialism in epistemology, see Resnick and Wolff (1987) and Wolff and Resnick (2012).

20 Throughout the history of the neoclassical tradition, the two tendencies had a dialectical relation of sorts: up to WWII, the Marshallian skein took the lead; after WWII, up to the 1970s, the Walrasian skein, perhaps due to the impact of its forceful and rapid mathematization, gained prominence; and since the early 1980s, partly due to the efforts of the proponents of the Chicago School, partly due to the ascendancy of the Coasean new institutional economics, and partly due to the increasing spread of the use of evolutionary metaphors (a distinctively Marshallian theme, as we will see), the Marshallian influences have been giving shape to the character of late neoclassical economics. Not

much seems to have changed in this regard since the 2008 Crash. It is important to note that the Marshallian approach and Marshall's analyses are different from each other. While Marshall's own work has influenced, and continues to influence, Marshallian neoclassicism, the latter is shaped by the entire history of neoclassical tradition and not just by Marshall's writings.

21   There is indeed a debate over whether the Adam Smith of the Chicago School is really the Adam Smith of *The Wealth of Nations* (1776) and *The Theory of Moral Sentiments* (1790) (Evensky 2005; see also Sen 1987: 15–28). Similarly, we should also ask how important the invisible hand theorem is for the Marshallian skein of the neoclassical tradition. Nonetheless, even if the Marshallian/Chicago appropriation of the invisible hand theorem does injustice to Adam Smith's and subsequently the Walrasians' formulations of the problem, both the Marshallian and the Walrasian skeins share the problem of the social reconciliation of the diverse demands of rational individuals, and focus on the competitive price mechanism as the privileged means for achieving social reconciliation.

22   According to Becker (1962), changes in the opportunity sets (budget constraints), induced by the changes in relative prices, will force "the average economic actor" to behave according to neoclassical theorems, even when each actual actor in the market may behave irrationally.

23   For Walras, a *crieur* is not really an auctioneer, but merely an announcer of prices. The term *auctioneer* began to be circulated only subsequently due to an incorrect translation by Jaffé (Walker 1996: 82). Also note that this volume will mainly consider *tâtonnement* models of general exchange equilibrium. Even though the auctioneer-led *tâtonnement* is the main metaphor for conceptualizing the price-adjustment process in an A-D exchange economy, non-*tâtonnement* (i.e., search) models of price adjustment have also been explored (Diamond 1971). For a survey of the literature, see Hahn (1982: 788–91).

24   Throughout the book, the term *microfoundationalism* will refer to the theoretical practice of explaining all social phenomena by referring them back to a mathematically tractable conceptualization of individual choice. From a microfoundationalist perspective, the auctioneer construct, to the extent that it is a *deus ex machina* that cannot be explained by the preferences, choices, and actions of rational individuals, fails to be a convincing representation of the invisible hand theorem.

25   In addition to being a euphemism for the Central Planning Board, another terrifying implication of the auctioneer metaphor for the pro-market neoclassical economists was that, given the relational structure of the Walrasian conceptualization of the economy, the Walrasian agents were autonomous neither from each other nor from a supra-individual agency, such as the auctioneer. The auctioneer metaphor was rather challenging for the methodological individualist presuppositions of the tradition.

26   In this sense, when Bowles and Gintis (2000) claim that the Walrasian approach was an unnecessary detour that delayed the development of "nonwalrasian economics" (their term for late neoclassical economics), they are missing the constitutive importance of the A-D model for late neoclassical economics. When they argue that "all of the underpinnings of a nonwalrasian economics had been set in place by 1960" (2000: 1429), it is impossible not to detect a quasi-Darwinian understanding of science as the progressive unfolding of better tools for representing the truth of reality. Walrasian economics can only be "an unnecessary detour" if "nonwalrasian economics" is superior to (i.e., more realistic than) the former according to some objective criteria; otherwise, economists would not return to these earlier concepts, nor would the concepts make a comeback! In other words, Bowles and Gintis assume that "nonwalrasian" concepts that were elaborated "in the period from 1937 to 1957" (e.g., transaction cost, Nash equilibrium solution concept, bounded rationality) were bound to replace the Walrasian concepts, because they are superior according to some objective and universally agreed criteria. There are many things to be criticized in this chain of reasoning. Let us just mention

four. First, according to which criteria are we going to decide whether nonwalrasian concepts are superior to the Walrasian concepts? For instance, if we embrace the notion that concepts are always inevitably partial representations of reality, according to what criteria are we going to decide whether one partial representation is better than another partial representation? Moreover, if the concepts do not only represent but also help shape reality, then the *veridical* nature of the concepts may even be complicated by their *performative* effects: if the concepts shape the reality that they represent, according to what reality are we going to adjudicate the representational superiority of a set of concepts over another set? Second, if some nonwalrasian (but, in my opinion, neoclassical) concepts are rediscovered and deployed by late neoclassical economists following the demise of Walrasian economics, many others (and, more often than not, those that are more damaging to the neoclassical problematic, such as Harvey Liebenstein's concept of X-efficiency) are forgotten! Third, there is no reason to believe that these nonwalrasian (yet neoclassical) concepts became attractive in the 1970s due to their inherent and objective superiority. They became valuable only retroactively, and precisely because they were nonwalrasian, after a number of influential neoclassical economists had become convinced that the Walrasian program was a dead end. And finally, the fact that these nonwalrasian (yet neoclassical) concepts pre-date the full development of the Walrasian program is yet another proof that there has always been more to the neoclassical tradition than the Walrasian program, that late neoclassical economic approaches, in criticizing the Walrasian program, are drawing from those other skeins of the neoclassical tradition.

27 The irony (which will be further explored in Chapter 5) is that the Chicago formulations that are usually referred to as the sources of late neoclassical responses to the Walrasian "structuralisms" were themselves saturated with structuralist moments! In other words, despite the fact that both the full axiomatization of the general equilibrium theory in the 1950s and 1960s *and* the "selectionist arguments" of the proponents of the Chicago School were saturated with influences from various types of structuralism, in the subsequent late neoclassical literature, they were read and interpreted in diametrically opposite ways. While the theoretical developments in the Walrasian general equilibrium theory are usually treated as a moment of "maturity," "culmination," or even "breakdown" (Davis 2006: 14–17), the "selectionist arguments" of the Chicago School are construed as the constituents of an "originary" moment when the "foundations" of the new institutional economics, evolutionary economics, and evolutionary game theory were laid down (Vromen 1995; Samuelson 2002).

28 To complicate the matter even more, each approach has a number of different versions, each addressing a different concern. For instance, there are a number of different versions of experimental economics: some focus on the nature of preferences, while others focus on the limitations of the human mind in processing information. Similarly, there are different uses of evolutionary game theory. For some approaches, it provides an explanation for the survival of altruistic preferences; for others, it provides a new and more versatile concept of equilibrium (i.e., evolutionary stability); and for yet others, it provides an explanation for the emergence of institutions.

2 Towards an anti-essentialist Marxian critique of theoretical humanism

Theoretical humanism is a decidedly post-Enlightenment philosophical orientation that cuts across not only numerous schools of thought within the discipline of economics but also other disciplines of social and human sciences (e.g., political science, sociology, anthropology, psychology). Theoretical humanism is a post-Enlightenment phenomenon because it displaces God from the central ontological position (*logos*) that it has enjoyed for centuries, only to put humanity, the human subject, in its place. And precisely for this reason, because it neither questions nor deconstructs the centered architecture of the pre-Enlightenment ontological universe and the place of God therein, theoretical humanism fails to carry through to the end the secular promise of the Enlightenment. The defining theoretical humanist operation, therefore, is the insertion of humanity, the human subject, or the collectivities of the human subject, into the void left by God at the apex of the centered architecture of the pre-Enlightenment ontology, epistemology, and ethics.

The constitutive problematic of theoretical humanism is the reconciliation of the pre-given interests of self-conscious, rational, and autonomous human subjects. This chapter will first discuss the two theoretical presuppositions that underpin the constitutive problematic of theoretical humanism, namely, the concept of the human subject and the ideal of social reconciliation. Following this discussion, the chapter will outline the basic contours of a truly secular critique of the theological idea of social reconciliation and the concept of the subject qua autonomous and rational consciousness that underpins the idea of reconciliation. And finally, the chapter will elaborate on the concept of a theoretical problematic and distinguish it from the particular theoretical positions *within* a theoretical problematic.

2.1 The notion of the human subject and the ideal of social reconciliation

The notion of the human subject that is found at the core of theoretical humanism is a centered, rational, and autonomous self-consciousness. She is a consciousness who possesses or who can eventually possess the full knowledge of her "true" interests (ends) and who has the capability to employ the necessary means to realize these ends. In this sense, the subject of theoretical humanism is simultaneously an epistemological and an ontological entity. As an epistemological entity, she is assumed to be equipped with the wherewithal "to know" her "true" interests (ends) and "to know" how to satisfy those interests (ends). As an ontological entity, she is assumed to have an intentional "agency" (the capacity to cause effects) to employ purposefully the necessary means to realize these ends. In defining theoretical humanism, North American economists David Ruccio and Jack Amariglio also refer to the epistemological and ontological qualities attributed to the human subject by theoretical humanism:

> Placing humans at the center of schemas of progress and history and meaning is what distinguishes theoretical humanism, as the human subject is thus the beginning and ending point of all movement from the growth of knowledge (which is now understood as undertaken by, for, and through human subjectivity) to the transformation of the natural world (through science and technology oriented to human desires and ends, such as happiness).
>
> (Ruccio and Amariglio 2003: 48)

Theoretical humanism inserts the human subject into the place of logos once occupied by the Divine Being. Yet, such insertion of a modern notion (human subject) into a pre-modern (theological) conceptual architecture has the potential to lead to what German philosopher Hans Blumenberg (1983) has called "reoccupation." Blumenberg articulated the concept in the context of the passage from pre-modernity to modernity in order to make sense of the way the problems of pre-modernity resurface in modernity. Expanding the domain of applicability of the concept to all social phenomena, and in particular to the political logic of hegemony, Argentinean political philosopher Ernesto Laclau defined "reoccupation" as

> the process by which particular notions, associated with the advent of a new vision and new problems, have the function of replacing ancient notions that had been formed on the ground of a different set of issues, with the result that the latter end up imposing their demands on the new notions and inevitably deforming them.
>
> (Laclau 1990: 74)

In this precise sense, to the extent that theoretical humanism fails to dispense with the centered architecture of the pre-Enlightenment ontology, a process of "reoccupation" begins to take over, and a number of theological constructs continue to exert their deforming influences on the Enlightenment discourse. Among those theological constructs is the utopian vision of a harmonious and contradiction-free social order (e.g., a paradise on earth) that would accommodate the postulated essence of the human subject in the best possible way. In other words, an important corollary of the centered, purposeful, and self-conscious human subject of theoretical humanism is the imaginary of a harmonious and contradiction-free social order: if there is an essence of the human subject that the human subject can become fully conscious of, then there must be a social order that would accommodate this essence—if it is not already the very embodiment of this essence. Regardless of the fact that such a social order can never be achieved in this world, such a notion is always present in theoretical humanist discourses and serves the function of a point of reference with which to compare the actually existing states as its imperfect approximations.

It is possible to find variations on this theoretical humanist theme of social reconciliation in the post-Enlightenment political theory, political economy, and philosophy. In the field of political theory, the post-Enlightenment idea of social reconciliation manifests itself in the various ontologies of concordance and harmony found in Thomas Hobbes, John Locke, and Adam Smith, who thought of discordance, disharmony, conflict, and antagonism as those aspects of the social that need to be banished from it (Connolly 1987; Mouffe 1992; Stavrakakis 1999). Similarly, in the field of political economy, the post-Enlightenment idea of social reconciliation manifests itself in the various concepts of equilibrium: the Walrasian concept of general equilibrium, the Marshallian concept of partial equilibrium (which always implicitly presupposes general equilibrium), the Nash equilibrium concept in classical game theory, the concept of evolutionary stability in evolutionary game theory, and even the notion of spontaneous order advanced by the Austrian School. Needless to say, the notion of a rational, self-transparent, and autonomous human subject underpins ("microfounds") all these political and economic notions of social reconciliation. Due to their "normative microfoundations," these theoretical humanist discourses, more often than not, function in the legitimization of the institutions of liberal democracy and the capitalist market economy. The very existence of the institutions of liberal democracy, capitalism, and market society becomes the proof of their legitimacy, for if they were bad for humanity, they would not be affirmed and internalized by human beings who are assumed to be rational and autonomous.

Indeed, there is much to be said about the "coincidence" of the epistemological role attributed to the human subject in the emergent Enlightenment philosophical *episteme,* the Age of Man, with the formulation of political liberalism around the concept of citizenship and the growing importance of "the contractual fiction" as the vital condition of existence of the market exchange.[1] Let us take a closer look at the precise nature of this "coincidence."

In order to be able to recognize the relation between the epistemological and ontological moments as one of "coincidence," we need to be able to distinguish them from one another. This is precisely what Belgian political philosopher Chantal Mouffe (1992) does when she distinguishes between the idea of "self-foundation," the epistemological project of the Enlightenment, and the idea of "self-assertion," the political project of the Enlightenment. "Self-foundation" refers to the epistemological grounding of knowledge in either the body (empiricism) or the mind (rationalism) (or a "balanced" combination of the two) of the human subject. "Self-assertion," on the other hand, is the emergence of the human subject as a citizen-subject through historical political acts such as the Declaration of the Rights of Man and of the Citizen (1789). Mouffe argues that there is no necessary relation between these two aspects.

Consider, for instance, the subject of political liberalism, the citizen-subject. The citizen-subject is the subject of Law; it is the subject who not only actively participates in the making of the Law (self-assertion) but also obeys this human-made Law. The idea of political democracy relies on this idea of the citizen-subject who is both constitutive of and constituted by the democratic polity. The citizen-subject is neither above nor below the Law—she is at the same level with the Law. To position the citizen-subject below the Law would be to return back to the pre-Enlightenment universe where the subject was supposed to be subjected to the Divine Law. To position the citizen-subject above the Law would be to conflate the political project of Enlightenment (self-assertion) with its epistemological project (self-foundation)—a mistake made by theoretical humanism. Indeed, the idea of the citizen-subject is a decidedly political concept that intends to establish (rather than presupposing as a given) a new political ontology (way of being); that is, it is not a concept that describes the essence of human beings but, rather, a concept that informs the Enlightenment project of enacting a new democratic political *way of being* (Mouffe 1992; Balibar 1994).

It is possible to extend this manner of reasoning to the subject of contractual law. The notion of *subject* that informs the contractual law does not describe the essence of human being; it simply establishes the prerequisites of a contractual arrangement. In order to function properly, it is argued, the contract law, "the core of the legal system in a market-dominated society," must assume that the individuals who enter into a contractual agreement are well-informed, purposeful, and autonomous (free) persons (Hodgson 1986: 214). Here, one must refer to "self-ownership" rather than "self-assertion." This assumption, this contractual fiction, of course, does not mean that actual human beings are "well-informed, purposeful, and autonomous" persons. Precisely for this reason, its status is one of "fiction"—even though it is indeed a fiction with material effects.

In this sense, neither the citizen-subject of the political law nor the contractual subject of the economic order has to rely on an essentialist conceptualization of the human subject to function. The political project of "self-assertion" and its objective of achieving "equality and freedom for all" do not require the epistemological "self-foundation" of the subject (Mouffe 1992: 10).[2] The conflation of the two is a theoretical humanist gesture. Analogously, the economic project of "self-ownership" and the necessity of contractual fiction for conducting market exchange do not require the epistemological "self-foundation" of the subject. In fact, Karl Marx's account of "commodity fetishism" is precisely about this non-coincidence. In the opening chapter of *Capital* (Vol. 1), Marx, describing the act of exchange from the perspective of traders, writes: "They do this without being aware of it" (1976[1867]: 166–7).[3] In the act of exchanging "by equating their different products to each other ... as values," Marx argues, "they equate [unknowingly] their different kinds of labour as human labour" (166). According to Marx, the act of exchange is not grounded in the self-knowledge of the exchanging subject. Or, more properly, it does not matter whether the subjects know what they are doing; the very act of exchange imposes equality (assuming there are no extra-economic factors causing commodities to be exchanged above or below their values) retroactively, and it is the task of critical political economy "to decipher the [social] hieroglyph" (167). (More in the next section on Marxism's relation to theoretical humanism.)

Nevertheless, as a decidedly post-Enlightenment philosophical orientation, theoretical humanism does make that additional, *legitimizing*, step by linking these Enlightenment notions of the citizen-subject and the contractual subject to an essentialist conceptualization of the human subject as a centered, rational, and autonomous self-consciousness who is responsible for the choices she makes.[4] And, precisely because it can serve a *legitimizing* function, the essentialist conceptualization of the human subject as a centered, unified, rational, and autonomous self-consciousness has important political and normative implications.

Consider, for instance, the idea of *equilibrium* in a perfectly competitive economy. An equilibrium is a state of this economy in which no one could be better off without making someone worse off. The concept of equilibrium derives its normative force as a Pareto optimum state of the economy from the assumption that individual agents who buy and sell goods and services do so in a rational and autonomous manner. Here, the concept of *autonomy* implies that the choices of the subjects reflect their preferences, and the concept of *rationality* implies that the preferences of the subjects are consistent and reflect the individual welfare of each (Sen 2002). In this sense, the essentialist conception of the human subject as a rational and autonomous self-consciousness functions as the normative foundation of the market economy. A similar argument can easily be made for the theoretical humanist appropriation of the concept of democracy and its corollary concept of the citizen-subject. It is possible to essentialize democracy and the outcomes of democratic processes, such as elections, if one understands the idea of citizenship as a natural right and interprets the political choices of the citizen-subjects as being reflective of their true preferences, and these preferences to be reflective of their individual welfare.

Therefore, the theoretical humanist *anchoring* of the secularizing, and in a certain sense pragmatic, fictions of the Enlightenment (e.g., the citizenship, the contractual subject) to a centered, rational, and autonomous notion of the human subject is a partisan restoration of the theological logos that should have been radically displaced by the Enlightenment. Within this vein, it is possible to read the history of post-Enlightenment philosophy as a history of the struggles between those who insist on re-centering the displaced logos around a foundationalist understanding of the human subject *and* those who remain in fidelity to the secular promise of the Enlightenment by criticizing not only the concept of God but also the very centered conceptual architecture of the pre-Enlightenment onto-theological universe. Accordingly, while a theoretical humanist discourse always presupposes a philosophical notion of the subject as a self-consciousness, as a unity, as a self-mastery, as a site of epistemological certitude, a thoroughly secular discourse of the post-Enlightenment era takes the critique of the very category of the subject as its entry point.

2.2 An anti-essentialist Marxian critique of the subject

It is possible to trace the genealogy of this secular "critique of the subject" back to the writings of Karl Marx, Friedrich Nietzsche, Sigmund Freud, Martin Heidegger, and Ludwig Wittgenstein, as well as to those of Jacques Lacan, Michel Foucault, Louis Althusser, and Jacques Derrida. According to French philosopher Jean-Luc Nancy, what this radically secular tendency has persistently aimed to accomplish is "the critique or deconstruction of interiority, of self-presence, of consciousness, of mastery, of the individual or collective property of an essence" (1991: 4). In articulating the contours of a secular and anti-essentialist Marxian critique of theoretical humanism, Foucault's critique of the category of the subject and Althusser's concept of ideological interpellation will be the point of departure.[5] More recent post-Althusserian analyses of the ideological conditions of existence of capitalism in the US will serve to illustrate the concrete implications of these theoretical constructs.

The term "subject" has a dual meaning. On the one hand, it connotes agency, autonomy, freedom, mastery, and consciousness. On the other hand, the term "subject" (qua *subjectus*) connotes subjection, submission, unfreedom, and powerlessness. In stark contradiction to the notion of the subject that the aforementioned critics of theoretical humanism have aimed to deconstruct, the latter notion of subject lacks autonomy and freedom, for it is subjected to a higher authority. This paradoxical situation begs the following question:

> [W]hy is it that the very *name* which allows modern philosophy to think and designate the *originary freedom* of the human being—the name of "subject"— is precisely the name which *historically* meant suppression of freedom, or at least an intrinsic limitation of freedom, i.e. *subjection*?
>
> (Balibar 1994: 8–9)

Perhaps, this coincidence of two radically opposite meanings is not as paradoxical as it initially appears. In order to be able to see why this may be so, we need to ask whether the subjection of the subject is simply a relation of brute force, an external constraint imposed upon an always already constituted subject? What if along with *subjection* (a political process) comes *subjectivation* (i.e., the constitution of the subjectivity of the subjected entity within the cultural processes of meaning production and dissemination)?[26] What if the cultural construction of the subjectivity of the subject, i.e., her/his *subjectivation*, is a condition of existence of her political subjugation, i.e., her/his *subjection*? Or, is there no room in this relation for the solicitation of the consent of the subject in her/his subjection? Moreover, what if, for subjectivation and subjection to succeed, the individual has to perceive herself (and to be perceived by others) as an autonomous subject? Foucault was articulating precisely this conjunction of the political and cultural processes when he was writing about a particular *technique* or *form* of power that

> applies itself to immediate everyday life which categorizes the individual, marks him by his own individuality, attaches him to his own identity,

imposes a law of truth on him which he must recognize and which others have to recognize in him. *It is a form of power which makes individuals subjects.* There are two meanings of the word *subject*: subject to someone else by control and dependence, and tied to his own identity by a conscience or self-knowledge. Both meanings suggest a form of power which subjugates and makes subject to.

(Foucault 1983: 212; emphasis in line 4 added)

According to Foucault, therefore, the political process of *subjugation* of human beings (individuals) and the cultural process of their *subjectivation* are interwoven. While the politico-juridical processes designate the individual as a legal subject who is subjected to laws, the cultural processes produce and disseminate meanings that enable the individual to perceive herself, and to be perceived by others, as an autonomous self-consciousness who is in total control of her identity. Subject-hood (in the sense of being a subject qua agency, unity, self-consciousness, and mastery), for Foucault, is not an inherent attribute of the individual but a product of the political and cultural processes of subjection and subjectivation. In other words, Foucault historicizes the notion of subject qua autonomous self-consciousness as both a condition and an outcome of the mechanisms of subjection.

While acknowledging the *equally* relevant status of economic processes, Foucault himself never developed a systematic analysis of the overdetermination of economic, political, and cultural processes in the making of "subjects out of individuals." Althusser, on the other hand, did articulate a way to conceptualize the relations between political subjection, economic exploitation, and cultural subjectivation. Instead of the concept of power that swallows up the political and the cultural, Althusser has chosen to distinguish between the politico-juridical processes of subjection, the economic processes of production, appropriation, distribution, and realization of surplus value, and the ideological processes of reproduction.

Even though Althusser uses the concept of ideology, he carefully distinguishes the concept from the theoretical humanist notion of *false consciousness.* False consciousness is a theoretical humanist concept because it presupposes the existence of a true consciousness. To argue that a representation is a *false* representation of the *reality* is to imply that there can be a *true* representation that will adequately "mirror" the reality. And the idea that there can be a true representation, true consciousness, presupposes the existence of a rational and self-transparent subject of theoretical humanism. For Althusser, ideology is neither *false* nor *consciousness*; there is nothing false or true about ideology. Rather, ideology "is a representation of the *imaginary* relationship of individuals to their *real conditions of existence*" (Althusser 1971: x; emphasis added). Let us try to unpack this highly sealed definition, treating each part separately.

First, "the real conditions of existence" of individuals refers to a structuralist notion of *relational* totality governed by a new understanding of causality. Althusser's name for this notion of causality was structural causality. This notion was carefully differentiated not only from the Cartesian notion of mechanical causality but also from the Hegelian notion of expressive causality (Althusser and Balibar 1970 [1965]; Cullenberg 1994). Structural causality implied that the causal chain is irreducible: the whole cannot be "microfounded" in its atomistic parts; the parts cannot be seen as expressions of a totalizing logic that governs the whole. Structural causality resides in between, in the very relationality of the parts. Yet, it is important to underscore that neither the parts nor the whole precedes the relational structure. Each part is always in a process of becoming, in a relation of mutual constitutivity with the totality of all the other parts. In fact, following North American political economists Stephen Resnick and Richard Wolff's (1987) interpretation of Althusser's conceptual innovations, it is probably better to speak about *processes* rather than parts. Resnick and Wolff define processes (natural, cultural, economic, and political) as the very basic building blocks of the relational structural totality. Pushing forward with Althusser's appropriation of the Freudian notion of *overdetermination* as yet another name for the irreducible concept of structural relational causality, Resnick and Wolff argue that each process is an overdetermined site of the contradictory push and pull of all the other social processes (Resnick and Wolff, 1987).[7]

This overdetermined totality could not be represented in discourse because the overdetermination implies that the totality is un-totalizable, that it cannot be made into a whole, a bounded and closed set.[8] Any attempt to represent it as a coherent whole is bound to fail, for the ceaseless becoming means that the overdetermined totality does not exist as a fixed and stable entity. In this sense, according to Althusser, individuals are bound to have an *imaginary* (read partial) relationship to the overdetermined totality, to their "real conditions of existence." And finally, an ideology is *one among many necessarily partial representations of the relationship of the individuals to the overdetermined totality*, because there are many different representations—none of which can be claimed to be truer than the rest, and every single one of which is necessarily partial. In this sense, Althusser distinguishes his notion of ideology from the theoretical humanist notion of *false* consciousness.

But Althusser also rejects the idea that ideology is another word for *consciousness*. On the contrary, for Althusser, ideology is "profoundly unconscious":

> Ideology is indeed a system of representations, but in majority of cases these representations have nothing to do with "consciousness": they are usually images and occasionally concepts, but it is above all as *structures* that they impose on the vast majority of men, not via their "consciousness."
>
> (Althusser 1969: 233)

Therefore, ideology is not a form of consciousness but a *structure*. Althusser uses the term *structure* in order to designate ideology as a relational element of the social totality. For Althusser, a social formation is a complexly overdetermined (structural) totality of regularized and concrete social practices.[9] In other words, ideology is not an "idea" but a system of representations that materialize in regularized and concrete social practices, which are, in turn, inscribed within the institutional materiality of what Althusser calls "ideological state apparatuses." As examples of the ideological state apparatuses (ISAs), Althusser refers to institutions such as the Family, the School, the Church, the Military, the Law, the Media, the Trade-Union, and so on.[10]

In short, for Althusser, the process of subjectivation, or the process of manufacturing of the particular subjectivities of individuals, i.e., the production of meanings and representations pertaining to who they are, what their attributes are, what their needs and desires are, and so on, occurs within the ISAs, and the individuals are simultaneously subjectivated and subjected by virtue of participating in the complex rituals and practices that are inscribed in particular ISAs. Subjection, as Judith Butler eloquently formulates it, "carries the *double meaning* of having submitted to these rules, and becoming constituted within the sociality [as subjects] by virtue of this submission" (1995: 14). According to Althusser, Butler reminds us, "subjection to the ruling ideology" is equivalent to "the *mastery* of its practice" (Althusser 1971: 133, cf. Butler 1995: 14), to becoming someone within the frame of reference of the ruling ideology (e.g., a good worker, an upstanding citizen, a good businessperson).

In this sense, both Foucault and Althusser argue that the process of subjectivation/subjection makes "subjects" out of individuals.[11] Althusser calls this process *interpellation*. He uses this term metaphorically to describe how the ISAs subjugate, subjectivate, and even make "subjects" out of, individuals by "calling" and "inviting" them to the practices within which particular ideologies materialize. In fact, a condition of existence of the process of subjectivation is that the individual conceives of herself, and is conceived by others, as a "subject." To put it differently, the interpellated individual, by responding to the interpellation, recognizes her/himself as an autonomous "subject," as the addressee of the "hailing" or the "invitation."

> The individual in question behaves in such and such a way, adopts such and such a practical attitude, and, what is more, participates in certain regular practices which are those of the ideological apparatuses on which "depend" *the ideas which he has in all consciousness freely chosen as a subject.*
>
> (Althusser 1971: 167)

Without doubt, Althusser, like Foucault, exploits the irony that inheres in the dual meaning of the term "subject." On the one hand, each time an individual is interpellated by a particular ISA (the Church, the School, etc.), her self-understanding as an autonomous subject is being reinstated. On the other hand, as discussed above, the participation of the "subject" in the ISAs simultaneously entails subjectivation and subjection. In this sense, the belief of the individual in her subjecthood, autonomy, and agency provides an important condition of existence for the reproduction of particular ideologies. In an essay on the role of ideology in the contemporary US social formation, Richard Wolff highlights the importance of this irony when he writes:

Individuals are shaped by ISAs to believe that their conformity to the needs of capitalist class structures is something quite different, a life path freely chosen by an independent and autonomous subject.

(Wolff 2005: 226)

As a Marxist philosopher, Althusser was particularly interested in the way in which particular ISAs secure (or fail to secure) the conditions of existence of class structures. For instance, while the family turns the children into docile subjects, the education system serves the purpose of preparing the young adults for the labor market. If these ISAs, by preparing the individuals to be docile and versatile workers, provide certain conditions of existence for the production and appropriation of surplus, others enable the realization of surplus:

Workers in the US had somehow to be interpellated systematically—in their families, schools, churches, civic and labor organizations, the mass media, and so on—as consumption oriented and driven. They had to be called to think of (identify) themselves and everyone else as free market participants striving to maximize the consumption they could achieve from work. They have to define themselves as above all "consumers" who willingly suffered "disutility" of labor to acquire the "utilities" embodied in consumption.

(Wolff 2005: 230)

Wolff's analysis of the reproduction of the ideology of "consumerism" in the US within and through ISAs highlights the importance of how subjectivation and subjection of individuals are predicated upon and perpetuated by their belief in their freedom and autonomy. In his analysis, Wolff highlights the role played by a particular economic discourse in the reproduction of the ideology of consumerism: "The neoclassical economics that so totally dominates academia, the media, and politics in the United States theoretically formalizes this interpellation" (2005: 230).

Indeed, Althusser's critique of the notion of the subject as an autonomous self-consciousness implicates theoretical humanism in all social sciences. According to Althusser, "the ideology of man as a subject whose *unity* is ensured or crowned by consciousness is not just any fragmentary ideology; it is quite simply *the philosophical form of bourgeois ideology*" (1996: 114). This ideology, according to Althusser, "still reigns over large sectors of idealist philosophy and constitutes the implicit philosophy of psychology, morality, and even political economy" (ibid.). For instance,

this ideology of the conscious subject constituted the implicit philosophy of classical political economy and [...] Marx was criticizing its "economic" version in rejecting any idea of "homo economicus," in which man is defined as the conscious subject of his needs and that subject of need is defined as the ultimate and constitutive element of every society. With that Marx rejected the idea that one could find in man as subject of his needs not only the ultimate explanation of society but also, and this is crucial, the explanation of man as subject, that is as a self-identical and self–identifiable unity, one identifiable in particular by that "self" par excellence which is self-consciousness.

(Althusser 1996: 115)

It is also possible to find parallel embodiments of "this philosophical category of the self-conscious subject" in the fields of sociology, psychology, law, and politics as well as "in *practical* formations such as morality and religion" (Althusser 1996: 116). These various "conscious subjects of" economics, politics, law, religion, and so on are "*unifiers of the social identity of the individual insofar as they are unified as so many exemplars of an ideology of 'man,'*" a being 'naturally endowed with consciousness,' to apprehend the profound unity of that ideology and its theoretical and practical formations" (Althusser 1996: 116). In other words, the conscious and unified subject of a theoretical field is a necessary correlate of the unity of that particular theoretical framework.

In the case of neoclassical as well as late neoclassical economics, the concept of *homo economicus* functions as the concept of conscious and unified subject that holds together the discipline of economics around the hegemonic reign of the neoclassical tradition. In turn, from a secular Marxian perspective that problematizes not only the production of surplus labor but also the reproduction of its conditions of existence, neoclassical economics, to the extent that it provides the theoretical foundations of a normative justification of exploitation, functions as an ideological state apparatus that contributes to the *reproduction* of the liberal democratic capitalism.

Nevertheless, given the central role that the concepts of overdetermination and aleatory contingency play in Althusser's thinking, it would be wrong to assume a functional relationship between the ISAs and the liberal democratic capitalism (or any other socio-economic order, for that matter). Wolff notes that "the social contradictions working on the ISAs provoke the formation of different and oppositional conceptions of subjectivity that complicate how the ISAs actually function" (2005: 226). In this sense, the concept of overdetermination removes any functionalist understanding of ideological interpellation. Every ideological state apparatus (the School, the Church, the Military, or even the neoclassical tradition within the discipline of economics) is a site of countless and contradictory influences, including those emanating from the counter-hegemonic ideologies that question and criticize not only the injustice of capitalist exploitation but also the "hegemonic ideology of 'free subjects' for ignoring/denying its social constitution and, in particular, for supporting capitalist exploitation" (Wolff 2005: 226).

To conclude, the secular critique of the category of the subject emphasizes how the concept of subject qua autonomous self-consciousness disavows the possibility of understanding the subject "as a site of countless and contradictory influences which plays its own overdetermining role on those very constituent influences."[12] However, no disavowal is innocent. In this case, it is not innocent because the decentered concept of the subject does not lend itself to a theoretical humanist morality that attributes positive normative value to the idea of reconciling the individual and the collective rationality. Theoretical humanist morality of reconciliation and order is premised upon the idea of the subject as an autonomous and rational self-consciousness. The autonomous and rational subject of theoretical humanism provides the normative microfoundations of a social order which will be *simultaneously* acceptable to each of its members as autonomous and distinct individuals. But, such a social order can only be justified if it is grounded in, and sanctified by, the authentic, rational, and welfare-increasing choices of the "individual" agents. In contrast, conceiving the subject as "a site of countless and contradictory influences" will make it difficult to argue that the subject is "the master of her own house," that the subject knows what would improve her welfare, that there can be a clear-cut and unique understanding of what his welfare is, that his preferences will reflect his "welfare," and that his choices will necessarily reflect his actual preferences.

It is important to emphasize the epistemological premises of the secular Marxian critique offered in this section. The critique does not criticize theoretical humanism for misrepresenting the truth of the subject. Rather, the critique offers an alternative to the theoretical humanist conception of the subject and criticizes the latter from the perspective of this alternative notion of the subject. This book is written from the latter perspective that decenters the subject, and as such, it is engaged in a partisan theoretical struggle with theoretical humanism in the discipline of economics.

2.3 The constitutive theoretical problematic of neoclassical humanism

In this section, I will briefly discuss the concept of the theoretical problematic in the context of neoclassical humanism. To begin with, within the neoclassical tradition, there are many ways to formulate the theoretical problematic of neoclassical humanism. In fact, the following chapters will offer a detailed study of the different ways in which the same theoretical problematic is formulated.

One of the most lucid and "economic" formulations of the theoretical problematic of neoclassical humanism can be found in Kenneth Arrow's *Social Choice and Individual Values* (1963). In this study, which single-handedly inaugurated social choice theory, Arrow makes a very pregnant analogy between voting and the market mechanism:

> In a capitalist democracy there are essentially two methods by which social choices can be made: voting, typically used to make "political" decisions, and the market mechanism, typically used to make "economic" decisions. [...] The methods of voting and the market are methods of amalgamating the tastes of many individuals in the making of social choices. [...] Can we find other methods of aggregating individual tastes which imply rational behavior on the part of the community? [...] In the following discussion ... the

distinction between voting and the market mechanism will be disregarded, both being regarded as special cases of the more general category of collective social choice.

(Arrow 1963: 1–5)

This is the sense in which I wish to understand the central theoretical problematic of neoclassical economics: the study of the conditions of existence of the reconciliation of the individual and the collective rationality. Or, to put it slightly differently, the neoclassical problematic is the study of the ways of achieving the social reconciliation (e.g., equilibrium) of the diverse demands of the rational and autonomous individuals.

Let me immediately note that within the neoclassical tradition, as will be demonstrated in the following chapters, no agreement exists on the exact meaning of individual rationality. Nor there is agreement as to what collective rationality entails and how the social reconciliation can be achieved.[13] In fact, what gives the neoclassical tradition its color, its vitality, its richness is precisely the absence of an agreement on the exact meaning of these terms. The heterogeneity of the neoclassical tradition results from the fact that there are important politico-normative, methodological, and conceptual differences among the various skeins of the neoclassical tradition. Nevertheless, despite these important differences, all these particular neoclassical approaches share the same theoretical problematic.

Let me also note that, even though it constitutes the horizon within which particular theoretical positions function, a theoretical problematic does not pre-exist the particular theoretical positions that inhabit its conceptual terrain. It is, rather, a retroactive effect of the theoretical interactions among the various theoretical positions that share a commitment to a common set of theoretical presuppositions. In other words, the theoretical problematic of neoclassical humanism is a by-product, an after-effect, that has only become possible to discern today, when the neoclassical tradition has matured into late neoclassical economics. As the neoclassical tradition splintered into multiple sub-approaches, as it branched out into applied fields, and as the themes explored and the research methodologies deployed became diversified, it became more and more clear that these approaches are united not around an object of analysis (e.g., the markets), or a core model (e.g., the A-D model), or even a research methodology (e.g., mathematical modeling), but around a theoretical problematic.

And, more importantly, the theoretical problematic itself is a site of hegemonic struggle between the various skeins of the neoclassical tradition. Even though the neoclassical tradition constitutes itself as a unified field, it does not do so around an explicit set of core attributes that every neoclassical economist agrees upon. In this sense, and perhaps ironically, the tradition does not establish its unity through reconciliation, harmony, or concordance. Rather, the unity of the neoclassical tradition emanates from the fact that the neoclassical problematic functions as a field of hegemonic struggle where the various skeins of tradition clash with each other in defining the meaning of individual rationality, equilibrium, collective rationality, and efficiency and in determining the "correct" way to achieve social reconciliation. It is important to appreciate the contradictory effects of the turbulence caused by this hegemonic struggle over determining the "correct" formulation of the neoclassical problematic. The tradition is simultaneously undermined and revitalized by this turbulent struggle for hegemony among its various skeins. For instance, when the struggle between the Walrasian left liberals and the pro-market Chicago neoclassicals led to the dissolution of the mid-century consensus, a space for alternatives that reject the basic presuppositions of the neoclassical humanism was opened. The foundation of institutions such as the Union of Radical Political Economics in the 1970s (harboring throughout its first two decades voices that explicitly criticized theoretical humanism from an anti-essentialist Marxian perspective) and the Association for Economic and Social Analysis in the 1980s, the revitalization of "old" Institutionalism on both sides of the Atlantic in the 1990s (finding its institutional home in the Association of Evolutionary Economics in the US and the European Association for Evolutionary Political Economy in Europe), and the institution of more recent international formations such as the Association of Heterodox Economics and the International Confederation of Associations for Pluralism in Economics all owe something to the weakening of the neoclassical tradition in the 1970s and 1980s. Yet, on the other hand, the hegemonic struggles among the various skeins of the neoclassical tradition, to the extent that they convey a richness and sense of openness and to the extent that they entail repetition and re-assertion of the same theoretical problematic through newer (imported) methodologies and concepts and in newer contexts, reinforce and reproduce the disciplinary prevalence of neoclassical humanism.

Notes

1 On *epistemes* and the discourses on value and exchange, see Foucault (1973[1966]) and Amariglio (1988). Here, the Age of Man refers not only to an emergent positivist epistemology that foregrounds human reason and senses (ranging from the Cartesian rationalism to the Humean empiricism) but also to an ontological vision that foregrounds Man (*laboring body* in Classical Political Economy and *desiring body* in Marginalist Economics). See also Ruccio and Amariglio (2003).

2 "Once we acknowledge that there is no necessary relation between these two aspects, we are in the position of being able to defend the political project while abandoning the notion that it must be based on a specific form of rationality... [T]he challenge to rationalism and humanism does not imply the rejection of modernity but only the crisis of a particular project within modernity, the Enlightenment project of self-foundation. Nor does it imply that we have to abandon its political project, which is the achievement of equality and freedom for all" (Mouffe 1992: 10).

3 Compare this with the original German version: "Sie wissen das nicht, aber sie tun es" (Marx and Engels 1968: 88). Slavoj Zizek translates the sentence as "they do not know it, but they are doing it" (1989: 28).

4 Even though the contractual law has to assume that the subject is autonomous, rational, and so on, these assumptions do not describe the ontology of the subject. The underlying assumptions pertaining to the subject are always open to debate and negotiation. In this sense, the legal debates on the socio-economic causes of crime, for instance, attest to the fact that the "autonomy" postulate is not an ontological attribute but a discursive and pragmatic device that everyday contracts deploy.

5 Many would contest treating Foucault as a part of the Marxian tradition. And Foucault himself has been vocal about his criticisms of the Marxian tradition (e.g., its theory of State, its conceptualization of capitalism, and the various concepts of power and subjectivity that circulate under the banner of Marxism). Nevertheless, Foucault, to the extent that his central theoretical problematic is structured around the antagonistic constitution of the social as well as the subject, along with other post-structuralist and psychoanalytical critics of capitalism, should be considered as a part of a broader theoretical and practical field that is, in part, shaped by the Marxian tradition.

6 It is important to distinguish the political processes of domination and subjection from the cultural processes of production and dissemination of meaning. While it would be wrong to line them up respectively with coercion and consent, it is important to acknowledge that elicitation of consent is only possible through cultural processes.

7 The concept of overdetermination has a complex genealogy. Freud (1965 [1900]) uses the notion in the context of the interpretation of dreams as the logics of condensation and displacement that characterizes the process of the formation of dreams. Althusser (1969) first used the concept in his essay "Contradiction and Overdetermination" to conceptualize the irreducible condensation of determinants at any given historical conjuncture that opens up to the possibility of revolutionary rupture. In Althusser's conjunctural use of the concept, overdetermination always comes with its corollary, underdetermination. If overdetermination brings forth the conjunctural possibility of revolution, underdetermination designates the failure of such a possibility. Ernesto Laclau and Chantal Mouffe mobilize the concept to describe "the symbolic character of social relations" and the absence of "an ultimate literality which would reduce [social relation] to necessary moments of an immanent law" (1985: 98). What is common to all these conceptualizations is the absence of a (causal) essence and the relational fabric of social relations.

8 French psychoanalyst Jacques Lacan (1998) calls this *pas tous*. A possible translation would be non-all, meaning as that which cannot be constituted as a whole.

9 Let us immediately note that each social practice itself is a site constituted by the endless push and pull of the totality of social processes (Resnick and Wolff 1987).

10 Equally important is the fact that the notion of ideology as a system of representations that materialize in regularized practices that are inscribed within particular ISAs has made it possible for Althusser to invert "the order of the notional schema of ideology," according to which the autonomous subject (*subjectum*) first decides to believe in an idea and then practices it. In contrast to this idealist/humanist notion of ideology that privileges ideas and consciousness and posits a "subject" that pre-dates the interpellation (an always already constituted subject who can voluntarily "choose" her particular subjectivity), Althusser argues that ideologies precede the individuals and are therefore, in a sense, imposed on individuals who participate in concrete practices; belief in a particular ideology, accordingly, comes only later as a performative after-effect of repetitive participation in ideological practices. Althusser is particularly fond of paraphrasing Christian theologician Pascal: "Kneel down, move your lips in prayer, and you will believe" (Althusser 1971: 168). In this context, it may be useful to think of the Freudian category of "rationalization," as the effort of the already subject(ivat)ed subject to come to terms with and to make sense of a traumatic cut. Belief, just like rationalization, always comes *après coup*. Or, to be more precise, first comes the trauma of being forced to pray ("I pray …"), then comes the belief ("I pray because I believe …"), and finally comes the rationalization ("I pray because I believe because …").

11 "[I]deology … 'recruits' subjects among the individuals, or 'transforms' the individuals into subjects by that very precise operation … called *interpellation* or hailing" (Althusser 1971: 174). Althusser explains the notion of interpellation by way of an imaginary scene that takes place in the street. When an everyday police officer hails "Hey, you there!" to an individual, *the moment* the hailed individual turns around,

because he has turned around, *because* by turning around "he has recognized that the hail was 'really' addressed to him, and that 'it was *really him* who was hailed' (and not someone else)," the individual finds himself in the position of a "subject," a distinct and autonomous unity (Althusser 1971: 174).

12 This sentence is a quotation from one of the exam questions that the late Steve Resnick asked in the midterm for his graduate seminar on Marxian political economy (Economics 709: Political Economy II, Spring 1995). The entire question goes as follows: "'The "human being," "human subject" or the "I" can be conceived as a site of countless and contradictory influences which plays its own overdetermining role on those very constituent influences.' Prepare an essay that explains what this statement means. What are its implications for approaches that tend to essentialise the role of the human subject in theories of society and of knowledge?" This book, as a study of the integral role that an essentialist notion of the human subject plays in the neoclassical tradition, is intended as a partial answer to this question.

13 On this last question, I am prepared to grant that the market mechanism is the privileged (but certainly not the only) method of achieving social reconciliation for the neoclassical tradition.

Part II

Neoclassical economics

Under the shadow of structuralism

To fully appreciate the complexity of the conditions of emergence of late neoclassical economics, it is necessary to return to the post-war North American context to take a closer look at two important theoretical developments that triggered tectonic changes in the shape of neoclassical tradition. The first one was the thorough formalization of the general competitive equilibrium model in the 1950s and 1960s by those mathematical economists associated with the Cowles Commission. This development has not only transformed the level of mathematics used in the discipline, as many have argued, but also, in an ironic manner, led to a deep crisis in the very mainstream of the tradition. The second was the articulation of the "selectionist arguments" whereby evolutionary metaphors were mobilized to make sense of the competitive process, again in the 1950s and 1960s, by the proponents of the Chicago tradition. This second development was itself a response to a series of theoretical challenges that can be traced back to the interwar years and was appreciated by the larger discipline only after the fact, in the 1980s and 1990s, as the late neoclassical condition began to take shape.

An important condition of existence of these two developments was the emergence of a tendency in the early 1930s to assume as little as possible about the preferences of the agents—a process that began with the ordinalist turn (the transition from cardinalism to ordinalism) and in particular with Samuelson's (1938) revealed preference approach, but took on a life of its own with Arrow's (1963) re-activation of the welfare economics in the language of mathematics. This minimalist impulse has propelled these neoclassical economists, albeit in different ways, increasingly away from grounding their theories in substantive notions of human subject and towards formulating models that attribute causal priority to structures—whether they resemble the linguistic (as in the case of the Walrasian model) or the biological (as in the case of Chicago selectionism) schema. In contrast to this structuralist drift in post-war neoclassical economics, the late neoclassical condition is characterized by an accentuated reversal of this tendency, with a significant amount of attention being devoted to the study of both the motivational and the cognitive aspects of human rationality (accompanied by an increasing number of assumptions being made about the human mind). Hence the restoration of theoretical humanism in late neoclassical economics.

To complicate matters, however, in the subsequent late neoclassical literature these two developments (i.e., the full development of axiomatic general equilibrium theory and the "selectionist arguments" of the Chicago approach) are read and interpreted in diametrically opposite ways. And this was despite the fact that both developments were saturated with influences from the various types of structuralism that characterize the disciplines from which these neoclassical economists were borrowing models, metaphors, and methodologies (mathematical and linguistic structuralism in the former case, and biological and evolutionary structuralism in the latter). While the theoretical developments in general equilibrium theory are usually treated as moments of "maturity," "culmination," or "breakdown" (Davis 2006: 14–17), the "selectionist arguments" articulated by the likes of Armen Alchian (1950), Milton Friedman (1953), and Gary Becker (1962) are construed as the constituents of an "originary" moment whereby the "foundations" of the new institutional economics, evolutionary economics, and evolutionary game theory are laid down (Vromen 1995; Bowles and Gintis 2000; Samuelson 2002).

What accounts for the discrepancy in the reception of these two developments in the late neoclassical literature? The neoclassical tradition is a series of reformulations, re-enactments, re-statements, and re-iterations of a constitutive theoretical problematic through different methodologies and modeling techniques, in different theoretical and empirical contexts, with different, and sometimes conflicting, policy implications. In other words, the different skeins of neoclassical economics and the different research programs or theoretical approaches of late neoclassical economics are nothing but so many different ways of formulating the same theoretical problematic. This is not to discount the important differences among various theoretical positions within the tradition: the way a theoretical problematic is formulated, how its constituents are specified, and what aspect of the problematic is accentuated have material consequences. And precisely in this sense, the discrepancy in the reception of these developments should be understood in the context of an ongoing and paradigmatic internal antagonism between the pro-intervention and the pro-market skeins of the neoclassical tradition (as embodied, roughly, in the general equilibrium approach of the Walrasian skein and the "market" approach of the Marshallian skein in its North American incarnation, respectively).

Read from this perspective, the perception of a "break" between neoclassical economics and late neoclassical economics itself becomes a symptom of a foundational *internal split* within the neoclassical tradition. A discourse (i.e., late neoclassical economics) that sees "the death of neoclassical economics" in the full development of axiomatic general equilibrium theory is also a neoclassical discourse—albeit one that does not recognize itself as such. Perhaps more frustratingly, this discourse fails to recognize itself as a part of the neoclassical tradition despite the fact that it finds its "foundation" in another neoclassical discourse, in the "selectionist arguments" of the Chicago School. Late neoclassical economists' claim to a break from neoclassicism, then, is premised on these two operations: the reduction of the neoclassical to the Walrasian model, on the one hand, and the reformulation and re-staging of the neoclassical problematic in purportedly non-neoclassical ways, on the other hand, even when these new trajectories had the imprimatur of none other than the Nobel Laureate neoclassical economists themselves.

In Part 2, these two developments will be discussed against the background of a widespread tendency within the neoclassical tradition to assume as little as possible about the human subject—motivated, in part, by the prevalent positivism of the tradition, and, in part, by a deeply normative sense of subjectivism. Chapter 3 will argue that the ordinalist turn in neoclassical tradition, while preparing the conditions that facilitate the incorporation of structuralist ideas into the mainstream, in the final analysis, failed to entail a break with theoretical humanism. Tracing the genealogy of the mid-century (1950s and 1960s) developments back to the "psychologism" controversy, the socialist calculation debate, and the marginalism controversy of the inter-war years, chapters 4 and 5 will demonstrate that both the Arrow–Debreu model and the selectionist arguments of the Marshallian Chicago School entailed, paradoxically, an eclipsing of the purported individuality and the supposed agency of consumers and producers. Nevertheless, in the final analysis, both developments, despite the clear presence of recognizable structuralist tropes, remain within the confines of the theoretical problematic of neoclassical humanism.

3 Neoclassical economics: shedding "psychologism"

Standard histories of neoclassical economics trace the origins of neoclassical economics to three key texts published in the nineteenth century as the loci of a theoretical break from late classical political economy: in Manchester, William Stanley Jevons' *Theory of Political Economy* (1871); in Wien, Carl Menger's *Principles of Economics* (1871), and in Lausanne, Léon Walras's *Elements of Pure Economics* (1874–1877).[1] There is indeed some grain of truth in this narrative of a "revolutionary break" occurring simultaneously across distinct geo-philosophical locations. These texts, each developing a variant of the idea of diminishing marginal utility, do indeed map onto "the utilitarian-empiricist tradition of British philosophy, the neo-Kantian philosophical climate of Austria, and the Cartesian philosophical climate of France," respectively (Blaug 1972: 269).

Yet this narrative also conceals a lot. The "revolution" trope conceals the gradual nature of the emergence of the neoclassical tradition out of the late classical political economy of the likes of John Stuart Mill, Nassau Senior in England, or Jean Baptist Say and Fréderic Bastiat in France. Similarly, the "simultaneity" trope also conceals a significant number of differences among these three traditions (British, Austrian, and French) that will be become much starker as the subsequent developments in each tradition further delineate their respective theoretical formations.[2] In particular, there are enough reasons to consider the Austrian tradition (especially after Menger) as a distinct school of thought with its own epistemological and methodological priorities. And if there is an important commonality, it is with respect to the role that late-nineteenth-century developments in physics had over both Walras and Pareto on the one hand, and Jevons and Edgeworth on the other (Mirowski 1984: 363–5). In that regard, let us note that Philip Mirowski argues that Menger should be separated from the rest because his theoretical orientation "effectively prevented the introduction of the physics analogy into economic theory" (1984: 372).[3]

Yet, even when the Viennese lineage is distinguished from the broader neoclassical tradition, there is still a significant fault line that separates the French and the British lineages. In fact, it is not possible to understand either the emergence or the heterogeneity of late neoclassical theory without taking into account this rather deep-running fault line that separates the French Walrasian and the

British Marshallian wings (and their North American counterparts, the so-called "saltwater" economists affiliated with the Cowles Commission and belong to the Samuelsonian MIT tradition, on the one hand, and the so-called "freshwater" economists of the University of Chicago tradition, on the other, respectively) of neoclassicism. This chapter will function as an archaeological excavation into the origins of the neoclassical tradition by way of introducing its Walrasian and Marshallian skeins. Rather than highlighting the marginal revolution as an important moment in the history of neoclassical tradition, the chapter will focus on the ordinalist turn, as this is precisely when the theoretical conditions that led to the aforementioned structuralist drift in the post-war years were set in motion. Under the influence of various forms of positivism, and in reaction to the accusations of psychologism, neoclassical economists of the inter-war years strongly desired to purge their theoretical models of "unobservable" assumptions regarding the human psyche that rely on the "pre-scientific" notions of the eighteenth-century utilitarian psychology. The notion of cardinal utility was one such category, and the ordinalist turn was precisely this theoretical gesture of purging economic models of consumer choice of such assumptions regarding the human psyche. This particular moment of theoretical break in the neoclassical tradition is important not only because it enables us to understand the subsequent "structuralist drift" in the post-war years, but also because the different variants of this ordinalist turn enable us to make sense of the theoretical diversity that characterizes the late neoclassical condition (which will itself be theorized in the subsequent chapters, in part, as a response to this "structuralist drift").

The chapter, while it will begin from the European context, will quickly proceed to the North American context to discuss the various variants of the ordinalist turn, including the Samuelsonian revealed-preference approach, the Arrovian preference orderings, and the pragmatism of the Chicago School. Here, the intention will be to prepare the reader to appreciate not only the troubling implications of the full axiomatization of the general equilibrium theory for the normative project of neoclassical humanism, but also the discrepancy between the subsequent receptions of the Arrow–Debreu model and the "selectionist arguments" of the Chicago School.

3.1 Early neoclassicism: Walrasian and Marshallian

The theoretical problematic of neoclassical humanism is one of reconciling the autonomously and rationally defined demands of the centered economic agents at a societal level. This shared problematic, as most neoclassical economists would argue, could be traced back to Adam Smith's *invisible hand theorem*.[4] While it is certainly true that neoclassical economists tend to attribute the status of an entry point to the invisible hand theorem, there is no agreement even among neoclassical economists as how to formulate the theorem.

Even though it is usually argued that Adam Smith's theorem received one of its earliest mathematical formulations at the end of the nineteenth century, in the writings of Léon Walras (1954; first published between 1874 and 1877) and Vilfredo Pareto (1971 [1906]), Bruna Ingrao and Giorgio Israel (1990) argue that it would be wrong to reduce the Walrasian general equilibrium model to a formalization of Adam Smith's invisible hand theorem. They identify, along with Smith and his notion of the *invisible hand*, Montesquieu and his notion of "equilibrium of social forces," Quesnay and his *Tableau économique*, and Condorcet and his *mathematique social* as the antecedents of general equilibrium theory. Therefore, even though Adam Smith and the naturalism of the Scottish Enlightenment were indeed an acknowledged influence, it is more appropriate to consider the Lausanne tradition as a product of the French rationalism, the Cartesian philosophy of science, and a constructivist worldview that considers society as an object of "engineering."

In Walras, we find the formulation of the *possibility* of an equilibrium price vector that will clear simultaneously all the markets in a market economy and the concept of *rareté*—a subjective measure of the last need satisfied (Ingrao and Israel 1990: 92). On the other hand, the concept of efficiency that corresponds to the general equilibrium, even though it gained general currency only in the post-war era after the ordinalist turn, is attributed to Pareto (Screpanti and Zamagni 1993: 206–7; Backhouse 2002: 279). A *Pareto efficient* allocation of resources refers to the state of a full-employment economy in which there is no way in which to reallocate the resources to make one person better off without making someone else worse off. These two concerns (the existence and the efficiency of equilibrium) would find their precise mathematical formulations elsewhere in North America, after WWII, in a series of papers and monographs written by the likes of Kenneth Arrow, Gérard Debreu, Frank Hahn, and Lionel W. McKenzie. In these high modernist mathematical studies, not only was the existence of an equilibrium price vector mathematically proven, but also the efficiency (in the sense of Pareto optimality) of such an equilibrium was established.[5]

Any genealogy of neoclassical economics, however, would be far from complete if the utilitarian lineage that stretches from Jeremy Bentham to William Stanley Jevons and then to Alfred Marshall were not also traced. Bentham's hedonistic calculus of pain and pleasure did not only rely on an introspective, subjective, and substantive theory of human action but also offered a cardinal index, a common denominator to compare and to add and subtract the magnitudes of different individuals. Indeed, the main concern of utilitarianism was to maximize the total utility of the community (Sen 2002: 70). In Jevons (1970 [1871]), we find an early formulation of the utility calculus (which predates Walras's notion of *rareté*); in Francis Ysidro Edgeworth (1932 [1881]), we find the concept of the indifference curve; in Marshall (1920 [1890]), we find a textbook version of the utility-based theory of demand and a discussion of elasticity. Since it was Marshall who consolidated this tradition and gave shape to its overall philosophical and methodological outlook, it is usually referred to as the Marshallian tradition (De Vroey 1999). In the 1930s and 1940s, as the center of gravity of the discipline began to shift from Europe to North America, the tradition would establish its headquarters at the Economics Department of the University of Chicago (Emmett 1997).

Even though the invisible hand narrative does not hold an important place in Marshall's formalization of the utility theory of demand and the real-cost theory of supply, the neoclassical problematic still dominates his concerns. The distinguishing characteristics of Marshallian economics are its partiality to the analysis of individual markets or industries (as opposed to general equilibrium analysis), its use of representative agents (as opposed to the idealized agents that populate the general equilibrium analysis), and its incorporation of temporality into the analysis of market equilibrium (as opposed to the synchronic non-temporality of the general equilibrium model).[6] A useful, albeit brutally simplistic, way of distinguishing the two traditions could be the following: in the Walrasian system, a *general* equilibrium is reached through a process of *price* adjustment whereby the adjustments are made in the price vector so that all excess demand functions equal zero; in the Marshallian understanding, a partial equilibrium is reached through a process of *quantity* adjustment whereby those who cannot survive in the equilibrium price leave the market. But despite these very important differences, Marshall's (and Jevons') policy prescriptions were guided by "the utilitarian principle [which defines] the ultimate goal of economic activity [as] the maximization of collective welfare" (Screpanti and Zamagni 1993: 182). In this sense, the Walrasian and the Marshallian traditions are different from, and opposed to, each other only in how they define and formulate the same neoclassical problematic. As I have argued in the last section of Chapter 2, this is a struggle internal to the neoclassical tradition. In fact, the neoclassical tradition is not only undermined by but also, to certain extent, thrives on such struggles over how to define and formulate its constitutive problematic.

Therefore, there are not one but (at least) two neoclassicisms: Walrasian and Marshallian. In fact, this internal division, which marks the tradition at its very origins, makes it possible to discern the contours of the theoretical humanist problematic around which the subsequent trajectory of the tradition is structured to this day. Early neoclassicisms were premised upon a similar concept of a centered and unified human subject who knows what she wants, whose wants improve her well-being, and whose choices reflect what she wants. Without doubt, for early neoclassicals, the concept of utility was not only an introspective, psychological "substance" upon which one could construct the theory of demand and consumption, but also a universal "measure" of happiness and well-being (Lewin 1996).[7] Accordingly, given the central role that the concept of (general or partial) equilibrium plays in these neoclassical analyses, the normative objective of all early neoclassicals, not unlike subsequent neoclassicals, was to maximize the social welfare (in utilitarian terms, in the case of the British tradition) through the reconciliation of the diverse wants and needs of autonomous and rational individuals.[8] Let us conclude by noting that the tradition was internally differentiated and structured around a theoretical problematic (and not around a single core model or theory and a universally agreed-upon set of concepts) even at the very moment of its inception.

3.2 The ordinalist turn in neoclassical economics

In the 1930s, with the advent of logical positivism and operationalism within the neoclassical camp (Blaug 1980: 99–103; Hausman 1992: 283–5) and the mounting criticisms from the "old" (or American) institutionalist camp (Rutherford 1994: 55–67), many neoclassical economists began to more rigorously question the "psychologism" that undergirds the Marshallian theory of the demand (Lewin 1996).[9] The renowned British economist Lionel Robbins was one of the first neoclassical economists to publicly criticize the notion of utility as a universal measure of well-being: "Every mind is inscrutable to every other mind and no common denominator of feelings is possible" (1932: 636). In two years' time, John Hicks and R. D. G. Allen (1934) would publish their version of the theory of demand, in which the preferences of the individual subject are represented through the indifference curves.[10] Based on the pair-wise ordering of commodity bundles (i.e., preference orderings), and thereby evading the cardinal comparison of marginal utilities, the concept of indifference maps eliminated the need for interpersonal comparisons of well-being (Arrow 1963). Moreover, with this ordinalist turn, *the utility function* lost its role as the universal index of well-being and traded its foundational place as the subjective foundation of the theory of demand with *the pair-wise preference orderings*. In this new architecture of choice, the concept of utility began to serve a secondary, supporting role to the preference orderings. The utility values are now assigned to different commodity bundles only in order to represent their rankings, but not the magnitude of "well-being" on the intensity of preference. And of course, the concept of efficiency that corresponds to the ordinalist architecture of choice could not be the utilitarian concept of efficiency whereby the idea was to maximize the total utility of the community by adding the utilities and disutilities of each and every member of the community. The concept of Pareto optimality, describing the state of the economy where no one can be better off without making someone worse off, would soon become the favored concept of efficiency of the neoclassical tradition after the ordinalist turn.[11]

In the North American context, there were at least two versions of the ordinalist turn: whereas Paul Samuelson's "revealed preference" approach for developing "the theory of consumer's behaviour freed from any vestigial traces of the utility concept" (1938: 71) was the empiricist version, the Arrovian social choice theory and the theory of consumer choice that underpins the Arrow–Debreu vintage general equilibrium models was the rationalist version. This is, of course, not to claim that the two approaches were mutually exclusive—in fact, even today, a quick look at the recent economic literature would reveal that the established practice, true to the spirit of a positivism that harmonizes empiricism and rationalism, is to assume that the ordinal utility functions based on the axioms of rationality can themselves be derived from the actual choices of the economic agents. Along with these two versions of the ordinalist turn, as a third variant, the pragmatist approach to the theory of demand as entertained by the proponents of the Chicago School will be discussed. The Chicago response to the psychologism controversy differs from the other two responses by its explicit rejection of the foundationalism of Samuelsonian operationalism and Arrovian formalism.

3.3 The empiricism of the revealed-preference approach

According to Samuelson, the foundational concept of the neoclassical theory of consumption (and therefore, the theory of demand) cannot be either the cardinal notion of utility or the ordinal preference orderings unless they are "revealed" and empirically observed by economists. Samuelson's "operationalist" program demanded that the scientificity of an economic theory (or any theory) should be assessed on the basis of its intersubjectively observable, empirical consequences. Empirically invalid or untestable portions of a given theory should be discarded.[12] For Samuelson, preference orderings, given their introspective nature, were empirically unobservable, and therefore, they were neither "operationally" useful nor methodologically sound (Hausman 1992: 19). Instead, he argued, the primitive concept of the theory of demand should be nothing but the empirically observable "choices" (i.e., the actual behavior) of the consumer.[13] If an individual chooses the commodity bundle x over another bundle y (when she has sufficient resources to buy either), she has directly revealed a preference for x over y. In particular, according to the Weak Axiom of Revealed Preference (WARP), if the subject *directly* reveals a preference for x over y, she must not reveal a preference for y over x.[14] The pair-wise choices of this subject will be *consistent* and *transitive* as long as they satisfy the WARP (Sen 1973: 244–47). Nevertheless, subsequent research demonstrated that the WARP was not sufficient to construct all the standard assumptions regarding consumer preferences (Katzner 2006: 99).

It is, however, important to distinguish between two distinct interpretations of the revealed-preference approach. Whereas one interpretation claims that the choices *reveal* the underlying preferences, a second interpretation claims that the actual choices make dispensable any reference to the underlying preferences (see for instance, Little 1949). The second interpretation, to the extent that it dispenses with "motives," claims to be thriftier with regard to the assumptions it makes regarding consumer behavior, and therefore should be considered to be "scientifically more respectable" (Little 1949: 97). As long as the conditions of consistency were obtained, it was argued, it would be possible to derive demand functions from the actual choices of the consumers without a need to peep into their underlying preferences.

In contrast, when Nobel Laureate Indian economist and philosopher Amartya Sen argues that "[the] rationale of the revealed-preference approach lies in the assumption of revelation and not doing away with the notion of underlying preferences" (Sen 1973: 244), he endorses the first interpretation. In fact, Sen argues, the second interpretation is logically untenable, as the WARP has to presuppose the existence of underlying preferences for the consistency of the ranking:

> Preferring x to y is inconsistent with preferring y to x, but if it is asserted that choice has nothing to do with preference, then choosing x rather than y in one

case and y rather than x in another need not necessarily be at all inconsistent. What makes them look inconsistent is precisely the peep into the head of the consumer, the avoidance of which is alleged to be the aim of the revealed preference approach.

(Sen 1973: 243)

In other words, the choices can be consistent only with respect to an underlying preference ordering. For if one does not refer to an underlying preference ordering (a relation that satisfies the axioms of connectedness, reflexivity, and transitivity), there is no reason to assume that the choices are "inconsistent"—for the supposed inconsistency can easily be explained away by referring to an infinite number of other factors (e.g., change of opinion, commitments; see also Sen 1993).

Yet the choices made by individuals depend not only on preferences, as Sen so eloquently argues, but also on beliefs. American philosopher of science Daniel Hausman (2000: 102), targeting the "extreme empiricism" of the revealed-preference approach, argues that, unless we assume that choices are made "in contexts in which unproblematic a priori information about beliefs is available," it is impossible not to refer to the "'unobservable' subjective states" including, for instance, subjective probability distributions. Both Sen and Hausman argue that the empiricist variant of the ordinalist turn, despite its operationalist aspirations, could not evade making psychological assumptions about the human mind. Even though Sen and Hausman articulated their critiques against the "extreme" empiricism of the revealed-preference approach, their arguments implicate the concept of preference ordering as well. As we will see in the next section, as long as the concept of preference ordering is used to theorize the human subject within the theoretical problematic of neoclassical humanism, it will inevitably be charged by a normative content that refers to the "'unobservable' subjective states." Let us now turn our attention to the concept of preference ordering.

3.4 The rationalism of preference orderings

The rationalist variant of the ordinalist turn was articulated by the economists associated with the Cowles Commission, which is perhaps best known for providing the requisite institutional and financial support for the inauguration of the social choice theory (Arrow 1963) as well as the axiomatization of the Walrasian general equilibrium models (Arrow and Debreu 1954; Debreu 1959).[15] Rather than beginning from the "observable choices" of the economic agents, in a truly rationalist spirit, the approaches of social choice theory and the general equilibrium theory take an axiomatic definition of rationality as their point of departure and embark upon establishing the conditions under which individual and collective rationalities can be reconciled. Let us consider both strands in more detail.

Both strands entertain a claim to have a generalized scope. In fact, social choice theory does not limit its domain of study to markets; it considers the market mechanism as one of the many methods of aggregating individual preference orderings.

In this sense, social choice theory defines its domain very abstractly and broadly as the study of the formal aspects of the construction of social welfare functions by aggregating individual preference orderings. In doing so, social choice theory redefines and expands the scope of applicability of the neoclassical problematic: is it possible to reach a social preference ordering (which satisfies the consistency criterion of transitivity) that aggregates the individual preference orderings in a manner that satisfies a "reasonable" number of the assumptions regarding the aggregation procedure? This reasonable set of assumptions comprises universality (unrestricted domain), Pareto inclusiveness (positive association of social and individual values), independence of irrelevant alternatives, citizen sovereignty (non-imposition), and non-dictatorship.

> The condition of *unrestricted domain* states that the aggregation procedure should be able to accommodate all logically possible orderings by individuals.
>
> The condition of *Pareto inclusiveness* states that if all individuals prefer x over y, then society should also prefer x over y.
>
> The condition of *independence of irrelevant alternatives* states that the social preference between two alternatives should depend solely on how individuals rank these two alternatives.
>
> The condition of *citizens' sovereignty* states that social welfare functions are responsive to individual preferences.
>
> The condition of *non-dictatorship* states that the social ordering should not coincide with the ordering of a single individual regardless of what others may think.[16]

Arrow's impossibility theorem states that there is no aggregation procedure that can simultaneously satisfy the five conditions listed above *and* produce a social preference ordering that is complete and transitive.[17]

To be able to understand the significance of Arrow's impossibility theorem in terms of the trajectory of theoretical humanism in neoclassical economics, it is necessary to understand not only the implications of the "reasonable" assumptions regarding the aggregation procedure, but also the concept of the human subject that informs this reformulation of the problematic. To begin with, Arrow took the individual preference ordering to be inviolate. In particular, the condition of unrestricted domain, as it permits all possible preference orderings, is an indicator of the importance of the autonomy of the agent for the social choice theory.

Second, Arrow, echoing the general ordinalist concern with falling into "psychologism," was not very keen on making assumptions regarding the motivations that underpin the preferences of the agent:

> It is assumed that each individual in the community has a definite ordering of all conceivable social states, in terms of their *desirability* to him. It is not assumed here that an individual's attitude toward different social states is determined exclusively by the commodity bundles which accrue to his lot

under each. It is simply assumed that the individual orders all social states by whatever standards he deems relevant.

(Arrow 1963: 17; emphasis added)

To put it differently, the concept of preference that underpins social choice theory is intended to be indifferent to the motivational basis of the agents. All that is required of the preferences are that they are connected, reflexive, and transitive, that is, that they constitute an "ordering" (Arrow 1963: 12–17). Needless to say, this does not mean that Arrow achieved what Samuelson intended. On the contrary, Sen's dissection of the revealed-preference approach discussed above applies to the Arrovian concept of preference orderings as well. Any concept of rational choice, even if it is defined solely in terms of the internal consistency of choice, cannot escape referring to some underlying preferences:

> [T]he very idea of *purely internal* consistency is not cogent, since what we regard as consistent in a set of observed choices must depend on the *interpretation* of those choices and on some features *external* to choice as such (e.g., the nature of our preferences, aims, values, motivations).
>
> (Sen 1987: 14)

And finally, the condition of independence of irrelevant alternatives rules out any form of cardinalization of preference orderings. For instance, if a society chooses *x* over *y* when the choice set include only *x* and *y*, then that society should also choose *x* over *y* when the choice set includes other alternatives. If the presence of other alternatives changes the final choice, then this could be thought to mean that the outcome is dependent on the relative intensity of preferences, and hence we introduce *a form of cardinalization*. For instance, the Borda count, because it is a method of aggregation that assigns weights to individual orderings, violates the independence of irrelevant alternatives.

Referring to Arrow's aversion to assigning intensity to the individual preference orderings and his deliberate broadening of the motivational basis of the preference orderings, North American economist John B. Davis (2003) argues that the conceptual apparatus of social choice theory does not need to specify the "mental" composition of the human subject, or even refer to a human subject. According to Davis (2003: 92),

> Arrow put a new slant on the old ordinalist conception of a preference. Mathematically speaking, a preference is simply a formal relation between an agent and the objects to which the agent's preference applies. However, in excluding information about preference intensity, this formal conception of a preference also eliminates the need for saying anything about the individual actually *experiencing* having a preference. Indeed, this conception of preference makes no necessary reference to the idea of preferences being part of a "mental" apparatus, this allowing "mental" processes to be modeled as computational processes. Thus, whereas in earlier ordinalism preferences

always belonged to individuals, with Arrow's formal conception preferences in principle can be implemented in any sort of hardware.

If we translate this to the concepts used in this book, Davis is claiming that the theoretical humanist notion of the human subject is not a necessary component of the concept of preference. In other words, Davis reads Arrow's reconceptualization of the notion of preference as an important moment in the transformation of economics into a post-human, cyborg science throughout the second half of the twentieth century (see also Mirowski 2002). Yet this is a highly contestable proposition, as the exclusion of "preference intensity" in itself is not sufficient for the concept of preference to be liberated from any reference to mental apparatus. Following Sen's line of reasoning developed earlier, to be able to count "internal consistency of choice" as a form of rationality, one has to refer to some underlying notion of "aims, values, motivations, etc." to impart some sense to consistency. Otherwise, we would have to consider an agent that "does exactly the opposite of what would help achieving what [it] would want to achieve" (1987: 13) to be a rational agent. Whether such sense-imparting directionality is entertained by an actual human being or programmed into a computational process does not matter; in either case, because it refers to an underlying notion of human intentionality, it remains within the problematic of theoretical humanism. Nevertheless, the question of whether this ordinalist-formalist turn in preference theory turns the neoclassical tradition into a post-human science is a persistent one, and will be further explored in Chapter 8, in the late neoclassical context.

This resistance towards "cardinalization" of orderings may, in part, be explained by referring, as Arrow does, to the conceptual difficulties involved in the measurement, comparison, and aggregation of utilities—the age-old empiricist critiques of the concept of utility applied to this context. Nevertheless, a historically relevant condition of existence of the Arrovian ordinalism may be found in Arrow's aversion to "non-democratic" central-planning models of socialism.[18] When combined with Arrow's well-known market-skeptic leanings, it is possible to see the contours of a modernist vision of market socialism. The project of aggregating individual preferences without reverting to "dictatorship" or "customs" is informed neither by a conservative impulse to legitimize capitalist liberal democracies nor by a "socialist" impulse to legitimize central planning, but by a modernist impulse to design social and economic institutions that can facilitate the rational governance of the society. In other words, Arrovian social choice theory reveals a theoretical humanist impulse to study formally the conditions under which autonomously and rationally defined preferences of individual actors can be rationally reconciled at the aggregate level of the social.

What is the significance of Arrow's impossibility theorem, then? Perhaps the significance of the theorem is not so much in its conclusions and implications, but rather, in the debate that it has generated. In the years that followed the publication of Arrow's *Social Choice and Individual Values,* a substantial literature that wrestles with the various aspects of Arrow's impossibility theorem has emerged. Sen, whose *Collective Choice and Social Welfare* (1970) provides an excellent companion to Arrow's text, argues that it is quite easy to circumvent the impossibility theorem by changing any single one of the assumptions regarding the aggregation process. For instance, Sen considers relaxing the independence of irrelevant alternatives assumption in order to be able to use an aggregation procedure that would assign intensities to individual preference orderings (e.g., the Borda count). Indeed, Sen argues that Arrow's impossibility theorem and the other "possibility theorems" should be "viewed not as arguments for nihilism, but as positive contributions aimed at clarifying the role of principles in collective choice systems" (1970: 199). In other words, Arrow's impossibility theorem functioned as a "Hitchcockian McGuffin," a plot device that does not mean much in itself but gets the story rolling (Zizek 1991: 26). It is not the actual theorem articulated therein, but its particular reformulation of the neoclassical problematic in terms of symbolic logic, that made Arrow's *Social Choice and Individual Values* a milestone text.

Moreover, the purported indifference of the Arrovian concept of preference ordering to the motivations of the individuals is much more explicitly compromised when the concept is used in the context of the general equilibrium theory. In the Arrow–Debreu models, the preferences of the agents are defined over consumption plans. Given all the relevant information about the commodities, consumers would choose the consumption plan that would best satisfy their preferences. Building up the architecture of the theory of demand on the ordinal utility theory, a significant attribute of these models, at least for the purposes at hand, was the persistent necessity to refer back to the subjective and introspective realm of the human psyche in order to motivate the normatively charged efficiency claims about the general equilibrium outcomes. The *preferences* of the economic agents were not only taken as the rock bottom of the theory of demand, but also assumed to be reflecting the *welfare* of the subject. This also, of course, requires a "peek into the head" of the individual and a reference to the subjective and introspective realm of the human psyche. To put it differently, in the context of general equilibrium theory, the concept of preferences is associated with a particular motivation: preference orderings that reflect the well-being of the individual constitute the normative microfoundations for the welfare properties of the equilibrium outcomes.[19]

In conclusion, the ordinalist turn in the neoclassical tradition does not entail an abandonment of theoretical humanism. On the contrary, the centered, autonomous, and rational concept of the human subject continued to underpin the normative implications of both social choice and general equilibrium theory. Even though it is impossible to compare the states of well-being of each individual with one another (hence the ordinalism), the individual is still assumed to know what her/his preferences are and to be able to articulate these preferences in his/her choice. In general equilibrium theory, in contrast to Arrovian social choice theory, it is additionally assumed that the preferences of the individual reflect her/his well-being. In the case of social choice theory, while no assumptions need be made regarding the motivations informing the preferences, a sense of directionality and intentionality must be presumed for the preferences to be deemed rational in some meaningful sense. Moreover, this indifference of the concept towards motivations could also be read as a sign of a deep-seated respect for the presumed individuality and singularity of human subjects. By remaining indifferent towards the motivations informing the preferences of an individual, Arrovian social choice theory articulates its own take on the neoclassical problematic, which is no less humanist for that.

3.5 The pragmatism of the Chicago school

For the proponents of the Chicago approach, such as Frank Knight, George Stigler, Milton Friedman, and Gary Becker, neither the Samuelsonian revealed-preference approach nor the Cowlesian formalism was necessary. Rejecting both variants of foundationalism, the proponents of the Chicago School distinguished themselves by their peculiar sort of pragmatism (McCloskey 1988: 288). In his famous methodological essay, for instance, Friedman argued that it does not make sense to ask whether the assumptions of a theory "are descriptively 'realistic,' for they never are" (1953: 15). Instead, he argued, we should judge a theory by the accuracy of its predictions: "Its performance is to be judged by the precision, scope, and conformity with experience of the predictions it yields" (Friedman, 1953: 4).

In order to be able to see the implications of this positivist/pragmatist methodological approach to the neoclassical theory of price, it is sufficient to recall that for the proponents of the Chicago School, there is no reason to go behind the demand curve. Indeed, the downward-sloping demand curve is the last instance of the Chicago version of the neoclassical theory of price. For instance, in his 1949 discussion of the Marshallian demand curve, Friedman (1953: 47–99) does not refer to the preference orderings of the individual. Whenever he invokes the assumption of utility maximization subject to budget constraint, he does not bother either to reveal it retroactively from the choices or to reconstruct it axiomatically. The disregard of the proponents of the Chicago School towards the microfoundational concerns of other neoclassical economists went so deep that, only a decade later, another Nobel Laureate Chicago economist, Becker (1962), argued that in order to derive the downward-sloping aggregate demand curve for a commodity, no assumptions regarding their rationality need be made as long as the budget constraint limited the opportunity set of the individual subjects. And if the Chicago economists continue to rely on the optimization assumption, they would argue that they do so only because of its convenience.

Given its pragmatist methodology, it is usually suggested that, for the Chicago School, the utility concept is simply a useful, expository device, a "convenient fiction" (Mirowski 2002: 204). Nevertheless, to claim that the concept of utility is dispensable for the proponents of the Chicago School would entail neglecting the importance of the notion of utility (or wealth) maximization for the derivation of the welfare implications of the market outcomes. The normative authority derived from the welfare properties of the market outcomes underpins their commitment to markets. As suggested above, the Chicago School is committed to the idea that markets always produce *efficient* outcomes. But more specifically, the markets can maximize "social" welfare only to the extent that they enable individual subjects to maximize their own welfare. As such, to be able to derive their welfare conclusions and policy recommendations, they must rely on a notion of preferences that reflects a subjective and introspective notion of individual welfare. The fact that the proponents of the Chicago School do not explicitly acknowledge this link is beside the point. The concepts of utility and the underlying and implicit assumptions regarding human psychology remain indispensable for the Chicago-style neoclassicism.[20]

3.6 Conclusion

Let us recapitulate the discussion so far. Up to the 1930s, there were two basic formulations of the neoclassical problematic. On the one hand, there was the general equilibrium tradition, which originated at Lausanne and was marked by the rationalist Cartesian philosophy of science. On the other hand, there was the tradition of the utility calculus, which originated in Britain, constituted by a Humean empiricism and a Benthamite utilitarianism, and was consolidated in Marshall's theory of demand and supply. Their differences notwithstanding, in both traditions we find a variant of the marginalist analysis of equilibrium states. In the Walrasian tradition, there is the concept of *rareté* and the idea of general competitive equilibrium. In the Marshallian tradition, there is the concept of utility and the idea of market equilibrium.

As the neoclassical tradition began to assert its disciplinary hegemony, especially through Marshall, Edgeworth, and Pigou's efforts, the other traditions within the discipline of economics began to question its assumptions. In particular, American institutional economists such as Thorstein Veblen, W. S. Mitchell, and J. R. Commons began to criticize the "psychologism" of the neoclassical concept of utility (Rutherford 1994: 52–66). These and other controversies (e.g., the marginalism controversy, which will be further discussed in Chapter 5), combined with the positivist aspirations of neoclassical economists, have led neoclassical economists to try to minimize (and at the limit, eliminate) the assumptions that they make—implicitly or explicitly—regarding the mental capacities and the psychological attributes of the human subjects. The first move in this direction was to substitute the ordinal indifference maps for cardinal utility function. In Samuelson's hands, the ordinalist turn took an operationalist twist, aiming to discard the empirically invalid or untestable portions. Arrow, on the other hand, rendered the concept of preference orderings indifferent to the motivational basis of the agents. And finally, the Chicago approach attempted to by-pass the entire question of "psychologism" by arguing that it is not necessary to make realistic assumptions—or, in the case of Becker's 1962 article, any assumptions—regarding the "mental" states of the economic agents to derive the downward-sloping Marshallian demand curve.

Nevertheless, despite these various attempts at purging the embarrassing references to some substantive theory of the human psyche, the neoclassical tradition continued to betray a persistent need to peek into the mind of the human subject. What, then, accounts for this unwelcome persistence of "psychologism"? I believe that the answer, in part, can be found in the neoclassical problematic that informs all these efforts. As long as their constitutive theoretical problematic remains the aggregate reconciliation (e.g., equilibrium) of the autonomously and rationally defined demands of individual agents, these scholars will inevitably refer to "unobservable subjective states," because, unless the welfare attributes of these states of (partial or general) equilibrium are grounded in the rational choices of autonomous agents that reflect their welfare, it is impossible to establish the desirability of such equilibrium states of reconciliation. If the desirability of equilibrium cannot be established, the neoclassical project will lose its normative power.

The next two, relatively brief, chapters will build upon the historical context provided by the preceding discussion of the "psychologism" controversy and the subsequent ordinalist turn in neoclassical economics. By the immediate aftermath of WWII, in the early years of the Cold War, neoclassical economics was already split into two distinct skeins (Mirowski and Hands 1998; Mirowski 2002; De Vroey 2003). On the one hand, there was the Walrasian tradition, mainly consisting of socialist-leaning émigré economists who viewed society as an object of social engineering and represented the economy as an interdependent system of general competitive equilibrium. Among the institutional supports for the Walrasian tradition was the Cowles Commission (Mirowski 2002). Given the left-leaning profile of Walrasian economists, it should not come as a surprise that the most significant policy conclusion of this skein was that "markets are never enough." Precisely for this reason, Arrow and others found it necessary to develop social choice theory as a *general* theory of *all* forms of preference aggregation—market mechanism being only one of them. On the other hand, there was the Marshallian tradition, as embodied in the Chicago approach. The Chicago Marshallianism, in contrast, cultivated an unflinching belief in the motto that "there are never enough markets," focused on partial equilibrium analysis, formulated models with representative agents, and established itself as a tradition that survives even in the late neoclassical context. The next two chapters will discuss how the formalization of general equilibrium theory at the Cowles Commission and the articulation of the "selectionist arguments" by the proponents of the Chicago School have led to unexpected eruptions of "structuralist moments" in neoclassical economics.

Notes

1 It is possible to add John Bates Clark in the US as an important formalizer of marginal utility theory with further extensions towards a theory of marginal product.
2 "Was there a marginal revolution?" This is one of the most debated questions in the field of history of economics. Surely, there is a lot at stake from the perspective of the defenders as well as the critics of neoclassical economics. Almost all textbooks on the history of economic thought devote nearly a chapter to this question (e.g., Blaug 1997; Screpanti and Zamagni 1993).

3 Menger was against not only "any deterministic notion of equilibrium" (i.e., the idea that a commodity must have a unique price) but also quantification (i.e., the idea that there exists a homogeneous commodity space where goods are traded as equivalents) (Mirowski 1984: 371–2). These two critical positions can also help understand the hostility of the Austrian school towards mathematical formalism. On the difference between the Austrian tradition and the Marginalist School, see also Streissler (1972). For a Walrasian view on the differences between these three traditions, see Jaffé (1976).

4 According to a canonical interpretation of the theorem, the competitive markets and the private ownership of the means of production, if left on their own, can harness the independent, decentralized, and self-interested activities of economic agents and deliver a general, economy-wide equilibrium that maximizes social welfare. For a classical statement of this position, see Stigler (1965). This understanding of Smith as the father of economics is re-iterated in every kind of neoclassical text, from the highbrow mathematical ones (Arrow and Hahn 1971: vi–vii) to the run-of-the-mill mainstream introductory textbooks. Amartya Sen (1977; 1987), an early and notable exception among the mainstream "theoretical" economists, has insisted on a different reading of *The Wealth of Nations* with *The Theory of Moral Sentiments*: "The support that believers in, and advocates of, self-interested behaviour have sought in Adam Smith is, in fact, hard to find on a wider and less biased reading of Smith. The professor of moral philosophy and the pioneer economist did not lead a life of spectacular schizophrenia. Indeed, it is precisely the narrowing of the broad Smithian view of human beings, in modern economies, that can be seen as one of the major deficiencies of contemporary economic theory" (Sen 1987: 28). Note that Sen's reading of Smith is distinctively theoretical humanist in the sense that it searches for an underlying unity between *The Theory of Moral Sentiments* and *The Wealth of Nations*. An exclusive search for unity implies theoretical humanism, for it is premised on the idea that Adam Smith was a self-conscious and centered author who was the master of his entire oeuvre. Contrast this reading with more recent discourse analytical readings of Smith that find "difference" rather than (or as well as) unity in his work (Brown 1994; Perelman 2000; Ruccio and Amariglio 2003; Kozel 2005).

5 For sociologically rich and epistemologically sophisticated histories of Walrasian general equilibrium theory, see Weintraub (1985); Ingrao and Israel (1990).

6 In fact, for Marshall, "the Mecca of the economist lies in economic biology rather than economic dynamics" (Marshall 1920: xiv). In this sense, if the Walrasian understanding of the markets is based on the field theory borrowed from physics (Mirowski 1989), the Marshallian understanding of the markets is (loosely speaking) based on the selection theory borrowed from biology (Loasby 1999).

7 Let us immediately note that Pareto's formulations in his *Manuel di economica politica* gesture towards an ordinalist understanding (Ingrao and Israel 1990: 132–5). Indeed, the understanding of justice and efficiency associated with the concept of Pareto efficiency is decidedly different from the utilitarian understanding of justice and efficiency. In a sense, despite its widely acknowledged shortcomings, the concept of Pareto efficiency continues to survive, in part, because it fits with the modern ordinalist understanding of utility maximization.

8 Michael Mandler, a historian of economic theory, argues that philosophical utilitarianism enabled early neoclassicism to connect its scientific aspirations with political/normative concerns:

> The economic theory of utility maximization was, and remains, the model of extension of philosophical utilitarianism into the social sciences ... More generally, utility theory provided a mathematical link between unobstructed market activity and the satisfaction of individual welfare. Economists had long backed the liberal view that individuals were the best judges of their own interests, and that in the absence of countervailing considerations individuals should be granted wide latitude

in decision-making … In the theory, agents do not accept traditional or customary restrictions on what goals to pursue; they have specific individual interests and privileged knowledge of what those interests are. The case for agents being given authority over the allocation of resources gained immediate support.

(Mandler 1999: 73)

9 The term "psychologism" was used by the critics of the early neoclassical subjectivism in order to denigrate subjectivism for its "bad psychology" and was usually articulated from an "old" (or American) institutionalist perspective (e.g., Mitchell, Veblen) that considered then-nascent "behavioralist psychology" as the correct scientific method of understanding the functioning of the human mind. Behavioralist psychology emphasized the role of instincts and habits. Shira Lewin notes that, for the institutionalists, the psychological critique of neoclassicism was only "a springboard for [their] more important campaign for the increased study of economic institutions and evolutionary change, rather than the formulation of more and more [as they saw it] metaphysical, static economic theories with no empirical content" (1996: 1300).

10 While the indifference curves were first introduced by Edgeworth (1932 [1881]), it was Pareto (1971 [1906]), along with Irving Fischer (1925 [1892]), who first argued that cardinal utility could be dispensed with: "We have shown that, by starting from the indifference lines given directly by experience, it is certainly possible to determine economic equilibrium and thence certain functions, among which ophelmity, if it exists, will be included" (Pareto 1906: Appendix, Sec. 2, n. 1; cf. Ingrao and Israel 1990: 133). For succinct historical accounts, see Backhouse (2002: 256), Blaug (1980: 164–8), and Mandler (1999: 110–22).

11 Nevertheless, Paretian ordinalism was not the only way out of the psychologism underlying the utility construct. One alternative path had already been taken by early Marshallian economists such as Arthur C. Pigou and Edwin Cannan. While distancing themselves from the Benthamite notion of utility, and by extension from issues pertaining to the measurability of utility, these economists continued to subscribe to a notion of interpersonal comparability of "material welfare" (defined pragmatically in terms of access to "necessaries" such as food, clothing and shelter; see Cooter and Rappoport 1984). According to these "material welfare" economists, redistribution of the "national product" from the rich to the poor, by permitting more material wants to be satisfied, would increase total welfare. Underlying this idea was a substantive notion of common "good," namely, the notion that the satisfaction of more material wants is good for everyone. In other words, by recasting the meaning of utility as material welfare, these early Marshallians were able to remain within a cardinalist framework without falling into "psychologism."

12 For further discussions, see Mirowski and Hands (1998: 282), Blaug (1980: 99–103), and Hausman (1992: 156–8).

13 This description glosses over the twists and turns in Samuelson's own understanding of the "revealed-preference approach" and the role it plays in the neoclassical theory of demand. According to Wong's (1978) narrative, Samuelson began his journey in 1938 with a radically "operationalist" objective of constructing the demand functions without needing to refer to unobservable concepts like utility or preference. Ten years later, in 1948, abandoning the initial objective of complete eradication of "psychologism," Samuelson described the revealed-preference approach as a means to reconstruct the Hicks–Allen ordinal utility theory in an empirically grounded manner. And finally, in 1950, he would grant that the revealed-preference approach is observationally and logically equivalent to the ordinal utility theory. It is possible to read these re-interpretations and secondary elaborations as various attempts to domesticate the radical and somewhat traumatic nature of the 1938 purge. Similarly, Hicks, who initially endorsed the revealed-preference approach as "the study of human beings 'only as entities having certain patterns of market behavior; it makes no claim, no pretence, to be able to see

inside their heads,'" later became less enthusiastic and more doubtful (Sen 2002: 124; internal quote is from Hicks 1956: 6).

14 While direct revealed preference refers to those situations in which the agent chooses *x* over *y* when she can afford both, the *indirectly* revealed preference refers to situations in which no direct observation is available, but a sequence of direct revealed preference leads to the conclusion that *x* is revealed to be more desirable than *y*.

15 The Cowles Commission, a think-tank for statistical and mathematical research in economics, was established in 1932. It was based first in Colorado, then briefly at the University of Chicago, and finally at Yale University. Among some of the well-known affiliates of the Cowles Commission are Oskar Lange, Leonid Hurwicz, Jacob Marschak, Trygve Haavelmo, Tjalling Koopmans, Lawrence Klein, Armen Alchian, Arrow, Hahn, and Debreu. For brief assessments of the different ways in which the Cowles Commission has been instrumental in giving shape to the neoclassical formalism of the second half of the twentieth century, see Ingrao and Israel (1990: 255–7), Arrow (1991), and Backhouse (2002: 248–68). For a more detailed narration, see Mirowski (2002).

16 For a succinct statement of the conditions of Arrow's impossibility theorem, see Katzner (2006: 467).

17 The proof of the (Arrow's impossibility) theorem states that given the objective of constructing a rational (complete and transitive) social ordering out of individual preferences, it is impossible to construct a social ordering "without making that ordering coincide in all respects with the preference ordering of just one of the individuals" (Weale 1992: 210). A very useful and clear discussion of the subject can be found in Sen (1970). But also, see Weale (1992) and Mueller (1989: 384–407).

18 Dennis Mueller argues that, for Arrow, allowing public officials "to engage in cardinal, interpersonal utility comparisons would vest them with a great deal of discretionary power and might be something to be avoided" (1989: 394–5). The other three conditions, the conditions of Pareto inclusiveness, citizen sovereignty, and non-dictatorship, should also be considered in this light.

19 In particular, "the optimality of the equilibrium, i.e., whether the market can lead to a position which yields maximal social welfare in some sense, is [...] examined in terms of preference with the convention that a preferred position involves a higher level of welfare of that individual" (Sen 1973: 253). In other words, in order to substantiate its basic normative conclusions (i.e., the desirability of equilibrium), the Arrow–Debreu model has to rely on a residual argument pertaining to the psychic, subjective state of the agent: that the agent always makes choices that will improve her welfare.

20 In a revealing passage, Becker compares his approach with one of "modern psychology": "Moreover, the economic approach does not assume that decision units are necessarily conscious of their efforts to maximize or can verbalize or otherwise describe in an informative way reasons for the systematic patterns in their behavior. Thus it is consistent with the emphasis on the subconscious in modern psychology and with the distinction between manifest and latent functions in sociology" (1976: 7). This interpretation is in stark contrast with the concept of the unconscious in psychoanalysis. For psychoanalysis, the unconscious articulates symptoms in singular ways for each and every subject. There may be social symptoms (e.g., the "Jew" in Nazi Germany) that many subjects share at any given time, but even then, these social symptoms are conjunctural and not eternal, and they function as "social" symptoms only because they serve as blank screens on which the subjects project their own singular fantasies (Zizek 1991). In contrast, Becker's notion of the subconscious is nothing but a cognitive (rather than affective) unconscious, a particular behavioral pattern (optimizing behavior) unwittingly practiced by everyone in the same way. See also Lewin (1996: 1318–19).

4 Theoretical humanism in crisis

The case of Walrasian economics in the post-war period

In the late 1960s and the early 1970s, when the invisible hand theorem was fully formalized in the Arrow–Debreu general equilibrium models, a number of neoclassical economists swiftly recognized and acknowledged that there are indeed substantial and difficult-to-tackle problems with this comprehensive model of an economy-wide equilibrium (Hahn 1984; Arrow 1987; Kirman 1992; Katzner 1998; 2004; 2006). Essentially, the problem was the difficulty in bringing together, with a convincing level of generality and in a logically seamless manner, the two aspects of the neoclassical theoretical problematic. Neoclassical economists desired to establish the conditions of a *unique* and *globally stable* general equilibrium, and they wanted to do this by starting ground up from the autonomous and rational choices of individual agents. In line with the ordinalist turn discussed in the previous chapter, they desired to accomplish this by assuming as little as possible about the motivations of the individual agents. And precisely this last objective proved rather difficult to maintain in conjunction with the broader objective of establishing the desirable properties of an economy-wide equilibrium.

Nevertheless, despite the fact that many historians of neoclassical economics consider this particular impasse as the central problem leading to the occlusion of the Arrow–Debreu model as the centerpiece of the tradition (and even "the death of neoclassical economics"), the reading provided here suggests that the theoretical crisis should be read at a deeper level, at the level of ontological (structuralist) and political (interventionist) implications of the Arrow–Debreu model. Therefore, if one can speak of a crisis of neoclassical tradition circa 1970, it was not necessarily due to the failure of the Arrow–Debreu tradition to achieve its desired objective but, rather, due to a deeper crisis of theoretical humanism precipitated by the increasing structuralist drift of the tradition combined with the anxiety developed around the interventionist implications of the model. The aim of this brief chapter, after providing a basic overview of the general properties of an Arrow–Debreu economy, is to discuss the structuralist moments of the Arrow–Debreu model together with the perceived normative, political, and policy implications of these structuralist moments.

4.1 The Arrow–Debreu model: formalism without apologies

The Arrow–Debreu (henceforth, the A-D) model is neither the first nor the final reformulation of the Walrasian general equilibrium model. By the 1950s, there were already a number of different formulations articulated by, among others, Cassel (1924 [1918]), von Neumann (1928; 1937), and Hicks (1939). Moreover, there are important differences even between Debreu's *Theory of Value* (1959) and Arrow and Hahn's *General Competitive Analysis* (1971). For instance, while the latter text, written a decade later, tried to recast the A-D model so as to accommodate the concerns of the economic discourse of the day, Debreu was uncompromising with respect to the formalism of his method. In his introduction to the *Theory of Value*, Debreu wrote:

> The theory of value is treated here with the standards of rigor of the contemporary formalist school of mathematics. The effort towards rigor substitutes correct reasonings [sic] and results for incorrect ones, but it offers other rewards too. [...] It may also lead to a radical change of mathematical tools. In the area under discussion it has been essentially a change from the calculus to convexity and topological properties, a transformation which has resulted in notable gains in the generality and the simplicity of the theory. Allegiance to rigor dictates the axiomatic form of the analysis where the theory, in the strict sense, is logically entirely disconnected from its interpretations.
>
> (Debreu 1959: x)

"The contemporary formalist school of mathematics" that Debreu refers to is, of course, the Nicolas Bourbaki group (Weintraub 2002).[1] Formalism of this mathematical structuralism entailed "emptying the theory radically and uncompromisingly of all empirical reference" (Ingrao and Israel 1990: 285) and creating an abstract and universal "root" model that can be applied, with the appropriate modifications, to different theoretical and empirical contexts.[2] An important implication of this accentuated formalist effort was that it developed as a natural extension of the overall neoclassical impulse (discussed in the previous chapter) to assume as little as possible about the individual agents.

Given the importance of the book and the compactness of its expository format, the following discussion of the A-D model will refer mainly to Debreu's *Theory of Value*. Beginning with the definition of an A-D commodity, the discussion will proceed to the production and consumption decisions, and conclude with an evaluation of the concept of general equilibrium and the concept of Pareto efficiency.

Debreu defines the A-D commodity as "a good or a service completely specified physically, temporally, and spatially" (1959: 32). This notion of commodity is crucial for the A-D model to establish its domain, for the concept transforms the heterogeneous mass of "things" into logical "objects" that can be manipulated in the language of mathematics. In this precise sense, an A-D commodity is a "logical object" and not a "thing." Writing on the notion of "suture" (a psychoanalytical notion also developed on the basis of the mathematical structuralism of the Bourbaki collective), Joan Copjec (1994: 171–2) provides a rather exacting account of the difference between the two:

> Objects are defined as logical entities as opposed to things, which are empirical ... [T]he abolition of the thing, the suppression of all its attributes [gives] rise to a logical object.

The distinction is essential, as it enables us to understand how the political and cultural (and even the natural) attributes of the commodity are suppressed at a very foundational moment of theoretical construction. Through this concept of the commodity, the A–D economy establishes a commodity space. For empirical "things" (goods and services that are being exchanged among producers and consumers) to be brought into the purview of the general equilibrium model, they must be extracted from their concrete social context and properly specified with respect to their physical properties, location, and temporal coordinates (e.g., a black umbrella, on May 11, 2020, in Northampton, MA). Specification of the *temporal dimensions* of a commodity enables the A-D model to incorporate "saving, or lending of money [...] as the purchase today of a particular future dated commodity" (Geanakoplos, 1989: 44). Specification of the *location* provides the opportunity to incorporate the transportation costs into the price of the commodity. In this sense, for the A-D model, the commodity as a logical object is conceived to be free of the social ambiguities and uncertainties of the actual "thing." The commodity space, in turn, is constructed to be flexible enough to be infinitely inclusive and temporarily infinite. Let us take a closer look at the implications of these two attributes.

The multifarious ambiguities and uncertainties that characterize empirical things emanate from the political, cultural, and natural attributes of commodities that are suppressed when they are transformed into objects of the A-D economy. A commodity can be contested only if its definition involves a degree of opaqueness. The A-D commodity, to the extent that it does not allow for the ambiguities and uncertainties that characterize empirical things, suppresses this political dimension of contestability.[3] On some occasions, cultural conventions, social discourses, or professional codes of conduct may enable communities to make up for the ambiguities and uncertainties of empirical things (e.g., caring labor) and render them exchangeable with as little friction as possible. On other occasions, cultural mores and social norms may make it impossible for things (e.g., human organs) to be exchanged as commodities, period.[4] Even the inevitably variable natural attributes are suppressed, as the A-D model assumes that it is possible to delineate commodities clearly with respect to their "physical properties." Here, the critical point to underscore is the expulsion of all the attributes that involve ambiguity, uncertainty, and opaqueness as the "thing" is transformed into a "logical object."

In fact, even when a certain notion of "uncertainty" is incorporated into the model through an expansion of the definition of the commodity, this is done through a domestication of the dimension of ambiguity that is essential to the notion of uncertainty:

> A contract for the transfer of a commodity now specifies, in addition to its physical properties, its location and its date, an event on the occurrence of which the transfer is conditional.

(Debreu 1959: 98)

In this framework, "uncertainty" is explained through the metaphor of an *anthropomorphized* "nature" that makes choices among a finite number of alternatives. Each alternative is a possible *event*. Therefore, a black umbrella, on a *rainy* May 11, 2020, in Northampton, MA, will be a different commodity from a black umbrella, on a *sunny* May 11, 2020, in Northampton, MA. In short, the commodity space is *infinitely inclusive*—anything can be included as long as it is transformed into a logical object—and *temporally infinite*—as the commodity space flattens into a synchronic totality encompassing all the possible future commodities by assigning them to a corresponding possible state of nature into the future.[5]

The rest of the A-D economy builds upon this formal definition of the commodity space. The producers are conceptualized as economic agents that choose a *production plan* (into the future), namely, a plan that specifies the quantities of all its inputs and outputs that will maximize profits. As such, the process of production, as a process of transformation of inputs into outputs, is treated as a "black box." Similarly, the technology is exogenously given, and the production functions are assumed to be convex. The assumption of convexity imposes strong restrictions on the model: neither the indivisibility of outputs nor the increasing returns to scale in production are permitted. In short, for the A-D model, the production is a frictionless, automatic process of optimization that takes as its domain the entirety of the commodity space.

In a structure parallel to the production, the consumer in the A-D model does not choose a single consumption bundle but chooses a complete *consumption plan* according to her preferences. Preferences should be complete, reflexive, transitive, continuous, insatiable, and convex. While assumptions pertaining to completeness, reflexivity, and transitivity are considered to be the basic assumptions of economic rationality,[6] the insatiability and convexity are necessary specifically for proving the *existence* of the equilibrium price vector.

Which brings us to the matter of the existence and efficiency of the general equilibrium. The A-D model does establish the *existence* of an equilibrium price vector that would clear all markets. Needless to mention, this is an existence only in the mathematical sense of the term. In fact, the A-D model has very little to say about the functioning of the actual markets. But for a mathematical economist like Debreu, the formalism that underpins the A-D model was not a shortcoming, but rather, an asset. Yet, despite all the formalist aspirations (i.e., "the generality of the theory" or "the disconnectedness of theory from its interpretations") articulated by Debreu, there is still a privileged type of market that silently structures the A-D model: the auction market. Ingrao and Israel highlight this point when they write:

> Debreu's intention in the *Theory of Value* is to take the Walrasian description of the market as what we are tempted to call an empirical frame of reference but is more correctly defined as a *framework of images and intuitive figures*. Moreover, not content with the most orthodox form, he chooses a hyper-simplified version in order to obtain a simple and compact model description. [...] Debreu's point of reference is the theorization of the Lausanne school, *which appears only in the background as a set of intuitive images* since his is a full-blooded axiomatic theory. The Walrasian paradigm is thus revived in a new form: the phoenix rises again from the ashes, even though its wings now glitter with axioms.
>
> (Ingrao and Israel 1990: 300; latter emphasis added)

This is a fairly accurate depiction of the extent to which the A-D model is a high-modernist mathematical formulation of the Walrasian vision. Nevertheless, while it is important to note that Arrow and Hahn's (1971) treatment of the general equilibrium model was much more explicit in its acknowledgment of the Walrasian lineage and detailed in its treatment of issues of uniqueness and stability, the A-D model in general should be treated as an interpretation of the Walrasian vision. In other words, the formalist posture of Debreu's Bourbakism should be taken with a grain of salt, and the particular vision of market exchange (i.e., the auction market) that informs its purportedly general model should be acknowledged.

As for the efficiency of the general competitive equilibrium, the A-D model offers two important theorems (also known as the *Fundamental Theorems of Welfare Economics*) (Debreu 1959: 90–7). The first theorem demonstrates that under the given assumptions pertaining to the commodity space, production, and consumption, any competitive equilibrium is Pareto optimal. The achievement of Pareto optimality relies on the assumptions that the producers maximize profit and the consumers choose "a consumption plan to which none is preferred" (Debreu 1959: 50). The second welfare theorem, on the other hand, shows that there is an equilibrium price vector that corresponds to each Pareto optimum allocation. In other words, because there exists an equilibrium price vector that corresponds to each of them, it is possible to reach any of the possible Pareto optimal allocations by rearranging the initial distribution of wealth and re-enacting the (imaginary) *auction process* until the corresponding equilibrium price vector is reached. In the next section, we will be able to treat the philosophical and methodological implications of these results, as well as those pertaining to uniqueness and stability of the general equilibrium, in more detail, and explore how the post-war Walrasianism manifests itself as a structuralist drift within the neoclassical tradition.

4.2 Two "structuralist moments" of the Arrow–Debreu model

Even though it offered a formal proof of the *existence* (and Pareto *efficiency*) of an equilibrium price vector, the A-D model, perhaps as a result of its clearly delineated axiomatic expository format, revealed to its practitioners that the number and the scope of the assumptions necessary to prove the *uniqueness* and the *global stability* of a general equilibrium in a decentralized economy with rational economic agents were quite extensive (Ingrao and Israel 1990: 314).[7] Unless further restrictions were imposed on the type of preferences that the consumers can have in an A-D exchange economy with the standard price-adjustment rules, it was impossible to obtain a proof of the global stability and the uniqueness of the general equilibrium.[8] Imposing further restrictions, however, for many commentators (but not all), meant the loss of the intended generality of the general equilibrium model. Reverting to the assumption of identical agents (i.e., to the models with representative agents) was tantamount for many Walrasians, when combined with the auctioneer-based price-adjustment rules, to a complete abolition of the microfoundations project for the sake of the uniqueness and the global stability of the general equilibrium, for imposing further restrictions on the agents would make the model incapable of accommodating the uniqueness and the individuality of the agents (Kirman 1992; Rizvi 1994; 1997; Mirowski 2002; Davis 2003).

It is important to distinguish the mathematical question of stability from the process of price adjustment (price determination)—even though both constitute different facets of the same question: "Are there forces at work capable of ensuring the imposition of a price system that is an equilibrium price vector?" (Ingrao and Israel 1990: 25). The metaphor of an auctioneer is invoked in order to motivate the *tâtonnement* (a French word meaning "groping," as in "groping one's way in the dark") process through which the suppliers and the buyers modify their plans (in relation to everyone else's plans) until the equilibrium is finally reached. During the non-temporal process of *tâtonnement*, no transaction takes place. Every time the auctioneer announces a price vector, production and consumption plans are modified accordingly. In fact, the A-D model of the economy is a structuralist model precisely because each element (each production and consumption plan) is determined relationally, in conjunction with all the other elements. The equilibrium price vector is the one that clears all markets (or, to be more precise, n-1 markets) simultaneously. The *tâtonnement* process continues until the economy reaches a system-wide equilibrium.[9] Nevertheless, unless the auctioneer adjusts the price vector according to a set of laws (an algorithm), there is nothing that guarantees the convergence towards the equilibrium. For instance, if the excess demand for a particular good is positive, the auctioneer will increase the price, and vice versa. And it is precisely for this reason that the conditions for stability must be present. Otherwise, the market excess demand functions may fail to respond to the auctioneer in an appropriate amount and in the right direction!

These two clusters of problems (pertaining to the conditions for stability and to the conceptualization of the price-adjustment process) can be considered as the two "structuralist moments" of the A-D model. The auctioneer and its contradictory position within the purportedly individualist framework of the Walrasian system have already been identified by a number of scholars as a structuralist moment of an otherwise theoretical humanist discourse (Amariglio et al. 1990; Charusheela 1997; 2004; see also Hahn 1984).[10] S. Charusheela, for one, insists that Walrasian economics is structuralist only with respect to "the equilibrium requirements of the paradigm" (2004: 32). With respect to "the notion of economic subjectivity," she argues, Walrasian economics is an individualist framework.

Others push the envelope much further and claim that, in the A-D model, instead of the centered, coordinated, and hierarchically ordered body of the classical political economy and the much-criticized "psychologism" of early neoclassicism, they find "a diverse set of bodily surfaces that are written on and of *bodily functions* and orders that are invoked *as economic agencies* in their own right" (Ruccio and Amariglio 2003: 117; emphasis added).[11] In particular, while they do grant that "there is often an obligatory nod to the 'rational/desiring/maximizing subject'," David Ruccio and Jack Amariglio insist that the axiomatization of economic behavior and the treatment of preference orderings "as reflections of choice rather than [its] determinants" has led modern neoclassical economics to render the forms of behavior as "discrete and distributed" and "to attribute *agency* to these *forms* themselves" (2003: 110–11; emphasis added) rather than to the individuals who enact these forms of behavior. To put it differently, the disparate and heterogeneous set of bodily functions and activities (including, inter alia, on the side of production, accounting, bookkeeping, assembly, transformation, repackaging, and on the side of consumption, devising a plan of consumption, performing factor services, consuming leisure along with other commodities) that they identify in the A-D model do not refer to a central agency. While each of these functions/activities adheres to a very specific set of assumptions (such as that of the nature of technology and that of preference orderings), it is not necessary to treat these codes as inherent properties of the individual subject. Rather, they argue, "the body operates as a surface on which the requirements proposed by the theorists can be inscribed" (Ruccio and Amariglio 2003: 116).

In short, Ruccio and Amariglio claim that Arrow, Debreu, and others, in their attempt "to displace the deep, hierarchical ordering of the body in favor of theories of consumption, production, and distribution based on the horizontal linkages among a wide variety of bodily functions," have been led to produce a "differentiated and dispersed (what [they] prefer to call a postmodern) body" (Ruccio and Amariglio 2003: 119). Their reading makes it possible to argue that, by the mid-1950s, high-brow neoclassical economics had, for all practical purposes, abandoned methodological individualism and embraced mathematical structuralism *à la* Bourbaki (see also Weintraub 2002). In other words, the replacement of the modern unified body by the postmodern bodily functions is itself an (if you like, unintended and contradictory) effect of an underlying drift from the individualist humanism of fin de siècle neoclassicism ("psychologism") towards mid-century structuralism.[12]

Yet there is another way, and indeed in the opposite direction, to read structuralism into the A-D model. As the aforementioned Sonnenschein–Mantel–Debreu results suggest, under the standard price-adjustment rules outlined above, in order to be able to obtain the desired uniqueness and stability results, it is necessary to impose further restrictions over preferences. In this case, the structuralism can be found on the side of the "agencies," in the fact that they are limited to a narrow set of functional forms. Consider, for instance, a recent model of an exchange economy with individual agents who are endowed with Cobb–Douglas utility functions (Katzner 1998; 2004; 2006). With this particular assumption (which has almost a canonical status in the tradition) about the shape of the utility functions of the agents in this economy, Katzner is able to obtain the conditions for uniqueness and global stability. Nevertheless, because it imposes a particular structure on the preferences of the individual agents, it compromises on the desired level of generality.[13] In other words, from the formalist perspective of Debreu, to assume that the individuals are endowed with Cobb–Douglas utility function would be undesirable, for it would entail imposing an "ad hoc" structure on the model.[14] What distinguishes this second "type" of structuralism from the type that Ruccio and Amariglio identify (mainly) in Debreu's *Theory of Value* is the desire to establish, in addition to existence and efficiency, uniqueness and stability of the general competitive equilibrium. These latter two properties, as Sonnenschein–Mantel–Debreu results imply, require further restrictions on the range of agencies allowed to be represented within the economy.

4.3 The interventionism of Walrasian structuralism

By many a commentator, these two "structuralist moments" (the conceptualization of the process of price adjustment and the questions of uniqueness and stability) have been deemed the main culprits of "the demise of general equilibrium theory" (Davis 2003: 82; for similar assessments, see Screpanti and Zamagni 1993: 344–8; Backhouse 2002: 261–2). But more importantly, a significant number of late neoclassical economists identify "the demise of general equilibrium theory" with "the death of neoclassical economics" as such (see Chapter 6). This is a highly contestable proposition. For it is not appropriate to read these developments as evidence of "the demise of general equilibrium" (for there are a number of vital research programs within the neoclassical tradition that continue to operate within this framework, computable general equilibrium analysis being one of them) or to equate the loss of the disciplinary hegemony of general equilibrium analysis with "the death of neoclassical economics." If one defines the neoclassical tradition as an amalgamation of a number of theoretical positions inhabiting the neoclassical problematic, then it will be possible to interpret the loss of the disciplinary hegemony of the general equilibrium theory and the subsequent changes within the mainstream of the discipline as a set of developments within the neoclassical tradition, as a reconfiguration of the neoclassical tradition, rather than its death.

Therefore, it may be useful to propose and substantiate an alternative hypothesis: the reason for the loss of the disciplinary hegemony of the general equilibrium theory was not that it simply failed with respect to some particular methodological criteria (e.g., logical incoherence, empirical irrelevance, abandonment of methodological individualism, failing to achieve formalist purity). Rather, the problem with the post-war theoretical developments in axiomatic general equilibrium theory was their policy implications and normative consequences. In other words, to be able to understand the loss of the hegemony of the general equilibrium theory, it is necessary to situate it in the historical context of the pro-intervention versus pro-market debate within the neoclassical tradition.

Against this backdrop, it will be useful to reconsider the socialist calculation debate. Within the neoclassical tradition, the socialist calculation debate is not a historical curiosity but an ongoing debate—albeit changing its form and idioms over time. It is now well known that the Walrasian tradition has always attracted socialist-leaning economists who perceived the general equilibrium model not as a template of a competitive market economy but as a model of a command economy where the Central Planning Board replaces the imaginary auctioneer. While the broader neoclassical tradition has been celebratory of individual freedom and, to a large extent, minimal government control over the economy, the Walrasian tradition has repeatedly attracted neoclassical economists with a socialist bent. In particular, many of the émigré economists (e.g., Oskar Lange, Jacob Marschak, and Tjalling Koopmans) who were convened around the Cowles Commission and contributed in one form or another to the development of the A-D model had patent socialist and pro-government leanings.[15] This meant that the Walrasian model of the economy was open to two different (and radically opposed) interpretations. It could be treated, at one end of the spectrum, as an abstract model of a competitive market economy, or it could be treated, at the other end of the spectrum, as an abstract model of socialist command economy.

Let us begin investigating the matter by considering the policy implications of the Fundamental Theorems of Welfare. The first theorem shows that under the given assumptions pertaining to commodity space, production, and consumption, any competitive equilibrium is Pareto optimal. The A-D model specifies an idealized model of the economy. Consequently, to the extent that its assumptions cannot be met in real-world economies (e.g., when there are externalities, when certain public goods cannot be provided by the competitive markets), the model is usually used to sanction deliberate action (i.e., government intervention) to remedy these "market failures."[16] Much of what is considered as the domain of traditional Musgravean public economics and that of the post-war social-democratic consensus regarding economic policies of the welfare state—with the notable exception of merit goods—is captured under these types of "standard" market failures (Madra and Adaman 2010).

The second welfare theorem, on the other hand, shows that under overlapping but slightly different conditions there is an equilibrium price vector that corresponds to each Pareto optimum allocation. This theorem implies that "any desirable final allocation of resources and commodities requires 'only' a redistribution of private ownership rights in the means of production" (Roemer 1995: 112). That is, in order to be able to establish a particular Pareto optimum allocation, provided there is always an equilibrium price vector that would satisfy it, it is sufficient to rearrange the distribution of initial endowments and then let the agents trade towards that final allocation of resources. Once again, to the extent that its assumptions cannot be met in real-world economies, the model sanctions government intervention to lead the economy towards equilibrium.

In addition to these two channels (i.e., the government interventions that would remedy market failures and implement asset-redistribution schemes) theorized by the A-D model for the government involvement in the economy, the two "structuralist moments" discussed above gave another reason. Many scholars found in the Sonnenschein–Mantel–Debreu results, with their implications for the uniqueness and stability of the equilibrium (Kirman 1992) and the numerous logical difficulties involved in the various specifications of the *tâtonnement* process (Hahn 1984), a strong case for the necessity of actual non-market institutions to usher the economy towards the equilibrium:

> the foregoing models are [...] incomplete as competitive *tâtonnement* models, and [...] to make them complete it is necessary to provide them with a central market authority and the *tâtonnement* rules and procedures that it enforces.
>
> (Walker 1972: 353)

Indeed, the problem of *stability* offers an interesting litmus test for distinguishing pro-market Walrasians from their pro-intervention brethren. For those who wanted to conceptualize the economy along the lines of Adam Smith's "invisible hand," it was necessary "to show that the economy is capable of attaining this state spontaneously, that the system's variables of state—i.e., prices—vary and adjust in such a way as to arrive at a vector of equilibrium prices" (Ingrao and Israel 1990: 331). Ingrao and Israel further argue that "[t]he distance between those considering it essential to maintain the theories of existence and uniqueness together with that of stability and those who do not regard the last as indispensable is the same as that between those firmly convinced of the self-regulating virtues of a free market and those who believe that the only way to achieve compatibility between contrasting individual interests is to decree the 'final coherent state'—i.e., equilibrium—through planning" (1990: 331–2). No wonder, then, that the latter group found themselves attracted to some selection of Keynesian ideas and developed the neoclassical–Keynesian synthesis that dominated the post-war macroeconomics until the mid-1970s (Tabb 1999).

Precisely for this reason, it is necessary to distinguish the Fundamental Theorems of Welfare, which provide justification for government involvement in a market economy, from the Sonnenschein–Mantel–Debreu results and the auctioneer controversy, which provide justification for the substitution of the command economy with a market economy. To put it differently, post-war theoretical developments in general equilibrium theory tilted the balance too much in favor of government involvement in the economy, to the dismay of the pro-market camp. In the next chapter, we turn our attention to the Chicago approach, which rejected the auction metaphor of the Walrasian program and proposed an alternative metaphor for conceptualizing the competition process and market dynamics. Curiously enough, this alternative was also drifting towards a kind of structuralism—albeit an evolutionary one rather than a mathematical one.

Notes

1 See also Bourbaki (1950 [1948]). Weintraub (2002: 101–25) explores Debreu's formalism in its relation to Bourbakist formalism.

2 Ingrao and Israel (1990: 300) note that Debreu's "uncompromisingly formalist" exposition of the A-D model is indeed an aberration in a long line of efforts that concentrate on demonstrating "the existence, the uniqueness, and the global stability of the equilibrium" (1990: 3). They argue that unlike, for instance, Arrow and Hahn (1971), who explored the aspects of the questions of uniqueness and global stability of the equilibrium through introducing a number of "ad hoc" assumptions, Debreu, in his *Theory of Value*, given his commitment to formalism and aversion to "ad hoc" assumptions, did not address such questions. In fact, Ingrao and Israel argue, "[t]he clarity of Debreu's approach to the subject soon leads him to recognize that the other cornerstones of the Walrasian program—uniqueness and stability—present enormous difficulties or, are, in fact, blind alleys" (1990: 303). Let us register for the moment that the very concept of "ad hoc" assumptions is not without its own problems: what assumptions qualify as "ad hoc" and what assumptions do not? We will have a chance to return to this point.

3 The contested nature of commodities is one of the primary loci of attention in late neoclassical economics. See Chapter 7 for a detailed discussion of "contested commodities" in the broader context of the late neoclassical theories of market failures and economic institutions.

4 On the role of values in determining what can and cannot be exchanged as a commodity, see Anderson (1993). For collection of cultural perspectives on commodities, see Appadurai (1988).

5 For a helpful discussion of "contingent commodities," see Safra (2008).

6 In particular, if the axioms of reflexivity, completeness, and transitivity hold, then the individual is considered to have a *preference ordering*; if the axiom of continuity also holds, the individual's preference ordering can be represented as a utility function (Hargreaves-Heap 1992: 6).

7 The *uniqueness* of a general equilibrium refers to the situation in which an A-D economy has a single possible equilibrium price vector. The question of *stability*, on the other hand, aims to address whether or not there is a tendency towards equilibrium when the economy is not in an equilibrium state. The Sonnenschein–Mantel–Debreu results showed that the desired properties of uniqueness and stability of the general equilibrium "cannot be obtained from [the standard] assumptions on the individuals in the economy" (Kirman 1992: 122). In particular, Debreu (1974) establishes that the unrestricted individual utility functions of the kind found in Debreu (1959) do not imply anything about the market excess demand functions other than continuity, Walras's Law, and homogeneity of degree zero. This would mean that it would be possible to have a perverse situation in which the aggregate demand for a commodity goes up as the price of the commodity rises.

8 For instance, Katzner's recent model of an exchange economy shows that when all agents are endowed with Cobb–Douglas utility functions, uniqueness and global stability obtain (Katzner 1998; 2004; 2006). More on this below.

9 As Brian Loasby, an eminent post-Marshallian (but not Chicago) economist, eloquently puts it, in the A-D model, "all markets open simultaneously, and once only; when a complete set of equilibrium contracts is in place, they all close—forever" (1999: 108). Since both production and consumption plans are into the future, once they are chosen in a way that permits all markets to clear, there will be no need for markets anymore. The remaining task for each producer and consumer is to routinely carry on his or her already set plans into the future.

10 S. Charusheela argues that "the desire for closure in the face of contradictions creates collapses [into structuralism] for [a humanist] theory" (1997: 33). It should be noted, however, that it is not an abstract "desire for closure" that propels the proponents of a discourse to revert to structuralism; rather, the theoretical problematic of reconciliation of the individual and the collective rationality itself sets up "closure" as the objective of theoretical practice.

11 This and the following paragraph and their associate endnotes are based on the arguments developed in Madra and Rebello (2005).

12 Without doubt, the characteristic operation of structuralism is to dissociate the individual from agency. Nonetheless, in doing so, structuralists have failed to offer a thoroughgoing critique of agency as such and have associated the latter, in a pseudo-Hegelian manner, with the structure (Balibar 2003). In other words, the structuralist critique of the humanist subject has merely displaced what used to be on the side of the individual subject onto the structure, and thereby remained committed to a modernist and centered understanding of agency. For example, the auctioneer in the A-D model, standing in for that absent universal algorithm that will ensure the uniqueness and stability of equilibrium, is that piece of imaginary structure endowed with intentional agency (Amariglio et al. 1990). In this particular sense, the continuing normative centrality of the concepts of *equilibrium* and *efficiency* for the neoclassical vision for all practical purposes eclipses the postmodern moment that Ruccio and Amariglio identify in the A-D model.

13 The same argument holds for "the agent-price-adjustment-story" proposed by Katzner (2004: 13–16) as an alternative to the auctioneer story. The agent-price-adjustment story effectively decentralizes the function of the auctioneer to the individual agents. But, in doing so, the agent-price-adjustment story adds one more assumption to the "postulate of rationality." Katzner (2004) openly acknowledges this when he suggests lumping together price-adjustment rules with agent maximization "in what might be regarded as an expanded 'postulate of rationality'" (13). Interestingly enough, in the contemporary context of late neoclassical economics, especially considering the considerably expanded conceptions of rationality used in game theoretic contexts, this particular extension of the rationality postulate scarcely stands out.

14 On the other hand, if there is no such thing as "pure formalism" or "full generality," if there are nothing but "ad hoc" assumptions, what's wrong with "adding extra hypotheses"? In fact, in order to be able to begin rethinking, and perhaps revitalizing, general equilibrium theory, it is necessary to drop the formalist imposture: "However, the issue of how 'close' to full generality it is possible to come is still an open question. And to give up before answering it is to foreclose on the possibility of finding conditions of 'reasonable' generality" (Katzner 2004: 9). Without doubt, how to define a "reasonable" generality is also an open question.

15 Mirowski (2002: 232–308) traces the links between Lange's earlier work on market socialism and the subsequent works of a number of other affiliates (e.g., Marschak, Tjalling Koopmans, Klein, Arrow) of the Cowles Commission. These scholars were highly fascinated by the social engineering aspect of market socialism; their motivation

was to construct mathematically tractable models that would enable them to specify the appropriate ways in which to intervene in the economy.

16 Without doubt, what is "failure," and, therefore, what needs to be "remedied," is determined retroactively, only after establishing, within theory, what counts as the proper functioning of the economy. Consequently, the remedies are themselves designed to mimic the idealized vision of the economy. This constitutes a perfect example of the way in which the modes of intervention in the economy are overdetermined by the particular conceptualization of the economy.

5 Theoretical humanism in the evolutionary mode

The case of the Chicago School in the post-war period

In the 1950s, as the early versions of the Arrow–Debreu (A-D) model were being published, a number of high-profile proponents of the Chicago School, well known for their pro-market affinities, developed "Marshallian" models of market adjustment (Alchian 1950; Friedman 1953; Becker 1962; for surveys, see Vromen 1995; Loasby 1999). Curiously enough, these Marshallian scenarios of market adjustment were also structuralist models, albeit of a different sort than the mathematical structuralism of the A-D models. In these models, the intentional and rational human agency was replaced by the "impersonal market forces" that function as the central causal engine that generates equilibrium outcomes, or tendencies towards equilibrium.

It is important to recognize that, while they seem to jettison the assumption of marginal calculus (a core concept of Marshallian neoclassicism) conducted by rational economic agents, these essays were written in defense of neoclassical marginalism. In the late 1930s and 1940s, a number of non-neoclassical economists began to question the realism of the marginal calculus in the context of the theory of the firm. Two British economists, based on surveys that they conducted with actual entrepreneurs, argued that the pricing and output decisions of firms are not governed by the marginal calculus (Hall and Hitch 1939). On the other side of the pond, R. A. Lester (1946) claimed not only that the information that is necessary for the marginality calculations was not available to actual entrepreneurs, but also that the immediate reactions of the firms to increases in labor costs were not to reduce output and employment levels, but to search for ways to increase production efficiency and to implement labor-saving technological changes.[1]

Nonetheless, these critiques of the neoclassical theory of the firm were only a small sample of a broader critical countercurrent to neoclassicism. Since the beginning of the century, the proponents of American institutional economics had persistently questioned the realism and the relevance of marginalism. In Chapter 3, the "psychologism" controversy and its effects on the neoclassical theories of demand in general have already been discussed. In the field of macroeconomic research and policy-making, given its failure to successfully respond to the Great Depression, the legitimacy of the marginalist neoclassicism was seriously undermined by the Keynesian revolution and its immediate policy success. And finally, the Walrasian general equilibrium theory was coming into its own as the mathematically equipped émigrés (Lange, Koopmans, Marschak, von Neumann, Oskar Morgenstern, and even Debreu, who came to the US in 1948) began to settle into their careers in the North American academia (Mirowski 2002).[2]

The papers by Armen Alchian (1950), Milton Friedman (1953), and Gary Becker (1960), which articulate, with slightly different accents, the same "selectionist argument," should be read primarily as responses to this context. While they are indeed responses to those who question the realism of the marginal calculus, both in the sphere of consumption ("psychologism" and related criticisms) and in the production sphere (the marginalism controversy), it is important to recognize their function as an alternative, dynamic take on the invisible hand theory. Indeed, the Marshallian image of the market-adjustment process should be seen as an alternative to the static and timeless general equilibrium models that rely on the auction metaphor to theorize the price-adjustment process. In what follows, after providing a close reading of these selectionist papers that accounts for the differences among them, the chapter will proceed to explore the subsequent reception and the ideological implications of this new metaphor for imagining the way the "invisible hand" functions.

5.1 Selectionist arguments: anthropomorphizing the evolution

Alchian's (1950) intervention is usually referred to as the first neoclassical text to introduce a biological analogy in an explicit manner. Alchian's contribution is a characteristically Marshallian response to the criticism levied against the marginalist theory of the firm, as its argument revolves around the distinction between the individual and the representative firm. Alchian defined a "representative firm" of an industry as "a set of statistics summarizing the various 'modal' characteristics of" (1950: 217) that industry. In engaging with the criticism, Alchian begins by conceding that, under the conditions of uncertainty and incomplete information, it would indeed be wrong to assume that the individual firms will be able to undertake and follow the marginal calculations. But he insisted that, even if each and every individual firm followed a different (and non-marginalist) decision criterion, the industrial average would still tend towards the pattern of behavior as predicted by the neoclassical theory. And the mechanism that would make sure that the industry average, the non-existent "representative firm," would approximate the behavior of the profit-maximizing neoclassical firm would be *the selection mechanism of the market forces*. In response to one of Lester's criticisms, Alchian writes:

> in attempting to predict the effects of higher real wages, it is discovered that every businessman says he does not adjust his labor force. Nevertheless, firms with a lower labor-capital ratio will have relatively lower cost positions and, to that extent, a higher probability of survival. The force of competitive survival, by eliminating higher-cost firms, reveals a population of

remaining firms with a new average labor-capital ratio. The essential point is that individual motivation and foresight, while sufficient, are not necessary.

(Alchian 1950: 217)

This argument was based on the assumption that, in the limit, the hypothetical neoclassical firm represents the essential characteristics of the firms that will survive the selection mechanism of the market forces. In other words, for neoclassical predictions, explanations, and diagnoses to hold at the industry level, it is not necessary for the individual firms to consciously maximize profits by following the marginal calculus. As long as the market forces run their course unhindered, the only firms that will survive in the marketplace will be those that "realize positive profits." In other words, by *adopting* the firms that are actually realizing positive profits and eliminating the others, an "economic" selection mechanism will make sure that the standard neoclassical theorems about the directions of the changes, if not the actual amounts of the changes, will hold at the industry level (Alchian 1950: 220).[3]

A second and bolder formulation of the selectionist defense of marginalism was articulated by Friedman (1953) in his famous paper on methodology in economics. Friedman (1953: 22) argued that since the selection mechanism will make sure that the surviving firms will be the ones that "approximated behavior consistent with the maximization of returns", regardless of how actual firms behave, it is "not at all unreasonable" to construct models that assume that individual firms maximize expected returns. Sharing the same Marshallian premises with Alchian, Friedman argued that the predictions of the profit-maximizing model should be tested at the industry level rather than at the level of the individual firm. The difference between the two approaches, however, resides in the notion of the maximization-of-expected-returns hypothesis that informs Friedman's understanding of the behavior of the surviving firm. For Alchian, the actual motivations of the successfully selected individual businesses do not have to approximate a notion of profit maximization. For neoclassical theorems to hold as *tendencies*, it is sufficient to have an "economic" selection mechanism (i.e., competitive markets) that will force the industry average, or the representative firm, to move towards the predicted directions in response to changes in independent variables. For Friedman, in contrast, the selection mechanism *will* select those firms that behave according to the maximization-of-expected-returns hypothesis. To put it differently, the surviving firms must be the ones that have approximated the neoclassical firm: if they weren't maximizing their expected profits, they wouldn't be able to survive.

A final installment of the selectionist defenses of marginalism was Becker's 1962 essay, "Irrational Behavior and Economic Theory." In this essay, after distinguishing between the behavioral motivations of individual households (and firms) and the aggregate market outcomes, Becker argued that the markets will tend to produce rational results that will systematically satisfy the basic predictions of neoclassical economic theory, even if the consumers and the producers do not respond to the changes in prices in a rational manner. Becker defines irrational behavior as a spectrum of modes of behavior that range from "impulsive" to "inert": while impulsive behavior would entail randomness, inertia refers to resistance to change. According to Becker, changes in the opportunity sets (budget constraints), induced by the changes in relative prices, will force "the *average* economic actor" to behave in the way that neoclassical theory predicts he or she will behave, regardless of how the *actual* economic actors behave. In other words, for Becker, the shifts in the opportunity set provide sufficient "structural" conditions to ensure the law of demand, which specifies an inverse relation between price and quantity demanded. That is, the famous law of demand may still be reproduced at the level of the population average, without any reference to the well-behaved preferences of the individual actors.[4]

On the production side, Becker's narrative is quite similar to Alchian's: "firms could not continually produce, could not 'survive', outputs yielding negative profits, as eventually all the resources at their disposal would be used up" (1962: 10). Repeating the story he told on the demand side, Becker argues that changes in "relative input prices" will shape the production opportunity set in a manner that dictates "rational behavior": a rise in the relative price of an input will move the input mix of the industry average away from that input.[5] In short, according to Becker, the *structure* is embodied in the *scarcity* imposed on the economic subject by the budget line. The budget line itself, at the level of the market, is enough to derive the basic theorems of neoclassical economics.

Each of these three models explicitly claims that it is not necessary for individual agents to undertake optimization; they claim that market forces will make sure that the surviving agents will be the ones that meet or beat the average (Alchian 1950; Becker 1962), or, in the case of Friedman (1953), the ones that happen to be undertaking the predicted optimization calculations. Without doubt, these formulations are inconsistent with methodological individualism, for they privilege an aggregate mechanism as the casual essence that establishes the equilibrium market outcomes. Especially Alchian's and Becker's formulations of competitive dynamics, unlike Friedman's rather cavalier treatment, have quite bold structuralist accents, as their results require no actual actor to behave in a "rational" manner. But to what extent do these models break with the theoretical humanist problematic and drift into an "evolutionary" structuralism?

For at least two reasons, these models should still be considered variations on ultimately the same neoclassical problematic, i.e., theoretical humanism. The first reason has already been mentioned in Chapter 3: to be able to argue that the markets always produce *efficient* outcomes, it is necessary to assume that the surviving agents maximize their own welfare. As such, to be able to derive their welfare conclusions and policy recommendations pertaining to the desirability of (however generated) market outcomes, the proponents of the Chicago School must rely on a notion of preference that reflects a subjective and introspective notion of individual welfare. In this sense, the "selectionist arguments" of the Chicago School are similar to the false consciousness arguments found in traditional Marxism: the actual agents within a given economy may not know what is really good for themselves (they may be "inert" or "impulsive"); but through the help of the market forces (and the economists who advocate for the institution of more markets), they are forced to come to terms with what is really good for them. The competitive dynamics of markets do not only make sure that the survivors will be optimizers, but also teach the economic agents how to behave "rationally" and hence, "efficiently." In this sense, these selectionist models, to retain their normative force, must continue to refer to the idealized notion of rational actor that informs the theoretical humanist problematic of neoclassicism.

The second reason runs deeper. When Alchian (1950: 214) invokes "environmental adoption", he is, in effect, anthropomorphizing market forces. Indeed, all the "selectionist arguments" of the Panglossian kind[6] involve an anthropomorphization of evolution as an optimizer. But, if we could go behind this anthropomorphization of the structure, would we not find an essentialist concept of *anthropos* with a given (human) propensity to survive, to reproduce its existence? Indeed, it is this humanist presupposition that underpins this structuralist machine: what silently motivates the "scarcity" assumption used by Becker (1962) is the presupposition that human beings have unlimited (insatiable) wants and desires.[7] Without this (unarticulated) theoretical humanist presupposition, it is impossible to motivate the idea of scarcity as a reified condition of human existence.

5.2 Panglossian evolutionarism: an economic ideology of neoliberalism?

In their subsequent writings, considering the prevalence of evolutionary themes/ arguments in these seminal essays, none of these economists systematically explored evolutionary economics.[8] In retrospect, it is quite clear that they articulated these selectionist arguments as rhetorical tools to fend off criticisms against the optimization assumption.[9] Despite this lack of sincerity in mobilizing evolutionary models, late neoclassical reception of these "structuralist" texts has been exceptionally enthusiastic. Some consider them as the foundational texts of new institutional economics (North 1990; Vromen 1995); some consider them as the antecedents of evolutionary game theory (Samuelson 2002); some find inspiration for their simulation-based experimental economics (Gode and Sunder 1993; 1997). The enthusiastic reception of these singular texts by the late neoclassical camp is all the more surprising given their explicit privileging of "market forces" at the expense of individual intentionality and rationality: if the late neoclassical turn in economics is a restoration of theoretical humanism, how come such structuralist models are embraced and reclaimed by late neoclassical economists? Moreover, given the presence of "structuralist moments" in both the A-D model and the "selectionist arguments," why was the Walrasian structuralism seen as a dead end or unnecessary detour (see Chapter 6 for a more detailed discussion), whereas the Chicago structuralism is seen as a foundational precursor for late neoclassical approaches?

The answer, at least in part, lies, again, in the opposing normative implications and policy consequences of these two variations on the neoclassical problematic. The Walrasian conceptualization of the functioning of the markets privileges the *price-adjustment* path to equilibrium. In this model there is no entry or exit, but, rather, a *tâtonnement* process in which a fixed number of producers and consumers adapt their excess demand functions to the declared price vector. In the final analysis, a general equilibrium model is premised on an understanding of the economy as a bounded system without an outside, a static model that functions outside real time. In this sense, what makes the model attractive to modernist economists with socialist, social-democratic, and egalitarian leanings is its all-inclusive understanding of the economy. In an A-D economy, at the end of the *tâtonnement* process, no one will be left out.

In contrast, the Marshallian partial equilibrium analyses, in part due to their short-run focus, privilege the competitive dynamics of the markets. In the Marshallian model, equilibrium is arrived at through the exit and entry of the firms and consumers. Since there is an outside to the economy, the equilibrium state does not have to be all-inclusive. The equilibrium is not all-inclusive, because equilibrium can only be arrived at when there is no incentive left to *enter* into the economy (or equivalently, when the inefficient firms are forced to *exit* the market). This particular difference between the Walrasian and the Marshallian conceptualizations cannot be explained only by the difference between the multi-market focus of the former and the single-market focus of the latter. It is a difference that arises from their respective understandings of how markets function.

An important policy implication of this difference pertains to the relation between the state and the markets. The mobilization of evolutionary analogies furnishes these Chicago economists with a concept of selection mechanism that ensures that the markets will indeed tend towards equilibrium without any need for a central market authority. If the perceived poverty of the Walrasian model in explaining the process through which equilibrium is attained has rendered the economy susceptible to government intervention, the evolutionary metaphors mobilized by the proponents of the Chicago School have rekindled the neoclassical trust in the efficacy (as well as the efficiency) of the competitive markets economics. The stark differences between the late neoclassical receptions of the full development of axiomatic general equilibrium theory and the "selectionist arguments" of the Chicago approach must be made sense of in light of this definitive difference between these two rival conceptualizations of the functioning of the markets.

But there is another way in which the full axiomatization of general equilibrium theory and the "selectionist arguments" differ from one another. While the A-D model was intended to give the general equilibrium theory as much generality as possible (in part, to establish it as a root model for subsequent analysis and, in part, out of commitment to a methodological individualism that wishes to impose the minimal number of assumptions on the individual agents) through formalism, the selectionist arguments articulated by Alchian, Friedman, and Becker, by conflating the biological notion of "natural selection" with the Marshallian understanding of market forces, reified (or "naturalized") the latter into an overarching social ontology that explains, *mutatis mutandis*, everything. In this sense, the stark discrepancy between the late neoclassical receptions of these two post-war developments shows that, whereas the former project of making the A-D model the "root" model of the subsequent research has lost its disciplinary hegemony, the latter project of conceptualizing all social phenomena through the lenses of an ontology of competition (e.g., "the survival of the fittest/er") has gained a new-found prominence.

In the final analysis, the analogy between a Panglossian understanding of "natural selection" and the Marshallian conceptualization of market forces is far from an innocent metaphor. Certainly, the situation is not one of a pragmatic use of an idea borrowed from biology to better understand an economic phenomenon. Not unlike the way early neoclassical economics gained something extra (e.g., scientific credibility) by borrowing concepts from physics, the post-war and late neoclassical tradition has gained something extra from toying with biological analogies: the elevation of competition to an ontological status. Once competition is naturalized and ontologized, it can then be applied to all social phenomena, indiscriminately. I believe that a closer look at these post-war developments and their subsequent differential reception in the late neoclassical period can contribute to our understanding of the theoretical foundations of neoliberalism as the hegemonic ideology of contemporary times.[10]

5.3 Conclusion

The full development of axiomatic general equilibrium theory and the "selectionist arguments" of the Chicago approach should be read against the background of a widespread tendency within the neoclassical tradition to assume as little as possible about the human subject. Responding in their own ways to the after-effects of the psychologism and marginalism controversies of inter-war years, both the mathematical structuralism of the Walrasian A-D model and the "selectionist arguments" of the Marshallian Chicago School entail a similar destitution of the agency and the subjectivity of the individual consumers and producers. In order to be able to make sense of the subsequent late neoclassical turn towards the study of the mind of the individual agent as a response, a reaction, to the destitution of the role that the individual plays in the post-war neoclassical ontology, it is necessary to take these two "structuralist moments" as the point of departure.

On the other hand, however, it is also necessary to make sense of the discrepancy between the late neoclassical receptions of these two developments. If anything, their similarities make the diametrically opposed reception of these parallel developments in post-war neoclassicism all the more striking. However, making sense of the discrepancy between the late neoclassical receptions of these developments requires an appreciation of the internal struggles within the neoclassical tradition over how to formulate its constitutive theoretical problematic. In this vein, a third condition of agitation of the "selectionist arguments," along with the marginalism and psychologism controversies discussed above, was the disciplinary struggle between the pro-market Chicago approach and the pro-interventionist Cowles approach over how to define the neoclassical problematic. In Walrasian economics, the market is conceptualized through the auction metaphor, and the equilibrium is reached through an iterative adjustment of the price vector. By the 1950s and 1960s, in the aftermath of the socialist calculation debate, it became clear that the metaphor of the Walrasian auctioneer and its particular understanding of how markets function lend themselves almost too easily to government control over the economy. In contrast, according to the Marshallian conceptualization of markets that informed the economists of the Chicago School, market forces tended to produce efficient ("optimizing") outcomes if they were left alone. In the light of this internal struggle within the neoclassical tradition between prointerventionist social engineers and pro-market social Darwinians, it becomes possible to read the "selectionist arguments" not only as "belated" responses to the marginalism or psychologism controversies but also as a timely response to the Walrasian skein of the neoclassical tradition. The selection metaphor mobilized by the Chicago School is indeed a formulation of the neoclassical problematic that presents itself as an alternative to the auction metaphor of the Walrasian skein. Accordingly, the proponents of late neoclassical economics, to the extent that they define themselves in opposition to the A-D model, tend to affirm "selectionist arguments" and renounce general equilibrium modeling. Let us now turn our attention to late neoclassical economics.

Notes

1 For surveys of this early debate, see Lavoie (1990), Vromen (1995: 14–17), and Mongin (1998).
2 From 1939 to 1955, the Cowles Commission was based at the University of Chicago. In this period, a number of the affiliates of the Cowles Commission were also members of the Economics Department. Debreu describes his experience of the period to Roy Weintraub:

> [The conflict between the Chicago economics group itself and the Cowles people] must have been much more obvious in the department meetings which I did not attend. But I am sure when I say that tension occurred between, let us say, Milton Friedman and the Cowles group it must have been substantial from many different grounds. Because at Chicago the non-Cowles people were devotees of Alfred Marshall, and the Cowles group took a more general equilibrium viewpoint, and that was one difference. And I am sure that the non-Cowles group thought that the Cowles group used far too much mathematics. And then there were ideological differences. One of the issues of the day was rent control, and this found its way into our discussions. But occasionally antagonism flared up.
>
> (Weintraub 2002: 151)

3 Alchian did not discount "the likelihood of observing 'appropriate' decisions" (1950: 216). While his argument does not require ascribing non-random, adaptive behavior to the firms, Alchian did discuss two other mechanisms that provide some breathing space for some minimal intentionality: namely, "imitation" and "trial and error."
4 No wonder, then, that in some contemporary introductory textbooks, the discussion of preferences and indifference maps is relegated to the appendix of the chapter on consumer choice. For instance, in Stiglitz and Walsh (2002), the demand curve is first derived without referring to the utility maps of the individual. In other words, the changes in budget constraint are deemed sufficient to demonstrate the negative relation between the price and the change in quantity demanded.

5 One important criticism of Becker's formulation is precisely the unexplained nature of the changes in relative real prices. Israel Kirzner (1962) asks: if no one in the economy is behaving rationally, if everyone is a price-taker, what causes the shifts in relative prices? Interestingly enough, in the context of the Walrasian model, we observe a similar problem, and the fiction of the auctioneer is there precisely to fill up the exact same problem: "Each individual participant in the economy is supposed to take prices as given and determine his choices as to purchases and sales accordingly; there is no one left over whose job is to make a decision on price" (Arrow 1959: 43). If every agent in the economy is a price-taker, then who changes the prices? Of course, the *ex ante* nature of the allocation process obviates the need to think about the price-adjustment process as a real-time phenomenon.

6 "Panglossian modes of thought often involve the assumption, one that Darwin himself was sometimes keen to avoid, that evolution always means increasing progress, a beneficient journey from the lower to the higher form of organization of life, and from the inferior to superior" (Hodgson 1993: 224).

7 For a genealogy of the notion of scarcity in classical political economy as well as modern economics, see Xenos (1989).

8 Becker's (1976) evolutionary game theoretic model, which provides a rationale for the existence of altruism in a population inhabited by selfish agents, is the only exception. Nevertheless, the evolutionary game theoretic model used in the 1976 paper is different from the Marshallian evolutionary model articulated in Alchian's 1950 and Becker's 1962 papers.

9 The symptomatic unwillingness of these Chicago economists to pursue evolutionary theorizing further is also highlighted by Tjalling Koopmans (1957: 140): "if [evolutionary selection] is the basis for our belief in profit maximization, then we should postulate that basis itself and not profit maximization which it implies in certain circumstances." Eminent evolutionary economists Richard R. Nelson and Sidney G. Winter also lament the absence of rigorous and formal engagement in these early elaborations of economic selection mechanisms (1982: 141).

10 For a theoretical-historical discussion of the different forms of neoliberal reason in economic thought, including the Chicago School, see Madra and Adaman (2014).

Part III

Late neoclassical economics
Restoration of theoretical humanism

There is no doubt that the loss of the disciplinary hegemony of the general equilibrium theory in mainstream microeconomics has been productive of an abundance of new economic approaches and research agendas. Among approaches and research programs that gained prominence in the last three decades, the following can be mentioned: new institutional economics, new information economics, behavioral economics, social choice theory, experimental economics, classical game theory, and evolutionary game theory. There is indeed a proliferation of approaches and methodologies; yet to what extent have these new research agendas stepped outside the neoclassical paradigm? In contrast to a number of commentators who identify a radical break between neoclassical economics and the various contemporary mainstream microeconomic approaches, the central thesis of this book is that these late neoclassical approaches, even though they display a significant amount of internal diversity (which deserves to be studied and made sense of in its own right), have yet to occasion a paradigm shift. They all remain committed to the presuppositions of neoclassical humanism, and for this reason, this book proposes to gather them together under a term that signals their *philosophico-theoretical* and *historico-genealogical* continuity with, as well as their differences from, the neoclassical tradition: late neoclassical economics.

Part 3 of this book aims to provide a mapping of this proliferation of approaches and research programs by organizing the field around three nodal points: new conceptualizations of institutions as the other of markets; new notions of the human subject beyond *homo economicus*; and proliferation of notions of equilibrium in game theoretic contexts. In doing so, it aims to counter the "break" hypothesis articulated by many prominent proponents of the late neoclassical turn in economics.

Chapter 6 provides a select survey of these pronouncements that declare a radical rupture with the neoclassical tradition in general and the Walrasian general equilibrium framework in particular and advances three theses on late neoclassical economics: that it is an articulated formation of diverse theoretical approaches sharing a common theoretical problematic; that this shared problematic is the theoretical humanist problematic of how to reconcile the interests of the individual with those of the society; and that all these approaches are in some way a response to a perceived crisis of the Walrasian tradition.

Chapter 7 looks at the growing late neoclassical literature on *market failures* and *economic institutions* and asks whether or not the late neoclassical efforts in these areas represent a break with the theoretical problematic of neoclassical humanism. Focusing on two trademark late neoclassical themes (i.e., transaction costs and information imperfections) that are referred to in explaining market failures, the chapter argues that these concepts extend, rather than delimit, the scope of the commodity space. The extension of the logic of commodity exchange (even to non-market social phenomena) is premised upon the re-activation of the neoclassical humanist presupposition pertaining to the human subject, namely, the assumption of *opportunism* (self-interested non-satiation). In short, these late neoclassical approaches, not unlike the neoclassical tradition, view the world from the perspective of the sphere of exchange. The chapter illustrates this point with a critical evaluation of the late neoclassical theories of the firm and the labor contract, and demonstrates how late neoclassical economics, contrary to the claims of its proponents, continues to treat the sphere of production and the firm (the quintessential non-market institution), just as neoclassical economics did, as yet another (albeit imperfect) exchange relation.

Chapter 8 focuses on the treatment of the concept of the human subject in late neoclassical economics and offers a critical evaluation of the accentuated pre-occupation of the late neoclassical approaches with the various dimensions of the assumption of rationality. On the one hand, there is the question of the proliferation of the motivational orientations (selfishness, altruism, reciprocity, envy, etc.). While some segments of the literature ask whether there is indeed a motivational diversity, others, who are convinced of the existence of a diversity, focus on understanding and explaining the nature of this diversity. On the other hand, there is a growing dissatisfaction with the "unrealistic" assumptions made in standard neoclassical models regarding the cognitive capacities of human subjects. This dissatisfaction has led to the development of economic models based on agents with limited cognitive capacities (e.g., bounded rationality). The chapter demonstrates that the late neoclassical turn towards a "richer" and more "subtle" concept of the human subject, which incorporates bounded rationality, motivational diversity, and self-reflexivity, constitutes not only a rehabilitation of the theoretical humanist project of the earlier neoclassical economics but also a response to the impoverished concept of the human subject that was expounded by post-war neoclassicism.

Finally, Chapter 9 focuses on the concepts of *equilibrium, efficiency,* and *institutions* in the game theoretic corridors of the late neoclassical condition. The chapter traces the trajectory of a transition from the concept of Nash equilibrium associated with classical game theory to the concept of evolutionary stability associated with evolutionary game theory. In doing so, it differentiates between the left liberal, pro-market, and conservative variants of the paradigmatic late neoclassical idea of conceptualizing "institutions" as "solution concepts" for games with multiple equilibria or for games with Pareto inferior equilibrium outcomes. The chapter demonstrates how these concepts and their various refinements are developed for revitalizing, rather than abandoning, the central theoretical problematic of the harmonious reconciliation of the interests of autonomous and rational actors.

Organization of the literature around these three themes renders visible the continuity between the neoclassical tradition and the multitude of approaches that make up the late neoclassical condition. If one were to study each late neoclassical approach in isolation, it would become difficult to recognize the relation of each approach to the broader neoclassical problematic. In this manner, however, it becomes possible to demonstrate how seemingly different approaches are aiming to tackle a particular aspect of the neoclassical problematic (e.g., the definition of the commodity space, the theories of the firm, the aspects of rational choice, the idea of equilibrium) with the conceptual tools inherited from the neoclassical tradition (e.g., opportunity cost, arbitrage behavior, labor as disutility, choice as a reflection of welfare, and natural selection metaphors to explain the functioning of market forces).

6   Breaking with neoclassicism or restoring theoretical humanism?

The purpose of this chapter is to state the basic contours of the central argument of the book and to prepare the reader for the remaining three chapters, which offer a critical account of a number of the central theoretical themes and debates of late neoclassical economics. The chapter begins with a statement of three central theses that informs its reading of the late neoclassical condition: that it should be characterized as one of dispersion and unity; that it displays a continuity with neoclassical economics; and that it is a response to a perceived crisis of Walrasian neoclassicism. While Section 6.2 develops the idea that the late neoclassical context is characterized by unity and dispersion, Section 6.3 lends an ear to the writings of the prominent late neoclassical figures and documents their own representations of their relation to the neoclassical tradition in general and Walrasian neoclassicism in particular. A common theme that unites the self-representations of this diverse group of prominent economists is a claim to have occasioned a break with the neoclassical tradition, an accentuated wish to distinguish their position from that of Walrasian neoclassicism, and an equation of neoclassical economics with Walrasian economics.

6.1 Three theses on late neoclassical economics

Late neoclassical economics is constituted as a unified field, despite a significant degree of internal diversity, because it remains within the neoclassical problematic, even though it is a response to the purported crisis of Walrasian economics. For this reason, rather than occasioning a break from neoclassical economics, the late neoclassical turn entails a restoration, re-activation, and re-elaboration of its theoretical humanist presuppositions. Let me briefly unpack these theses.

The unity and dispersion thesis. The first thesis states that late neoclassical economics is an articulated discursive formation consisting of a diverse group of economic approaches and research programs that share a common problematic and a sufficiently common set of concerns and concepts that enable them to sustain—recurring failures in communication notwithstanding—an ongoing conversation among themselves even as they differ from one another methodologically, thematically, and politically. The central theoretical problematic of late neoclassical economics is the exploration of the conditions of existence of a harmonious and contradiction-free socio-economic order (i.e., an efficient and stable state of equilibrium in its various versions) that would best accommodate the needs of human subjects as they are postulated in theory (i.e., according to the axioms of rationality). As argued in Part 2, this was also the central theoretical problematic of neoclassical economics.

The continuity thesis. This brings me to the second thesis. Contrary to the claims of its many proponents (as will be documented shortly), late neoclassical economics does not constitute a radical departure from the neoclassical tradition. Late neoclassical economics inherits its constitutive theoretical problematic (the reconciliation of the individual with the collective rationality), its conceptual lexicon (e.g., opportunity cost, utility maximization, axioms of rationality, and labor as disutility), and its policy concerns, which continue to be limited to a spectrum that ranges from pro-market to market-skeptic, from the neoclassical tradition.

The response thesis. And finally, late neoclassical economics is a patchwork of *responses* (with a certain degree of internal diversity) developed by economists who were trained in the neoclassical idiom to the perceived crisis and fall from grace of the Walrasian skein of neoclassical economics. The most accentuated characteristic of these late neoclassical *responses* to the purported crisis and demise of Walrasian economics is that they all display a concerted effort to rehabilitate (albeit in different and sometimes conflicting ways) the two theoretical humanist presuppositions of neoclassical economics: the notion of the human subject as a unified and rational self-consciousness and the pre-destined vision of a harmonious socio-economic order. These rehabilitative efforts may take the following forms: more "realistic" models of the economy that take market failures into account, models that analyze the internal social organization of the firm, models with rational actors with other-regarding and non-selfish motivations, models with boundedly rational actors, the functionalist use of institutions as equilibrium selection devices for non-cooperative games with multiple Nash equilibria, the use of metaphors borrowed from evolutionary biology, etc. In these and other cases, the central concern of late neoclassical economists has been to explain why and how societies may fail to reconcile individual and collective rationality and how (already existing or to-be-designed) "institutions" (do or will) solve the problem of the mediation of the relation between the individual rationality and its aggregate counterpart—without ever questioning either the assumption of the human subject as a unified self-consciousness or the deeply normative concepts of equilibrium and efficiency.

In some ways, one is tempted to argue that if the unity is an outcome of the continuity with the neoclassical tradition, the dispersion is an outcome of the manifold ways in which late neoclassical approaches respond to the perceived crisis of Walrasian neoclassicism. Yet the picture is slightly more complicated. Perhaps most importantly, the continuity and unity pertain to the theoretical problematic rather than to the particular figurations (representations) of the theoretical problematic. For this reason, the continuity and unity are difficult to discern. Furthermore, responses are themselves structured around a shared problematic; hence, while they display a high degree of diversity (warranting "fragmentation" narratives), they are indeed structured around a common theoretical problematic. In other words, dispersion itself can be read as a condition of unity and continuity. For this reason, unity and dispersion, as well as continuity and response, theses have to be further elaborated.

Let us begin with the source of the *unity*: each late neoclassical approach positions itself in relation to (*responds* to) the concept of perfect competition and the invisible hand theorem as it is defined and formalized in the Arrow–Debreu (A-D) model. There are two ways in which a theoretical approach can position itself in relation to the A-D model. A late neoclassical approach can *either* focus on and isolate one or two assumptions of the A-D model and construct (local) economic models based on these weakened assumptions without questioning the constitutive presuppositions of neoclassical humanism *or* reformulate the neoclassical problematic in a new way. The latter, in turn, can be accomplished either by drawing upon the nonwalrasian skeins of the neoclassical tradition (e.g., the evolutionary themes of the Marshallian/Chicago approach, the concept of transaction costs of the neighboring Coasean tradition, or the Nash equilibrium concept of classical game theory) or by importing new concepts and methods from other disciplines (e.g., cognitive sciences, behavioral psychology, or cyborg sciences). These two moves, i.e., the weakening of the isolated assumptions and the reformulation of the problematic, allow late neoclassical economists to explain *either* why it is impossible to obtain the conditions necessary for the invisible hand theorem to hold true (i.e., "the markets are not enough") *or* why it is necessary to do something to institute the conditions necessary for the realization of the invisible hand theorem (i.e., "there are not enough markets"). In other words, the neoclassical problematic ("is it possible to aggregate in a rational manner the diverse needs and demands of rational and autonomous actors?") and its corollary policy debate between the pro-interventionist "liberal" position and the *laissez faire* conservative position is reproduced, albeit in new forms, in the late neoclassical context. (There will be more to follow on the contours of the late neoclassical policy debate and its similarities with and differences from the neoclassical policy debate.)

Some of the key late neoclassical concepts and strategies of containment that will be discussed in this and subsequent chapters will provide an excellent illustration of how late neoclassical economics remains within the theoretical problematic of neoclassical humanism: transaction costs, price dispersion, information failures, bounded rationality, rent-seeking behavior, and the ubiquitous treatment of non-market institutions as devices for solving market failures.

The concept of *transaction costs* relaxes the assumption of the effortless formulation and enforcement of contracts that informs the perfect competition model and explains why it may be more efficient to supersede the markets with other economic institutions (Coase 1937; 1960); the concept of *price dispersion* relaxes the assumption of price uniformity and explains why the same good can be bought and sold at different prices (Stigler 1961); the concepts associated with the *information failures* (i.e., moral hazard and adverse selection) relax (up to a point) the assumption of the perfect availability of all the relevant information and provide explanations for the existence of phenomena such as credit rationing and unemployment (Arrow 1974; Shapiro and Stiglitz 1984; Bowles and Gintis 1990); the concept of *bounded rationality* relaxes the assumption that the human subject as such has unbounded computational capabilities and provides explanations for why individual actors may fail to function as the standard theory predicts that they will behave (Simon, 1976); and the concept of *rent-seeking behavior* (*malfeasance, opportunism*) transforms the standard model of imperfect competition into a generalized theory of government failures and bureaucratic corruption (Krueger 1974). All of these late neoclassical conceptual innovations, in turn, feed into the ubiquitous functionalist treatment of "institutions" as devices that exist to solve the various failures of the price mechanism to deliver a unique Pareto efficient equilibrium outcome (Schotter 1981; Williamson 1985; North 1991).[1]

The common denominator of all these *late neoclassical concepts* is the investigation of the conditions that derail or prevent markets from conforming to the predictions of the perfect competition model. In doing so, all these approaches, while remaining within the overarching neoclassical problematic (i.e., the reconciliation of the individual and the collective rationality), produce concepts that explain *either* why the price mechanism (on its own) may fail to achieve such a reconciliation *or* why the only solution to achieve this reconciliation is the institution of new markets (e.g., privatization, trade liberalization, financial liberalization, marketable permits).

Let me emphasize, however, that the study of the aspects of *market imperfections*, the defining theme of late neoclassical economics, can only be thought in reference to the concept of *perfect competition*, a concept that can be found in all the skeins of the neoclassical tradition. Put differently, the model of perfect competition underpins all the late neoclassical treatments of market imperfections. All the key late neoclassical concepts that pertain to or lead towards market imperfections and failures (transaction cost, information failures, bounded rationality, interdependent preferences, corruption, coordination failures, etc.) serve the purpose of explaining *either* why perfect competition can never be realized (i.e., the liberal position) *or* what prevents perfect competition from being realized (i.e., the conservative position). In doing so, both positions take "the ideal state" of perfect competition as their point of departure. In this sense, all late neoclassical approaches are unified around a very particular theoretical humanist problematic: the theoretical problematic of *late neoclassical* humanism presupposes and positions itself in relation to the theoretical problematic of *neoclassical* humanism.

Let us now turn to the source of the *dispersion* that characterizes the late neoclassical condition. Indeed, the political (as hinted above), the methodological, and the thematic topographies of the late neoclassical condition in mainstream economics are internally differentiated and fragmented. As noted above, each late neoclassical approach is developed around the investigation of a particular assumption or set of assumptions of the A-D model. *New institutional economics*, for instance, uses the concept of transaction costs (which weakens the A-D assumptions pertaining to the commodity space) to explain the existence of economic institutions such as firms. *New information economics*, on the other hand, begins with the non-existence of many future markets and proceeds to weaken (but only in certain ways) the informational assumptions of the A-D model (e.g., moral hazard and adverse selection). The *behavioral economics* of Herbert Simon weakens the assumptions pertaining to the cognitive capabilities of the rational agent (i.e., bounded rationality). Other behavioral economists, using experimental methodologies borrowed from behavioral psychology, ask whether or not non-selfish preferences (e.g., altruism, reciprocity, multiple preference orderings) exist and, drawing upon evolutionary game theoretic models, try to predict their viability as motivational traits in mixed populations (which include selfish A-D agents along with non-selfish ones). And yet another cluster of game theoretic approaches tackles the questions of uniqueness and stability of equilibrium in various game theoretic contexts (e.g., Nash equilibrium solution, "institutions" as equilibrium selection devices, evolutionary stability). This specialization (and hence fragmentation) of research around the various assumptions of the A-D model is the source of the *thematic heterogeneity* of late neoclassical economics.

Moreover, each late neoclassical approach adopts a different research methodology for "unpacking" its particular pet "black box" (e.g., the contract, the firm, the mind, the preferences, the government). Some run laboratory experiments with college students, and others use computer simulations. Some borrow from engineering calculus, others from evolutionary biology. In other words, late neoclassical economics lacks a central research methodology and a central formal model, a "definitive analytic mother-structure" that could be "re-interpreted" in and adjusted for new theoretical and applied contexts (Weintraub 2002: 121).

Let us be as precise as possible here about how late neoclassical economists relate to the A-D model. Weintraub (2002: 121) argues that Debreu, inspired by the mathematical structuralism of Bourbakism, intended his *Theory of Value* either to function as "the definitive analytical mother-structure" or to be treated as an ideal model whose assumptions would gradually be weakened and contextually modified. Unfortunately, late neoclassical economists did not treat the A-D model as "the root structure" of microeconomic research, as an "abstract core model" to be adjusted for and applied to new theoretical and empirical contexts. In practice, they chose either to weaken the assumptions of the A-D model (i.e., Debreu's second route) or to reformulate the neoclassical problematic in nonwalrasian or new ways (e.g., by handling uniqueness and stability of equilibrium through the concept of "evolutionary stability"). In this sense, the A-D model served, and continues to serve, a central role, but, at best, as a point of departure, as a benchmark, as a reference point, and, at worst, as a "scapegoat." Therefore, when the students of mainstream economics study the A-D model, they do not do so in order to extract from it a particular way of doing economics. Rather, they treat the A-D model as the ultimate repository of a set of *assumptions* to be revisited, revised, and relaxed in order to re-activate and re-elaborate the neoclassical problematic.

In addition to this "negative" condition (i.e., the lack of interest in the A-D model as a root model or a source of research methodology), there is another factor that accounts for the *diversity of research methodologies* in late neoclassical economics. The growing importance of applied fields (e.g., labor economics, agricultural and resource economics, development economics, economic geography, environmental economics, public economics, financial economics, economics of transition economies, and area studies) has put the discipline of economics and those economists who were trained within the neoclassical idiom in touch with other disciplines such as sociology, political science, area studies, cognitive sciences, behavioral psychology, law, organizational theory, management studies, engineering sciences, applied mathematics, earth/environmental sciences, and biology. In the process, a certain amount of concept trading took place between late neoclassical approaches and those research programs in these adjacent fields that adhere to the theoretical humanist presuppositions and the modernist epistemology of neoclassical economists.[2]

The *political* topography of late neoclassical economics also presents itself as a realm of *heterogeneity*. Here, the two central policy positions within neoclassical economics, i.e., the pro-market conservative and pro-government liberal positions, are repeated, albeit with certain modifications. For instance, a late neoclassical but pro-market response to the emerging discourses on market failures was to develop extensive analyses of rent-seeking behavior in bureaucracies and produce an equally effective discourse of *government failures*. The concept of "good governance," a concept that is being promoted by the World Bank, is, in part, a product of this late neoclassical debate on government failures. Moreover, it will be misleading to refer to late neoclassical liberalism as pro-government. The late neoclassical liberal position argues for the necessity of "incentive compatible" non-market institutions to supplement the market mechanism in order to remedy its shortcomings.[3] These "incentive compatible" non-market institutions could range from social norms to non-governmental organizations (NGOs). In this sense, in late neoclassical conversation, theoretically speaking, the government has lost its credibility as a viable locus of agency for intervening in the economy. In this regard, the late neoclassical political topography is indeed different from the earlier neoclassical political spectrum. While the conservative position is still resolute in insisting on the necessity of further privatization and economic liberalization ("there aren't enough markets"), the liberals need to supplement the motto "the markets are not enough" with a series of qualifications that acknowledge the "shortcomings" of the government.

To recapitulate, the late neoclassical condition is characterized by both *unity* and *dispersion*. Late neoclassical economics is an articulated discursive formation consisting of a number of research programs and schools of thought that display a thematic, methodological, and political diversity, yet that share the theoretical humanist problematic of the reconciliation of individual and collective rationality. Moreover, each late neoclassical approach defines its research program in relation to, and as a response to the perceived demise of, Walrasian neoclassicism. Therefore, they are unified not only in their theoretical humanism, but also in their relation to neoclassical humanism. Chapters 7, 8, and 9 offer a detailed mapping of the late neoclassical condition and show why and how different contemporary mainstream approaches remain within the theoretical humanist problematic of, and define themselves in relation to, neoclassical humanism, and therefore should be counted as various skeins of late neoclassical economics. But before proceeding to this topic, let us turn our attention to the self-representations of some prominent figures of the late neoclassical program in order to juxtapose their self-representations with the representation proposed in this volume.

6.2 The so-called "break" thesis: the specter of Walrasian economics

It is important to note that many Walrasian economists themselves recognized and even encouraged this parasitical appropriation of the A-D model. Debreu's Bourbakist intentions have already been mentioned. Weintraub (2002: 121) reminds us that the "'weakening' of assumptions" was one of the paths of future research that Debreu would have encouraged. Another eminent Walrasian econo-mist, Frank Hahn, articulated a similar position only three years after the publi-cation of *General Competitive Analysis* (Arrow and Hahn 1971). According to Hahn, when confronting those who unequivocally believe in the powers of the price mechanism to allocate resources efficiently, the response of an economist should be

> to note that an Arrow-Debreu equilibrium must be an assumption that [the believer] is making for the economy and then to show that why the economy cannot be in this state. [...] This negative role of Arrow-Debreu equilibrium I consider almost to be sufficient justification for it, since practical men and ill trained theorists everywhere in the world do not understand what they are claiming to be the case when they claim a beneficent and coherent role for the invisible hand. But for descriptive purposes of course this negative role is hardly a recommendation.
>
> (Hahn 1984: 52)

Without doubt, this ascription of a "negative role" to the A-D model is premised upon the implicit assumption that the A-D model is the only way to represent Smith's theory of the invisible hand in a scientific manner. This assertion (per-haps deliberately) ignores the existence of the alternative treatments of the invis-ible hand scenario—a very prominent alternative formulation proposed by the Marshallian-Chicago tradition, in which the competition process was represented as a selection mechanism, has already been discussed in Chapter 5. In the pas-sage quoted above, when he chides "practical men and ill trained theorists," Hahn reduces "economics" to neoclassical economics and the latter to Walrasian economics.

It is possible to read an insecure undercurrent in Hahn's disregard for alter-native research programs and schools of thought (both neoclassical and non-neoclassical). By the 1970s, it was already clear—especially for the pioneers of the general equilibrium theory—that the conditions that are required to achieve the existence and efficiency of the general equilibrium, let alone its uniqueness and global stability, could not reasonably be satisfied by actual economies. By the 1970s, the very pioneers of general equilibrium theory (e.g., Hahn, Arrow, and Radner) were already trying to create a research project for themselves within the soon-to-change topography of the mainstream microeconomics. The Walrasian model was defended by the affiliates of the Cowles Commission, first from the Hayekian charge against the Barone–Lange–Taylor models of market socialism that were easily grafted onto the Walrasian general equilibrium models of the 1930s and 1940s (Adaman and Devine 1996; 1997; Mirowski 2002), and then from the attacks coming from the Marshallian-Chicago tradition in the 1950s and 1960s (De Vroey 2004). Once the limitations of the Walrasian model became the new consensus, perhaps ironically as a result of the very efforts of Walrasian economists themselves (i.e., the so-called Sonnenschein–Mantel–Debreu results), the only way to salvage the research agenda was to treat the model as an "ideal-type" and to re-orient the research agenda towards the study of the deviations from the model.

In short, Walrasian economists wanted the model to be treated as an "ideal-type." According to the "continuity" scenario articulated above, the A-D model was indeed treated by late neoclassical economists, in the precise sense described above, as an "ideal-type." Nevertheless, late neoclassical economists, and those who perceive a "break" between the neoclassical economics of the 1950s and 1960s and contemporary mainstream microeconomics, do not agree with this "continuity" scenario. For instance, Samuel Bowles and Herbert Gintis argue that the Walrasian model was a competition to, and not a precondition for the development of, the "nonwalrasian approach" (their term for late neoclassical economics):

> Perhaps the full development of the Walrasian model was a necessary precondition for developing analytical models of incomplete contracts and broader models of human behavior. [...] But the founding contributions to incomplete contracts, game theory, and behavioral economics did not await the development of the Walrasian model. Rather, the foundations of a nonwalrasian approach were laid down by prominent economists in the period from 1937 to 1957, precisely the period in which the Marshallian paradigm was displaced by the nascent Walrasian paradigm, subsequent to which two generations of economists were taught Walrasian general equilibrium as the core of modern economic theory. [...] In short, all of the underpinnings of a nonwalrasian economics had been set in place by 1960. Walrasian economics was not the precondition of these innovations—it was their competition.
>
> (Bowles and Gintis 2000: 1429)

According to Bowles and Gintis, Walrasian economics was an unnecessary detour, and there is practically no relation between contemporary mainstream microeconomics and Walrasian neoclassicism. Instead, they find the origins of contemporary mainstream economics in the Marshallian paradigm. Steven Cheung, a prominent new institutional economist trained in the Chicago tradition, constructs a similar narrative of antagonism between new institutionalism and Walrasian neoclassicism (here, coded as "welfare economics"):

> All this was subtly changing in late 1950s and the early 1960s. By the 1970s, the drive for economic explanation had gained such momentum that welfare economics has since been on the decline. The new institutional economics is a part of this significant development. *Of course, its ideas did not crop up overnight.* Knight (1924), Coase (1937), Hayek (1945), and Director had earlier done significant work in the field. *Yet these seminal contributions, scattered over a 30-year period, failed to break the field open.* It was a different era when, in 1960, Coase published his paper on social cost, followed by Stigler's paper on information (1961) and Arrow's on the appropriability of returns (1962). They had the support of the profession at large, because by this time interest in the real world was spreading. The joint effort ignited a fire.
>
> (Cheung 1992: 49; emphasis added)[4]

In these and other narratives, the disciplinary hegemony of Walrasian economics is seen not as a useful precondition of the development of contemporary mainstream economics, but rather, as a dark shadow that prevented its flowering.[5] In fact, if anything, the received wisdom regarding the contemporary state of mainstream economics is that its heterogeneity is a healthy and pluralist antidote to the monochrome austerity of the standard neoclassical model (see also Thompson 1997; Bowles and Gintis 2000; Colander 2000). Yet, at the same time, it is difficult to not to notice that even in their denial of a relation, even as they define themselves by differentiating themselves from the Walrasian model, they acknowledge the existence of a relation.

The late neoclassical emphasis on "institutions" is usually seen as being what renders it more open to pluralism. Since they purportedly do not impose a single model for the analysis of different social formations—since they take imperfect, rather than perfect, competition as the norm—it is argued that contemporary mainstream approaches made possible the flourishing of a variety of different economic models with contextualized assumptions pertaining to economic agents and institutional constraints.

Nevertheless, the reason for the internal diversity (and hence the purported pluralism of the late neoclassical context) is not so much that individual late neoclassical approaches have abandoned the "formalism" of neoclassical economics and embraced the "substantivism" of American institutional economics.[6] Far from it. Individual late neoclassical approaches continue to apply the same concepts (transaction costs, information failures, opportunism, etc.) universally, and even if they take market imperfection as the norm, the very concept of market imperfection itself presupposes perfect competition as its hidden norm. The diversity, therefore, does not arise from the substantive and context-sensitive analyses of institutions. As argued above, all late neoclassical approaches explain "institutions" as "person-made devices" that are intended to solve market imperfections. They differ only in the particular ways in which they theorize market imperfection.

Each late neoclassical approach (new institutional economics, new information economics, behavioral economics, etc.) posits its trademark concept of market failure (transaction costs, information failures, bounded rationality) as the reason why the "standard" neoclassical model was wrong and why "institutions" matter.[7] For instance, a founder of new institutional economics (also known as transaction-cost economics—an important late neoclassical approach), Ronald Coase, claims that the key concept that was missing from the standard neoclassical model was the concept of transaction costs:

> Adam Smith explained that the productivity of the economic system depends on specialization (he says the division of labor), but specialization is only possible if there is exchange—and the lower the costs of exchange (transaction costs if you will), the more specialization there will be and the greater the productivity of the system. But the costs of exchange depend on the institutions of a country: its legal system, its political system, its social system, its educational system, its culture and so on. In effect it is institutions that govern the performance of an economy, and it is this that gives the "new institutional economics" its importance for economists.
>
> (Coase 2000: 5)

Contrast this position with that of Joseph Stiglitz, a prominent figure in late neoclassical models of information failures. For him, the path forward lies in *new information economics*:

> The fundamental problem with the neoclassical model [...] is that [it fails] to take into account a variety of problems that arise from the absence of perfect information and the costs of acquiring information, as well as the absence or imperfections in certain key risk and capital markets. The absence or imperfections of these markets can, in turn, to a large extent be explained by problems of information. During the past fifteen years, a new paradigm, sometimes referred to as the information-theoretic approach to economics (or, for short, information paradigm), has developed. This paradigm is explicitly concerned with these issues. The paradigm has already provided us insights into development economics and macroeconomics. It has provided us a *new new welfare economics*, a *new theory of the firm*, and a new understanding of the role and functioning of financial markets. It has provided us new insights concerning traditional questions, such as the design of incentive structures.
>
> (Stiglitz 1994: 5)

Bowles and Gintis offer a more ecumenical perspective. They argue that the missing ingredient was the concept of *incomplete contracts*, a concept that brings together ideas culled from new institutional economics (transaction costs and social norms), new information economics (information failures), radical economics (power and social norms), game theory (strategic behavior), behavioral economics (bounded rationality), and experimental economics (bounded rationality and non-selfish motives). In doing so, they are careful not to alienate the *formalist* (in the model-building sense of the term) sentiments of mainstream economists:

> The first implication [of abandoning the familiar terrain of complete contracts] is that where some aspect of an exchange is not subject to a costlessly enforceable contract, social norms and psychological dispositions extending beyond the selfish motives of *Homo economicus* may have an important bearing on outcomes, even in competitive markets. The second implication is that market outcomes depend on strategic interactions in which something akin to "power" in the political sense is exercised. Where contracts are complete … there is nothing for power to be *about*, but where much remains to be determined after the handshake, the institutional details of the exchange process determine the strategic opportunities and effectiveness of the parties concerned. The result of these two consequences of incomplete contracts is that economic analysis must become more social and psychological in its treatment of the human actor, more institutional in its description of the exchange process, yet no less analytical in its model-building and no less dedicated to the construction of general equilibrium models.
>
> (Bowles and Gintis 2000: 1412)

In short, each late neoclassical approach positions itself in relation to the standard neoclassical model. In most cases, the standard neoclassical model refers to the Walrasian model. In doing so, late neoclassical economists represent their various research agendas (e.g., new institutional economics, new information economics, game theoretic approaches, behavioral economics) as genuine alternatives to the standard neoclassical way of thinking. According to the "break" narrative expounded by these scholars, while neoclassical economics lacked institutional content, late neoclassical approaches attend to institutional specificity; while neoclassical economics was monolithic and homogeneous, late neoclassical economics is pluralist and heterogeneous; while neoclassical economics was abstract and useless for real economies, late neoclassical models are easily applicable and useful for human beings; while neoclassical economics was static, late neoclassical approaches explain institutional change. And, most importantly for the purposes of this book, many of these scholars believe that late neoclassical approaches have occasioned a radical break from the "invisible hand scenario" that informed neoclassical humanism. For instance, Stiglitz argues that *the first fundamental theorem of the welfare*, which asserts the Pareto efficiency of every competitive economy,

> is the modern rendition of Adam Smith's invisible hand conjecture [and it] provides the intellectual foundations of our belief in market economies. Like any theorem, its conclusions depend on the validity of the assumptions.

A closer look at those assumptions, however, suggests that the theorem is of limited relevance to modern industrial economies.

(Stiglitz 1994: 28)

Similarly, in a recent lecture, economic historian Douglass North, a prominent figure of new institutional economics, announces that it is necessary to abandon the idea that price mechanism on its own can reconcile the uncoordinated actions of economic agents:

> We should begin by recognizing that there is no such thing as *laissez-faire*. Milton Friedman is a great man but we should realize that any society, economy or polity is structured and the structure is *a person-made* function of the way in which we order the society. The structure is a complex mixture of rules, norms, conventions and behavioral beliefs, all of which together form the way in which we operate and determine how successful we are in achieving our goals.
>
> (North 2000: 7; emphasis added)[8]

According to North's understanding, "we" have common goals (e.g., economic growth and efficiency), and there are various (in the final analysis, "person-made") institutions, means, and mechanisms, including the price mechanism, that mediate the uncoordinated actions of independent economic agents for "achieving our goals." "The most important" task of a new institutional economist is "to understand the process of economic change so that we can improve the performance of economies" (North 2000: 9). In other words, for North, the difference between *laissez faire* economics and new institutional economics is not so much in the question that they ask (i.e., "What are the conditions of existence of a harmonious socio-economic order that would best accommodate the needs and interest of rational subjects?") but rather, in *how* they *pose* the question and *how* they *answer* it.

Despite their differences, these late neoclassical figures are unified in finding a *discontinuity* between what they are doing and what neoclassical economists were doing up to the late 1960s and the early 1970s. Without doubt, there are differences between neoclassical economics and the various late neoclassical approaches. Moreover, there are important differences among the late neoclassical approaches. But, as much as there are discontinuities between the mainstream microeconomics of today and the mainstream microeconomics of yesterday, there are both *historico-genealogical* and *philosophico-theoretical* continuities. The important task is to try to study and understand both the discontinuities and the continuities.

To begin with, it has already been argued in Part 2, contrary to the representations of the proponents of the discontinuity narrative, that neoclassicism has never been monolithic or unified. In fact, an important condition of possibility of its disciplinary hegemony was its internal heterogeneity (see also Mirowski and Hands 1998). Second, the late neoclassical approaches emerged both from *within* the neoclassical tradition, in response to the perceived crisis of the Walrasian microeconomics research agenda, and from *without* the neoclassical tradition, as the latter began to enter into concept trading with the theoretical humanist strands of the neighboring disciplines. In this sense, neither a self-celebratory "clear break" nor a reductionist "there is nothing new here" narrative is useful. What is necessary is to understand the overdetermination of neoclassical concepts as mainstream economics goes through its changes and to assess whether new and borrowed concepts and methodologies reinforce or subvert the core presuppositions of the tradition.

Third, and most importantly, while it is indeed true that many late neoclassical approaches are not subscribing to the invisible hand scenario, this does not mean that late neoclassical economics breaks from the theoretical problematic of neoclassical humanism. In fact, there have always been market-skeptic neoclassical tendencies. Chapter 4 discussed the case of liberal- or socialist-leaning neoclassical economists who had serious reservations about what competitive markets can do. Moreover, the rejection of the invisible hand scenario does not mean giving up the possibility of the harmonious reconciliation of the rationally and autonomously defined interests of human subjects. For both neoclassical and late neoclassical economists, the so-called "invisible hand" of the market forces has always been just one of the numerous potential ways of reconciling the autonomously determined rational choices of human subjects.

For instance, Bowles and Gintis, who reject the invisible hand scenario, are committed to the policy objective of "getting the rules right." After informing the reader that "most modern economists see both market failures and state failures as common rather than exceptional" (2000: 1425), they claim that "markets and states are now seen not as *competing* but as *complementary* institutions in the quest to 'get the rules right,' and many formulations see a broader range of institutions of economic governance as essential in this task, including small-scale communities—neighborhoods, nongovernmental associations, and the like—as well as families" (2000: 1425–6). For Bowles and Gintis, "getting the rules right" means the design and implementation of the appropriate institution that would "improve allocative efficiency" (2000: 1427). Stiglitz is also committed to the idea of "getting the rules right":

> [In the absence of] formal models of the market process, it is not possible to assess claims concerning the efficiency of that process, and second (and relatedly), in the absence of such modeling, it is not possible to address the central issues of concern here, the mix and design of public and private activities, including alternative forms of regulations (alternative "rules of the game" that the government might establish) and the advantages of alternative policies toward decentralization-centralization.
>
> (Stiglitz 1994: 25)

The utopia of harmonious social reconciliation of individual interests is still articulated in key "normative" concepts of late neoclassical economics, such as "economic growth," "the performance of the economy," "the efficiency of institutions," "Nash equilibrium," "evolutionary stability," and so on. Even when the objects of inquiry are "inefficiencies," "path dependencies," "limitations of rationality in strategic interactions," "market failures," "government failures," and so on, in the backdrop there is still the ideal of social harmony that informs, motivates, and drives the late neoclassical research.[9]

6.3 Conclusion

Contemporary mainstream economics is an articulated discursive formation consisting of a number of research programs and schools of thought that, while displaying a thematic, methodological, and political diversity, continues to share the theoretical humanist problematic of the reconciliation of individual and collective rationality. In this sense, contrary to the claims of late neoclassical economists quoted above, despite the fact that each contemporary approach defines its research program as a *response* to the purported crisis of Walrasian neoclassicism, the contemporary mainstream has failed to occasion a substantial break with post-war neoclassicism, and should therefore be referred to as late neoclassical economics. These two sentences sum up the central argument of this volume.

The following three chapters aim to substantiate this central argument and the three theses that are simply asserted in this chapter: the representation of the late neoclassical condition as one characterized by *dispersion and unity*, the claim that late neoclassical approaches display *continuity* with the neoclassical tradition, and the reading of late neoclassical economics as a response to a purported crisis of Walrasian neoclassicism. In order to accomplish this task, how these late neoclassical approaches reproduce, reformulate, repeat, revise, and return to the theoretical problematic of neoclassical humanism—even when they seem to be diverging from it—has to be demonstrated.

Recall the invisible hand theorem, the most privileged version of the theoretical problematic of reconciling the individual and the aggregate rationality. Competitive markets, combined with the institution of private property, if they are allowed to function on their own, are supposed to reconcile the interests of selfish, autonomous, and rational individuals. Taking this scenario as their point of departure, the following three chapters will trace the trajectory of the three components of the "scenario": the concept of markets and the role of non-market institutions; the concept of selfish, autonomous and rational human subjects; and the idea of equilibrium as the harmonious reconciliation of diverse interests. Along the way, each chapter will trace out the contours of some key late neoclassical debates and controversies. For instance, the chapter on market failures and economic institutions will focus on late neoclassical theories of the firm and survey the different late neoclassical answers to the question of the non-existence of democratically run worker-owned enterprises in modern economies. The chapter on rationality will consider the debates on the causes of the diversity of motivational orientations and on how to incorporate the concept of bounded rationality into economic models. And finally, the chapter on equilibrium and efficiency will deploy game theory as a context to differentiate between three philosophico-political tendencies within the late neoclassical camp (the pro-market "invisible hand," the pro-interventionist "prisoners' dilemma," and the anti-interventionist "spontaneous order" positions) with respect to the particular way in which each conceptualizes social reconciliation.

Notes

1   The late neoclassical concept of *institution* is perhaps best formulated by Douglass C. North:

> Institutions are the humanly devised constraints that structure political, economic and social interaction. They consist of both informal constraints (sanctions, taboos, customs, traditions, and codes of conduct), and formal rules (constitutions, laws, property rights). Throughout history, institutions have been devised by human beings to create order and reduce uncertainty in exchange. Together with the standard constraints of economics they define the choice set and therefore determine transaction and production costs and hence the profitability and feasibility of engaging in economic activity. [...] Institutions provide the incentive structure of an economy; as that structure evolves, it shapes the direction of economic change towards growth, stagnation, or decline. [...] Effective institutions raise the benefits of cooperative solutions or the costs of defection, to use game theoretic terms. In transaction cost terms, institutions reduce transaction and production costs per exchange so that the potential gains from trade are realizable.
>
> (1991: 97–8)

It is commonplace to theorize games themselves as institutions. For instance, Samuel Bowles, another late neoclassical economist who considers game theory to be an indispensable tool for doing economics, defines institutions as "the laws, informal rules, and conventions that give a durable structure to social interactions among the members of a population" (2004: 47–8). Institutions qua games, therefore, determine the payoffs associated with each strategy, who will play when, who knows what, and so on. In this sense, institutions can be seen as durable environments that structure the choices of individuals; they are structures that individual subjects take as given. Nevertheless, late neoclassical economists tend to argue that games are *recursive* "in the sense that among the outcomes of some games are changes in the rules of this or other games" (Bowles 2004: 54). In other words, "the rules of the games" (or "institutions") that subjects take as given in making their (strategic) choices are themselves the outcomes of previous games, where the subjects had to have taken another set of rules as given, and so on .... It should be clear that this train of thought leads to an infinite regress. Unless we assume the possibility of an institution-free state of nature, or unless it is possible to conceive the act of "choice" without referring to a pre-given structure (qua a choice set and a reason to choose), methodological individualism has to interrupt the argument at some stage and assume the existence of a *piece* of structure (qua choice set) that cannot be reduced to prior choices and actions of individual agents.

2   To what extent this was largely a matter of applying neoclassical concepts (e.g., opportunity cost, scarcity, equilibrium, efficiency) in these applied fields, or of introducing new concepts and techniques culled from the field into economics, no doubt requires a detailed study. Nonetheless, such a study will not affect the basic point that is being made here. For even if the concept and technique trading was mutually enriching, the important point that should not be missed is that this "cross-fertilization" occurred only among theoretical humanist traditions. For instance, if there was any trading between psychology and economics, this happened between neoclassical economists

and the theoretical humanist traditions of psychology (e.g., American ego psychology, cognitive psychology, experimental behavioral psychology) and not, for instance, those Freudian and Lacanian traditions of psychoanalysis that are highly critical of the core of concepts of theoretical humanism, such as a unified and centered subject qua self-consciousness.

3 "Incentive compatibility" entails the design of institutions with the appropriate incentive schemes that would elicit the desired level of effort from the participating agents even when they are assumed to be self-interest seeking.

4 Note that Cheung is including Kenneth Arrow's work on the non-excludable character of research and development as a part of what he understands to be new institutional economics.

5 Joseph Stiglitz, a prominent figure of the new information economics, also makes a similar claim: "I want to argue [...] that the competitive paradigm [or, the neoclassical or Walrasian model] not only did not provide much guidance on the vital question of the choice of economic systems but what 'advice' it did provide was often misguided. The conceptions of the market that underlay that analysis mischaracterized it; the standard analyses underestimated the strengths—and weaknesses—of market economies, and accordingly provided wrong signals for the potential success of alternatives and for how the market might be improved upon" (Stiglitz 1994: 5).

6 For a discussion of the formalism–substantivism debate in economics and economic anthropology, see Adaman and Madra (2002).

7 For instance, in a brief yet revealing essay on new institutional economics (an important late neoclassical approach), Coase finds neoclassicism faulty for being too abstract and detached from what happens in the real world:

> Mainstream economics [microeconomics], as one sees it in the journals and the textbooks and in the courses taught in economics departments has become more and more abstract over time, and although it purports otherwise, it is in fact little concerned with what happens in the real world. [Harold] Demsetz has given an explanation of why this has happened: economists since Adam Smith have devoted themselves to formalizing his doctrine of the invisible hand, the coordination of the economic system by the pricing system.
>
> (Coase 2000: 3)

Contrast this position, however, with that of eminent economic historian Douglass North. North identifies continuity between neoclassicism and new institutional economics: he claims that the latter is not trying "to replace formal neoclassical price theory," but "to make it applicable and useful for human beings" (2000: 8). The common thread of both positions is the idea that new institutional economics is an economic approach that is more in touch with reality than neoclassical economics. More generally, whenever late neoclassical economists emphasize the continuity between their particular approach and neoclassical economics, they usually do this in order to underscore the superiority of the former over the latter.

8 Note that North is very careful in specifying that the ontological nature of the social, economic, or political structure is "person-made." This is because North, like all other late neoclassical economists, subscribes to the fiction of methodological individualism—the idea that it is possible to sustain a thoroughly individualist account of all social phenomena.

9 Moreover, the scenario of the "invisible hand" still continues to have a legitimate place within the late neoclassical conversation.

7 Market failures and economic institutions

Opening black boxes and introducing meta-markets

Neoclassical economics views the economy from the perspective of the sphere of exchange, as a nexus of mutually beneficial exchange relations, and whenever it articulates a theory of production it does so from this perspective. In fact, the inability of neoclassical economics to theorize the production process has been a recurrent critique of the tradition. In neoclassical theory, the critics argue, the firm, because its internal structure remains untheorized, is treated as a "black box." An important claim of late neoclassical approaches discussed in this chapter is that they distinguish themselves from the standard neoclassical model by addressing this criticism. These late neoclassical approaches propose to address this criticism by theorizing firms and other non-exchange institutions of "command" (non-choice) as social devices that "supplement" or "supplant" markets when the latter fail to function in the way predicted by the standard neoclassical models. Needless to say, these are functionalist theories of firms and institutions, and they continue to view non-exchange institutions from the perspective of exchange.

Nonetheless, late neoclassical debates on *market failures* and *economic institutions* (in particular, the institution of the firm as a site of production) provide significant insights with respect to the three theses advanced in the previous chapter: the characterization of the late neoclassical condition as one of dispersion and unity; the continuity of late neoclassical economics with neoclassical economics; and the status of late neoclassical economics as a response to a perceived crisis of Walrasian neoclassicism. Accordingly, the chapter aims to produce answers to the following three questions. To what extent do late neoclassical debates on market failures and economic institutions exhibit *unity and dispersion*? To what extent do late neoclassical treatments of the production sphere represent a *break* from *the exchange perspective* that defines the neoclassical tradition? This second question is particularly pertinent for the purposes at hand because the exchange perspective, with its underlying ontological presuppositions pertaining to the rational and autonomous agents and the harmonious reconciliation of their diverse interests in the contractual exchange, is yet another name for the constitutive theoretical problematic of neoclassical humanism. Precisely for this reason, a failure to break with the exchange perspective signals the *continuity* of late neoclassical economics with the neoclassical tradition. And finally, in order to shed light on the internal dynamics and divisions within the neoclassical tradition, the chapter will ask: to what extent does the late neoclassical turn towards theorizing market failures and economic institutions represent a *response* to the purported crisis of the Walrasian dominance during the post-war period?

The structure of the chapter is as follows. The next section offers a historical genealogy of the neoclassical tradition as a tradition that views the economy from the perspective of the sphere of exchange. The remainder of the chapter is divided into two main sections. Focusing on the sphere of exchange, Section 7.2 offers a discussion of the two alternative late neoclassical ways to theorize market failures: the Coasean and the post-Walrasian approaches. The concept of market failures is critical for late neoclassical economics, for it opens up a locus for the insertion of non-exchange institutions within the market-centric edifice of neo-classical economics. The discussion will highlight the differences as well as the similarities between these two approaches. With Section 7.3, the chapter moves from the sphere of exchange to the sphere of production, offers a discussion of the differences and similarities between the ways in which these two late neoclas-sical approaches make sense of the production process and theorize the firm (the quintessential non-exchange institution), and asks whether they have succeeded in moving beyond the exchange perspective that has structured the constitutive theoretical problematic of neoclassical humanism for so long. The chapter con-cludes with a discussion of the role of the debate on non-exchange institutions in providing the conditions for the increasing dominance of the selection meta-phor (now taking the form of an ontologized "meta-market") in the discipline of economics.

7.1 The exchange perspective in the history of economics

Maurice Dobb (1945) once noted that the line that divides the discipline of economics into two different camps is the one that separates the spheres of exchange and production. According to Dobb, one either speaks from the perspec-tive of the sphere of exchange and subscribes to a subjective (utility) theory of value, or speaks from the perspective of the sphere of production and subscribes to an objective (labor) theory of value. The realist epistemology that underpins the distinction between the "objective" and the "subjective" theories of value notwith-standing, Dobb's distinction has a remarkable validity in delineating the contours of a central theoretical debate that has given, and continues to give, shape to the history of economic thought since Adam Smith. Indeed, even Smith's *The Wealth of Nations* articulated two distinct, and contradictory, perspectives on the problem of value. On the one hand, Smith formulated a perspective that put the sphere of production at the forefront ("Labour was the first price, the original purchase-money that was paid for all things" (Smith 1991 [1776]: 36)), and, through his labor theory of value, articulated a discourse on social classes and class conflict (Hunt 2002: 41–65). On the other hand, in the pages of the same book, Smith pro-ceeded to formulate a perspective that centered on the sphere of exchange and, in stark contradiction to his discourse on social classes, viewed the society as being composed of individuals (and not of collectivities such as social classes) who are busily exchanging commodities with one another.[1]

In late classical political economy, this split in Smith transformed into a more accentuated disciplinary split embodied, on the one hand, in the writings of David Ricardo and the subsequent Ricardian socialists (e.g., William Thompson, Thomas Hodgskin), who teased out the political and ethical implications of the labor theory of value, and, on the other hand, in the writings of Jean-Baptiste Say and Nassau Senior, who gave a Benthamite utilitarian twist to Smith's "adding-up" theory of value. According to Dobb, Marx's critique of classical political economy and the subsequent marginalist counter-revolution in the late nineteenth century (Jevons, Walras, Menger) is yet another manifestation of this divide that splits the discipline of economics into two. Similarly, we can distinguish the production perspective articulated in the contemporary Sraffian and Kaleckian mark-up pricing theories of value (e.g., Lee 1998) from the exchange perspective found in the contemporary choice-theoretic approaches to value (as embodied in, for instance, Debreu's *Theory of Value*, discussed in Chapter 4), where production is conceptualized as a series of exchanges (i.e., the labor contract, the buying and selling of capital, and so forth). Following Dobb's framework, therefore, it is possible to categorize post-war neoclassical economics as a tendency that views the world from the perspective of the sphere of exchange, and whenever it articulates a theory of production, it does so from this perspective.[2]

In this sense, it may be useful to read the so-called "radical political economy" critique of post-war neoclassical economics and the late neoclassical response to this critique through the interpretative grid provided by Dobb. In the late 1970s and throughout the 1980s, a growing number of "radical political economists" began to question the absence, in neoclassical economics, of a theory of the production process, of a concept of "the internal social organization of the firm" (Bowles 1985: 16).[3] In a particular sense, late neoclassical developments in the field constitute a response to this critique: they claim to have addressed this criticism by theorizing firms as well as other non-exchange institutions of "command" (non-choice) as social devices that "supplement" *or* "supplant" markets when the latter fail to function in the way that the standard neoclassical models predict.

The aim at hand is to assess the validity of this late neoclassical claim and to ask whether or not the late neoclassical treatments of production represent a true break from the exchange perspective of the neoclassical tradition. Given that the concept of "the exchange perspective" that Dobb articulated is yet another name for the theoretical problematic of neoclassical humanism, to ask whether or not late neoclassical economics continues to be an exchange theory (despite its claims to the contrary) is to ask whether or not late neoclassical economics continues to remain within the theoretical problematic of neoclassical human-ism. Or, to put it in yet another way, through a reading of the late neoclassical theoretical debates on market failures and economic institutions, it is possible to assess the extent to which the late neoclassical analyses of market failures (i.e., the late neoclassical modifications to the concept of commodity) and of economic institutions (i.e., new theories of the firm and other non-market institutions) occasion a break with the neoclassical problematic and its theoretical humanist presuppositions.

In order to establish the humanism of the exchange perspective, it will be helpful to recall the two foundational presuppositions of theoretical humanism. On the one hand, theoretical humanism presupposes that the human subject is a centered, rational, and autonomous self-consciousness. On the other hand, it presupposes the existence of a social order that would enable the harmonious reconciliation of the diverse interests and demands of these rational agents at the level of society. Within the discipline of economics, and in particular within the neoclassical tradition, the (nebulous and ever-changing) concepts of (individual) rational choice and (social) equilibrium correspond, respectively, to these two presuppositions. The neoclassical conceptualization of market exchange (which can be traced all the way back to Jevons' early formulation of neoclassical marginalism) as an idealized process constitutes a paradigmatic example of the neoclassical version of theoretical humanism: two centered, rational, autonomous, and opportunistically motivated agents enter into an exchange that is destined to be mutually beneficial. The exchange must be mutually beneficial because, at the end of the transaction, the interests of both parties will be reconciled in such a manner that neither agent would desire to change their position. Notice that here the agents are assumed to be fully conscious of their true interests and capable of rationally seeking to improve their own lot by exploiting all available opportunities (i.e., the assumption of *opportunism*). Two basic presuppositions (pertaining to the rational and autonomous agents and the harmonious reconciliation of diverse interests in equilibrium states) of neoclassical theoretical humanism are indeed embodied in a distilled form in this highly idealized notion of exchange. In short, theoretical humanism, in its neoclassical mode, envisions the economy from the perspective of an idealized notion of exchange, as a nexus of exchange relations materialized in contracts.

In order to see how non-market institutions are inserted into this *contractual ontology* of the social in late neoclassical economics, let us recall the three basic assumptions of the standard neoclassical model as it was canonized in the mid-century Arrow-Debreu (A-D) general equilibrium model: economic agents are assumed to be "unboundedly" rational, contracts are fully specified and effortlessly enforced, and a unique and stable equilibrium is assumed to exist. According to a late neoclassical consensus, when these idealized conditions of market exchange are not met (when contracts are incomplete, when the agent rationality is bounded, or when there are multiple equilibria), it becomes necessary to supplement or even supplant markets with non-market social institutions (i.e., governments, firms, self-help organizations, norms, conventions, etc.) in order to reconcile the choices of individual agents and to establish a form of social order (taking the form of an equilibrium concept).[4] This is a rather general tendency. In this chapter, however, the focus will be on late neoclassical models, where it is too costly to write and enforce comprehensive contracts that would account for all the contingencies that could possibly arise from the opportunistic behavior of the contracting agents.

In such cases, late neoclassical economists claim that to the extent that *firms* (qua hierarchies) economize on the transaction costs of writing and enforcing contracts, they supplant markets by internalizing what could otherwise be handled through a nexus of contractual exchange.[5] Therefore, within the neoclassical tradition, in order to be able to open up the black box of the sphere of production, it is first necessary to open up a room for firms (hierarchies) within the sphere of exchange. In the next section, we will see how late neoclassical economists have done this during the 1980s.

7.2 The sphere of exchange: creating a room for institutions

Commodity space is, by definition, the very object of economics, if the latter is understood as the analysis of price formation. In other words, the scope of economic analysis for neoclassical as well as late neoclassical economics is coterminous with the scope of the commodity space. Accordingly, a precise definition of commodity space is a necessary condition of economic analysis for the neoclassical tradition.

In the A-D economy, for instance, the concept of commodity holds a central place. An A-D commodity is completely specified according to its physical, temporal, and spatial attributes, and, under uncertainty, according to the state of nature. There are two different kinds of late neoclassical criticisms of this theoretical construct: the *new institutionalist* "transaction costs" critique that descends from Ronald Coase's singular work in the British Marshallian tradition, and the "information failures" critique developed mainly by those economists who were trained within the tradition of general equilibrium theory (K. Arrow, J. Stiglitz, etc.). In order to highlight the genealogical and conceptual continuities, the latter critique can be referred to as the *post-Walrasian* tradition. It is important to note from the outset that, contrary to widespread opinion, these two skeins are not necessarily compatible with each other. In fact, there is a significant degree of incompatibility between the concepts of "transaction costs" and "information failures" and disagreement between the proponents of the two camps.

7.2.1 Explaining market failures: transaction costs vs. information failures

Both lines of criticism unpack the A-D concept of the commodity by focusing on the contract that specifies the nature of the commodity. The central thrust of the Marshallian-Coasean criticism was to remind economists that the exchange process itself is not without costs, that it is costly to write and enforce contracts, and that the maintenance of (market or non-market) institutions comes with costs.[6] The genealogy of this criticism can be traced back as early as 1937 to the writings of Ronald Coase on the theory of the firm, but also to his well-known critique of Pigouvian, pro-interventionist welfare economics (Coase 1960). In the former essay, the idea of *transaction costs* was used to explain the existence of firms: if the cost of conducting a transaction in the form of a market exchange exceeds the cost of conducting it through the form of a non-market institution, then there is an "economic" reason for the existence of the latter. (More on this below.) In the latter essay, Coase provided a verbal *reinstatement* of the first and the second fundamental theorems of welfare economics *in terms of legal rights and transaction costs.* To remind the reader, the first fundamental theorem of welfare economics (FFTW) states that under the A-D assumptions (discussed in Chapter 4) pertaining to commodity space, production, and consumption, any competitive equilibrium is Pareto optimal, and the second fundamental theorem of welfare economics (SFTW) states that there is an equilibrium price vector that corresponds to each Pareto optimal allocation. According to the second theorem, because there is an equilibrium price vector that corresponds to each of them, it is possible to reach any of the many possible Pareto optimal allocations by rearranging the initial distribution of wealth and then re-enacting the *auction process* until the corresponding equilibrium price vector is reached. The so-called "Coase theorem" states, analogously but in terms of legal rights and transaction costs, that as long as we let the markets run their course, traders will arrive at an efficient outcome (FFTW) and, from the perspective of Pareto efficiency, the initial allocation of legal entitlements does not matter (SFTW) as long as they can be traded in a perfectly competitive market (where there are no transaction costs, no market failures, etc.).[7] In Coase's view, markets run their course when the affected parties (those who hold the legal titles and those who bear the social costs (externalities)) negotiate over side-payments that would make up for externalities (the Pigouvian social costs).[8]

The first policy conclusion of the "Coase theorem" would be to delineate legal entitlements and private property rights as clearly as possible and to enforce private contracts. Many have read Coase's essay as the basis of a pro-market position that promotes ever-expanding private property rights. Yet, another, and perhaps more subtle, reading of "The Problem of Social Cost" found a second policy conclusion: to compare the different costs and benefits involved in deploying different institutional mechanisms (i.e., markets, firms, and governments) to address the problem of social cost (i.e., externalities) (Coase 1960: 15–19; McCloskey 1998: 240). One should resist reading these two policy conclusions (the "privatization" approach vs. the "cost–benefit analysis" approach) as being in opposition to each other. It is more important to recognize that these two policy conclusions are yet another manifestation of the way in which the two skeins of the neoclassical tradition are locked into an endless struggle with one another. In fact, the latter "cost–benefit analysis" approach itself can be considered as a theoretical "public sphere" within which pro-market and pro-government intervention positions can offer policy suggestions and debate their feasibility in terms of costs and benefits.[9]

This Marshallian-Coasean tendency has two well-recognized appellations: the *transaction costs approach* and *new institutional economics.* Today, while the latter appellation is more widely used, it unfortunately occludes the importance of the notion of transaction costs for this tendency. Among the economists within this tendency are George Stigler, who applied the concept of transaction costs to the study of the phenomena of price dispersion and search costs (1961); Harold Demsetz (1967), who crafted a theory of property rights out of the transaction-cost theory and the "Coase" theorem; Oliver Williamson (1975; 1984; 1985), who applied the concept of transaction costs to explain the raison d'être of "hierarchies" (i.e., non-market institutions); Steven Cheung (1982), who wrote extensively on comparative economic systems; and Douglass North (1990; 2005), who emphasized transaction costs in the historical study of institutional change and economic growth.[10]

In contrast to this Marshallian-Coasean lineage, which takes the notion of transaction costs as its entry point into the critique of the A-D notion of the commodity, those who were trained within the Walrasian tradition (e.g., Kenneth Arrow, Joseph Stiglitz, Michael Rothschild, Peter Diamond) levied a different criticism. These economists argued that the central problem with contracts is not simply that it is costly to write and enforce them. Rather, they highlighted the strategic dimensions involved in the informational requirements of any given contractual engagement. Beyond the simple cost of acquiring information, because of the absence of future markets and the existence of information asymmetries, there are two classes of widespread and generic cases of information failures: adverse selection and moral hazard. The problem of adverse selection results from the asymmetries of information among *contracting* agents (prior to the moment of exchange). Consider, for instance, the case of insurance markets. When insurance companies cannot discriminate between high- and low-risk groups, they raise insurance rates across the board. This has the undesirable effect of driving low-risk groups out of the market, leaving the insurance companies with only high-risk groups—hence the problem of adverse selection. The problem of moral hazard results from the difficulty of monitoring the *contracted* agent.

This late neoclassical tendency is usually known, due to its emphasis on information failures, as *new information economics*. This name recalls the institutional and disciplinary context of the emergence of this strand of research. It is now established that these Walrasian neoclassicals, on their way to becoming post-Walrasians, were interpellated by the mandate of the US military and its affiliated research think-tanks, such as the RAND Corporation, to explore the various aspects of C³I (command, control, communications, and information) (Mirowski 2002). Walrasian economists were mostly affiliated with the Cowles Commission, and the latter was the portal through which the US military financed economics research. But this institutional mandate was not the only reason that led these economists to develop their theories of incomplete information. They had to distinguish themselves from other neighboring schools of thought. On the one hand, there was the Hayekian challenge pertaining to the epistemic status of knowledge in the market process. If they had to produce a critique of the market mechanism that would somehow counter the Hayekian defense of markets, they had to account for the problem of information. On the other hand, there was the need to differentiate their understanding of information from the Stiglerian concept of information qua commodity, as this also had strong pro-market implications and lacked the strategic dimension. (More on this difference below.) In this post-war context, it seemed necessary for Walrasian economists to tackle the question of information and relax the perfect information assumption that undergirds the basic Walrasian model—especially if they wished to further substantiate the implicit critique of the market mechanism that they had already articulated in a negative manner in the A-D model.[11] In addition to these factors, as a part of the broader tendency to develop partial equilibrium models of factor markets with asymmetric information, we can also mention *new Keynesian* macroeconomists, who use the concepts of adverse selection and moral hazard in order to provide "microfoundations" for certain Keynesian insights pertaining to non-clearing factor markets (e.g., unemployment, credit rationing).[12]

7.2.2   Addressing market failures: more markets or institutional design?

Therefore, in late neoclassical economics, there are two distinct ways in which the neoclassical concept of the commodity is complicated and the concept of market failure is articulated. On the one hand, there is the concept of *transaction costs*, as elaborated by the Marshallian new institutional economists, such as Coase, Stigler, Cheung, and Williamson. On the other hand, there is the concept of *asymmetric information*, as articulated by the post-Walrasian new information economists, such as Arrow, Stiglitz, and Shapiro. Since these two tendencies articulate the concept of market failure in different ways, they also articulate different policy prescriptions to remedy it.

It is possible to demonstrate the points of disagreement between the two tendencies in stark terms if we begin the discussion with the way a Marshallian economist (George J. Stigler) treats the question of information. As argued above, an important policy implication of the "Coase theorem" is to clearly assign property rights and then let title-owners work out efficient economic arrangements. Similarly, if it is costly to gather information, the solution, according to the transaction costs economics, is to turn information into a commodity by introducing a new market for information! This theoretical maneuver constitutes the gist of Stigler's (1961) treatment of information.

In his well-known essay, Stigler (1961) investigates how the phenomenon of price dispersion (due to imperfect availability of information, "ignorance") will lead consumers to canvass various sellers. Alas, this "search" activity is not without its costs. Consequently, a rational consumer will continue to search only until the marginal cost of the activity of search equals its marginal benefit. Indeed, Stigler ingeniously introduces an implicit/shadow market for "information," where the price of information regarding the whereabouts of the cheaper commodity is the marginal cost of search. As long as the benefit from gathering information continues to compensate for the increasing marginal cost of search, the search will continue. In other words, if a consumer is purchasing a commodity at a relatively high price, this does not mean that she is irrational. Rather, it simply means that in maximizing her utility function, the consumer is incorporating the costs of information. Moreover, advertisement and "firms which specialize in collecting and selling information" (1961: 220) are nothing but two modalities in which shadow markets materialize as concrete institutions. In this treatment of information qua commodity, the absence of information does not undermine the smooth functioning of the markets; if anything, it leads to the emergence of new commodities and markets. Moreover, the problem of search may not be a problem at all. It may, indeed, be conceptualized as another mechanism through which competitive forces work: "the greater amounts of search will lead to a smaller dispersion of observed selling prices by reducing the number of purchasers who will pay high prices" (Stigler 1961: 218). Those consumers, who either "value the gains of search more highly or have lower costs of search," will, by rendering concerns of reputation credible, reduce the price dispersion.[13]

The post-Walrasian new information economics, in contrast, is much less optimistic about the flexibility of markets to accommodate less than perfect availability of information. Taking the A-D model as its point of departure, this approach has insisted that information failures of the markets are not incidental, but endemic to the system (Stiglitz 1994). In other words, for new information economics, the adverse effects of information failures cannot "be kept within tolerable even comfortable bounds" without supplementing markets either with "well-designed" government intervention or with non-market organizational forms. There are two main reasons for this. First and foremost, to solve information failures with markets for information implicitly assumes that somehow such markets themselves are immune to information failures. Second, when there is less than perfect information, new information economists argue, Coasean negotiations and side-payment arrangements between title-owners may not result in efficient economic outcomes, as Coaseans seem to claim.

> [I]ndeed mutually beneficial deals simply may not occur, as one party tries to convince the other the value of the relationship to him is small, in an attempt to appropriate a larger fraction of the surplus that accrues from the relationship.
>
> (Stiglitz 1994: 12)

The difference, therefore, between these two skeins is indeed a theoretical one, and the difference *does* have policy implications. Their difference arises from the particular way in which they formulate what they mean by "market failure," and, accordingly, while for the Coasean transaction costs economists, such as Stigler, Cheung, Demsetz, and Becker, "there are never enough markets," for the post-Walrasian new information economists, such as Arrow, Akerlof, and Stiglitz, "the markets are never enough." Moreover, it is also necessary to distinguish the post-Walrasian position from the earlier market socialist and interventionist Walrasian position. Subscribing to the generally agreed-upon late neoclassical thesis that the failures that haunt the markets would also apply to bureaucracies, new information economists are essentially concerned with "the *mix* and *design* of public and private activities, including alternative forms of regulations (alternative 'rules of the game' that the government might establish) and the advantages of alternative policies toward decentralization-centralization" (Stiglitz 1994: 25).

Nonetheless, these conceptual differences (transaction costs versus information failures) and divergent policy positions (pro-market versus market-skeptic) should not prevent us from identifying their shared theoretical problematic. In both sets of criticisms, we see a concerted effort to provide an explanation as to why an equilibrium outcome may not be Pareto efficient. In both cases, a notion of perfect competition as an ideal limit (respectively, the "Coase theorem" and the first fundamental theorem of the welfare) embodies the state of a Pareto efficient equilibrium outcome.

Moreover, both sets of criticisms, while relaxing, revising, and reformulating the assumptions of the perfect competition model, remain committed to the theoretical humanist presuppositions of the neoclassical tradition. First, both set of criticisms are still committed to the theoretical humanist idea(1) that it is possible for there to be an economic outcome that would be efficient for everyone in a given social formation—if only contracts could be fully specified and enforced. And second, in both cases, the failure to fully specify contracts arises from the "opportunistic" (i.e., selfish) nature of economic agents. Even though the term "opportunism" is articulated and deployed with a newfound enthusiasm by late neoclassical economists of different stripes, it is nothing but the assumption of "non-satiation" released from the narrow confines of the Walrasian auction or the Jevonsian exchange and applied to all imaginable social activities (from voting to governing, from gifting to child-rearing, from exchanging to contracting).

Let us take a closer look at this. As the transaction costs economists would argue, there are costs involved in writing and enforcing well-delineated and extensive contracts precisely because the contracting agents are assumed to be opportunistic (i.e., non-satiating and rational) in such a manner that they will be able to identify and be compelled to exploit the existing gray areas in the contract in their favor.[14] Similarly, new information economists would claim that asymmetrically distributed information will cause problems for the writing and the enforcement of contracts, because opportunistic economic agents will exploit their informational advantages in their favor and at the expense of their contractual partners.

To recapitulate, in these late neoclassical approaches, we do not only observe the presence of the model of perfect competitive markets as an ideal reference point; we also observe the re-assertion of the opportunistic rational economic agent as a central figure. In other words, we observe a return to the central theoretical construct of neoclassical economics, to a notion of *homo economicus* without bounds as the protagonist of both the Chicago-based, Marshallian transaction costs story and the post-Walrasian information asymmetry narrative. The theoretical disagreements pertaining to the nature of market failures and how to remedy them outlined above, therefore, should be understood as two positions that co-inhabit the same theoretical problematic: given that the economy is populated by rational economic agents, and given that it is impossible to fully specify and enforce the contracts (due to either transaction costs or information asymmetries), how can we achieve an efficient equilibrium outcome at the social level? Regardless of the answers they give (more markets or institutional design), the two late neoclassical tendencies share the problem.

In the next section, we will turn our attention to the corresponding ways in which the Coasean and the post-Walrasian economists theorize the sphere of production within the conceptual space that is opened through a relaxation of the concept of contract. The objective of this discussion is to assess whether or not late neoclassical economics departs from the exchange perspective in its treatment of the sphere of production. In posing this question, the intention is not to obscure the internal heterogeneity of late neoclassical economics. On the contrary, its unity is not simply weakened but, rather, strengthened by the extent to which its constitutive theoretical problematic accommodates different and opposing positions.

7.3 The sphere of production: opening the black box?

An important extension of the late neoclassical relaxation of the concept of commodity has been within the flourishing subfield of economics known as the theory of the firm. As noted earlier, a well-known criticism of the neoclassical tradition is that it lacked a theory of the firm, that the firm is treated as the proverbial "black box." In an influential essay that formulates the contours of a left-wing late neoclassical economics, Samuel Bowles claimed as much:

> [In] the simple Walrasian model [...] the production process is represented as a set of input-output relations selected from an array of feasible technologies by a process of cost minimization with respect to market-determined prices. The Walrasian model presents no analysis of *the internal social organization of the firm*.
>
> (Bowles 1985: 16; emphasis added)

One of the most prominent accomplishments of late neoclassical economics, at least in the eyes of its practitioners, is the wide range of contributions it offers in this area. In this sense, an important reason why various late neoclassical economists can claim to be doing a new kind of economics that "takes institutions into account" is the fact that they (claim to) theorize, to paraphrase the title of Oliver Williamson's book, not only *markets* but also *hierarchies* such as firms. Indeed, Coase first formulated the concept of transaction costs in the context of his paper on the nature of the firm. Similarly, Arrow explored the broader implications of his own post-Walrasian work on information failures in 1974 in a monograph titled *The Limits of Organization* and intended his explorations to be a general theory of markets *and* organizations (e.g., the firm, the military, and the polity).

7.3.1 Opening the black box: the Coasean and the post-Walrasian traditions

There are two skeins to the late neoclassical theories of the firm: the new institutionalist skein that descends from the Coasean tradition and, for lack of a better term, the "efficiency wage" skein that descends from the Walrasian tradition. While the former has the concept of transaction costs at its center, the latter has the concept of information failures (i.e., adverse selection and moral hazard). While there are some significant similarities and a good deal of room for conversation, there is one significant difference between the two skeins: the former aims to explain why firms exist, whereas the latter aims to explain "the internal social organization of the firm" in the context of labor market equilibrium with unemployment (Akerlof 1982; Shapiro and Stiglitz 1984; Bowles 1985). This important difference notwithstanding, both skeins remain committed to the theoretical humanist presuppositions of neoclassical economics. Let us take a closer look.

The very idea of transaction costs was first elaborated by Coase in the context of his influential paper titled "The Nature of the Firm" (1937). In this paper, Coase argued that firms come into existence (as "islands of conscious power in this ocean of unconscious co-operation") when the costs of using the price mechanism (e.g., the discovery of the relevant prices, the costs of negotiating and concluding a separate contract for each exchange, and the risk and uncertainty of the short-term contracts) exceed the costs of organizing transactions within a firm, through long-term contracts. As noted in the previous section, the implicit assumption here is that contracting agents are ruthless opportunists, and, given the opportunity to improve their own lot, they will default on the contract.

Armen Alchian and Harold Demsetz (1972) brought out what was implicit in Coase's incipient theory of the firm by incorporating considerations associated with metering and monitoring the performance of "cooperating inputs" in the context of "team production." According to Alchian and Demsetz, team production is production in which "several types of resources are used and the product is not a sum of separable outputs of each cooperating resource" (1971: 779). Nevertheless, since it is "costly to directly measure the marginal outputs of the cooperating inputs," and since individuals (i.e., input owners) are inherently selfish, and labor is a disutility, there are incentives to shirk. For Alchian and Demsetz, then, different types of firms (i.e., "forms of organizing team production") with their differential metering, monitoring costs, and arrangements of who should be the residual claimant (the manager who specializes in monitoring the performance of the members of the team, or the members of the team themselves directly) constitute so many different answers to the following question: how can the members of a team be rewarded and induced to work efficiently?

The assumption of opportunism is prominently made by Oliver Williamson (1975; 1984; 1985) as well. For Williamson, in order to render the individual the agent of the economic processes that s/he participates in, it is necessary to apply the assumption of opportunistic behavior consistently throughout. In this sense, for new institutional economics, opportunistic behavior (defined as the desire to improve one's own lot) becomes synonymous with economic agency as such. However, in addition to the motivational assumption of opportunism, Williamson's transaction costs economics incorporates the concept of *bounded rationality* as an important assumption regarding the cognitive capabilities of the contracting agents. (More on the development of the concept of bounded rationality will be offered in Chapter 8.) Deploying this definitive insight of behavioral economics, namely, the idea that economic agents are "*intendedly* rational but only *limited* so" (Simon 1961: xxiv), Williamson (1984: 198) asks the following question: "Given the limited competence, how do the parties organize so as to utilize their limited competence to best advantage?" In other words, Williamson understands the concept of bounded rationality as a form of constrained optimization. For new institutional economists, therefore, the firm as an economic institution is devised by human society to economize on transaction costs (which are, in part, caused by the opportunism of the contracting agents), to solve incentive problems arising from ubiquitous *opportunism*, and to make the best out of the limited competence of economic agents.

In contrast to the new institutionalist approach, the main concern of the second, post-Walrasian skein of late neoclassical theories of the firm, as noted above, is not simply to explain the existence of firms. Rather, new information economics focuses primarily on the information problems that prevent factor markets (for labor and capital) from clearing, and the consequences of this particular form of market failure (asymmetric information) on the internal social organization of the firm and the disciplinary mechanisms for the extraction "effort."[15] For instance, consider the case of labor market imperfections and the well-known scenario of the "efficiency wage" (for different versions of this argument, see Akerlof 1982; 1984; Shapiro and Stiglitz 1984; Bowles 1985; Bowles and Gintis 1990).

Since it is impossible to write and enforce comprehensive labor contracts, since it is costly to monitor the performance of each and every worker, or more specifically, since it is difficult to differentiate among the varying performance levels of workers (*moral hazard*), in order to elicit the cooperation of the worker, capital pays an efficiency wage that is higher than the market-clearing wage rate.[16] This rent makes sure that employed workers have something to lose. Moreover, the existence of employment rent means that there is an excess supply of labor. Since the higher the unemployment rate, the lower is the probability of an unemployed worker finding a new job, there are enough incentives for those who are employed to perform better so that they do not lose their jobs. Therefore, caught between the proverbial carrot of the *employment rent* and the proverbial stick of *the cost of job loss* (defined as a function of the rate of unemployment and the fall-back wage or the unemployment benefit), the worker's cooperation is elicited. And finally, since those who are bidding down the wage rate below the efficiency wage will lack credibility (*adverse selection*), market forces fail to pull the wage rate to the market-clearing level.

7.3.2 Sameness and difference in theories of the firm

The question, once more, is to see to what extent these late neoclassical innovations constitute a radical break from theoretical humanism in general and from the theoretical humanist presuppositions of neoclassical economics in particular. Or, to put it differently, do these late neoclassical theories of the sphere of production really break from the exchange perspective that has structured the neoclassical tradition since its origins in Adam Smith?

To begin with, the late neoclassical theories of the firm constitute a special case of the more general case of the late neoclassical theories of non-market institutions discussed in the previous section. In late neoclassical economics, institutions such as firms emerge as devices for reaping "the benefits of collective action" (Arrow 1974: 34) when the price mechanism (market exchange) is comparatively more expensive to conduct due to *transaction costs* or when the price mechanism simply fails due to endemic *information problems*. Underlying these failures, we find, once again, the paradigmatic theoretical humanist presuppositions of the neoclassical tradition, namely, the opportunistic behavior of economic agents and the teleological construct of efficient social outcomes. Accordingly, such theories reduce firms to a simple function: providing efficient solutions to market failures. In this particular sense, the late neoclassical theories of the sphere of production continue to understand and theorize production from the perspective of an idealized concept of exchange—as that which supplements the gaps within or offers solutions to the problems that arise throughout the contractual relations that are supposed to (under idealized conditions of perfect competition) fully determine the specifications of the commodity that is being exchanged. To put it differently, even though the markets may fail to deliver optimal social outcomes (given market failures), there exists a set of non-market institutions to make up for the failure of markets to deliver optimal social outcomes. The firm qua non-market institution is theorized as an answer to the problems that pertain to the idealized notion of market exchange that informed the neoclassical model of perfect competition as embodied in the A-D model.

Nonetheless, it is important to take note of the existence of a politically overdetermined theoretical conflict between the neo-Marshallian transaction costs and the post-Walrasian new information economists that manifests itself in two important areas pertaining to the question of efficiency, or more precisely, the *content* of efficiency. Before proceeding to the content of the disagreement, however, it is necessary to establish the status of the disagreement as one that is embedded within the context of a shared late neoclassical *belief* in a universal notion of efficiency as an indispensable attribute that renders equilibrium outcomes socially desirable.

Richard Wolff (2006), in a brief yet sharp analysis of the concept of efficiency and its practical correlate, cost–benefit analysis, after establishing from an overdeterminist perspective that "all efficiency analyses and results are relative" (304), distinguishes between two different ways of criticizing cost–benefit analysis. The first is to criticize a particular efficiency analysis—without questioning the idea of absolute efficiency analysis as such—for not taking into account certain effects and costs (gender- or ecology-related effects and social costs associated with them, monitoring costs that are necessary to extract effort from workers, and so on). The more radical second path is to criticize the very idea of an absolute efficiency analysis as such. In this particular sense, the difference between the two skeins of late neoclassical economics is in their respective "principles of selectivity in identifying their problems and solutions, their causes and effects" (305). Otherwise, they both subscribe to the existence of an "absolute efficiency calculus" (305).

To put it differently, the disagreement between these two approaches does not pertain to the necessity of an "absolute efficiency calculus" but rather, to their respective assessment of which institutions are efficient and which are not, which efficiency criteria should be used, and so on. In this regard, with respect to the theory of firms, we can highlight the two areas in which these two late neoclassical tendencies disagree: whether "hierarchical" or "democratic" firms constitute the most efficient response to market failures, and whether or not the existence of an institutional form (e.g., firms, norms, states) is the proof of the efficiency of that institutional form.

Let us begin with the first disagreement. For the new institutionalist camp, the firm with a *hierarchical* organizational structure is a transaction-costs-*economizing* response to the inherent opportunism of shirking workers (Williamson 1984).[17] For the second camp, information failures in the labor market (adverse selection) and the failure to extract the contracted level of effort from the worker (moral hazard) necessitate the use of various other institutional disciplinary devices (the employment rent, the cost of job loss, and so on). In fact, precisely because information failures necessitate the deployment of monitoring and disciplining devices that incur additional costs for the firms, imperfect factor markets "generally fail to implement socially efficient resource use, in the sense that there exist transactions that are Pareto superior to the competitive equilibrium" (Bowles and Gintis 1990: 80).[18] In other words, while, for new institutional economists, the capitalist firm with a hierarchical structure is an efficient response to market failures, for post-Walrasian economists, the costs that pertain to the range of institutional disciplinary devices that characterize the various aspects of contemporary hierarchical firms cause them to be dominated by other institutional arrangements—in particular, by worker-owned "democratic" firms in which the workers are "residual claimants." To put it differently, for post-Walrasian economists like Bowles and Gintis (1990), the democratic firm, in which the worker remuneration is directly linked to the success of the firm, constitutes a better (more "efficient") response than the hierarchical firm to the market failures that are caused by the opportunism of contracting agents who exploit information asymmetries.[19]

The second area of disagreement between the two approaches lies in the way they interpret the continuing existence, i.e., the survival, of the firms. Williamson (1993), for instance, holds that "institutions emerging from the competitive process will be *comparatively* efficient" (Williamson, 1993: 107). New institutional economists argue that, at any given moment in history, the distribution of institutional forms such as firms and markets, or hierarchical and democratic firms, is determined by their comparative efficiency. In other words, late neoclassical economics posits a meta-selection mechanism ("the competitive process") that determines the distribution of institutions: those institutions that are more effective than the average survive.

Some scholars, in their attempts to tone down the social Darwinian inflection of this idea, have suggested the concept of "path dependency." According to this notion, a particular constellation of events might end up protecting and enabling the reproduction of an inefficient institution in such a manner that after a while it becomes too costly to change paths, so to speak, and switch to the more efficient alternative (David 1985). Relying on this concept, Bowles and Gintis argue:

> The inference that survival entails efficiency is unwarranted, for it ignores the path dependent nature of evolution and the possibility of multiple equilibria. In any model with multiple stable equilibria, biological or economic, where you end up depends on where you've been, and whatever optimality properties may be claimed for the equilibria are at most local rather than global.
>
> (Bowles and Gintis 1993: 97)

In this sense, these two areas of disagreement are not unrelated. In fact, the two areas of disagreement are the two acts of a single debate pertaining to the comparative efficiency of hierarchical and democratic firms. The "path dependency" argument put forward by post-Walrasians is itself a response to the question posed by new institutionalist economists: if democratic firms are more efficient solutions to market failures, as post-Walrasians claim, why aren't there more of them?[20]

It is important to underline the shared conceptual terrain on which the debate is being waged. Just as the concept of "imperfect competition" relies upon the concept of "perfect competition," the concept of "path dependency" relies upon the idea that there is a central tendency of History, in this case, of the unfolding "competitive process," in the form of a meta-selection mechanism that would "choose" the more "efficient" institutions. In other words, even post-Walrasian late neoclassicals, who invoke the concept of "path dependency" in response to the Coasean new institutionalists, rely upon a concept of an overarching selection mechanism, a market-like meta-logic that governs the division of labor between markets and hierarchies, or the distribution of hierarchical or democratic firms, or the distribution of social norms, and so on.

Despite their many differences, post-Walrasians and the Coasean new institutionalists silently agree with each other with regard to their understanding of social ontology. This is the Panglossian social ontology of the Chicago approach that was discussed in Chapter 5. As already suggested there, the biological concept of natural selection is more than a merely pragmatic or useful metaphor to theorize the process of adjustment of the markets towards equilibrium. The analogy serves the purpose of turning the logic of competition into an overarching social ontology. Arguably, these late neoclassical debates around the concepts of "comparative efficiency" and "path dependency" demonstrate the extent to which the Walrasian metaphor of "price adjustment" through auctions has been supplanted by the Marshallian metaphor of "market adjustment" through selection as the dominant metaphor of the mainstream economic thinking.

7.4 "Meta-markets" beyond markets and firms

What McCloskey argues, apropos of the status of the difference between the new institutional economics of the Good Old Chicago tradition and the new information economics of Stiglitz, Bowles, Akerlof, et al., is quite accurate:

> The market is like a post-impressionistic painting. If one steps back and squints, then the gold points fade to insignificance, and there is effectively one world price for gold. [...] When one gets close enough to any market, on the other hand, the brush strokes appear. [...] The close view is no more real than the far view. It may be more or less convenient for this or that human purpose to take a close view or a far view. That is all.
>
> (McCloskey 1994: 158)

Both late neoclassical tendencies subscribe to an overarching meta-ontology of competition. They share a common framework and common lexicon; they speak the same language. The only difference between them is that while those who subscribe to the liberal (and radical) positions look closely and form a pessimistic opinion about the virtues of the "competitive process," those who subscribe to the conservative (pro-market) position enjoy the "competitive process" from afar and form an optimistic perspective. Or, to put it in terms articulated by Wolff (2006), they differ not in their belief in an absolute efficiency calculus, but rather, in the particular set of costs and benefits that they deem important in making their efficiency calculations.

Late neoclassical economists theorize firms (and other non-exchange institutions of "command") as "governance structures" or, more generally, social devices to supplement or supplant markets when the latter fail to function in the way predicted by the standard neoclassical models. Since they theorize market failures to be caused by the opportunism of the economic agents that enter into contractual relations, all late neoclassical treatments of the firm (or, all non-market institutions), whether they explicitly acknowledge it or not, rely upon the paradigmatic theoretical humanist presupposition of *homo economicus* as that which causes the problems to which institutions are supposed to be solutions.

Moreover, it is necessary to pose the following question to the late neoclassical economists: what propels communities to devise transaction-cost-economizing institutions (assuming momentarily, for the sake of argument, that this is the case)? The late neoclassical answer lies in the other presupposition of the neoclassical problematic: the teleological construct of harmonious reconciliation through equilibrium. Both of the late neoclassical approaches discussed in this chapter presuppose the existence of a meta-competitive process, a meta-selection mechanism that adopts "comparatively efficient" institutions and weeds out inefficient ones. (Antecedents of this elevation of competition into an overarching meta-ontology can be found in the "selectionist arguments" articulated by the proponents of the Chicago approach.) As noted above, the concept of "path dependence" does not break from these two presuppositions—it is a concept devised to "relativize" (within the bounds of "last instance determinism") the essentialisms of the theoretical presuppositions of the neoclassical problematic.

Before concluding, let us revisit the three theses on late neoclassical economics outlined in Chapter 6, but now in relation to the debates discussed in the present chapter. To begin with, the present chapter demonstrated that the late neoclassical treatments of market failures and economic institutions display both *dispersion* and *unity*. In terms of dispersion, we have seen that the Marshallian/Coasean and the post-Walrasian traditions have both theoretical and political incompatibilities. In terms of unity (and *continuity*), we have argued that both tendencies subscribe to the two theoretical presuppositions of theoretical humanism ("opportunism" and "reconciliation") and operate within the confines of the neoclassical problematic. Second, to the extent that late neoclassical theories of market failures and economic institutions remain within the neoclassical problematic of how to reconcile harmoniously diverse interests of self-transparent and unified human agents, they fail to break from the neoclassical tradition. And third, both late neoclassical approaches are, in their own ways, *responses* to the perceived "shortcomings" of the A-D model: the concepts of transaction cost and information failures are aimed at addressing the shortcomings of the A-D understanding of the commodity and commodity space; the concepts of "firm-as-a-nexus-of-principal-agent-relations" and "efficiency wage" are aimed at producing a theory of "the social organization of the production process"; and finally, the Walrasian understanding of the *ex ante* "price-adjustment" process has been thoroughly supplanted by the Marshallian metaphor of *ex post* "quantity adjustment" through selection.

In conclusion, late neoclassical economics, despite the fact that it presents itself as capable of taking the sphere of production into account, does so by universalizing the theoretical construct of a centered, rational, and autonomous subject presupposed in the contractual fiction to the level of an ontological truth about all human beings. For this reason, late neoclassical economics continues to see the world and its institutions (firms, bureaucracies, and so on) from the perspective of the sphere of exchange, that is, from within the theoretical problematic of neoclassical humanism.

Notes

1 For Smith, with the "appropriation of land" and the "accumulation of wealth," it became impossible to explain the value of a commodity only by referring to the amount of labor that goes into producing it. Accordingly, in Smith's second theory of value (the so-called "adding-up" theory of value), the value of a commodity is defined as the price at which labor, capital, and land are all receiving their "natural prices" as determined by the competitive dynamics of the market forces.

2 Nevertheless, this distinction is helpful only up to a point, because a third possibility (among numerous others) that escapes Dobb's classification—perhaps due to his realist epistemology—is a Marxian, and emphatically non-Ricardian, value theory, which theorizes the spheres of production and exchange as being mutually constitutive of each other and articulates a view that takes the question of the social organization of the production, appropriation, and distribution of surplus labor as

its entry point to social theory (Wolff et al. 1982; 1984; Roberts 1996; Zizek 2004; Kristjanson-Gural 2003).

3 Among these radical political economists and sociologists associated with the journal *Review of Radical Political Economics*, it is possible to mention Stephen Marglin (1974; 1975), Richard Edwards (1979), Michael Burawoy (1982; 1985), and Samuel Bowles (1985).

4 The introduction of non-market social institutions casts a dark shadow over the sacrosanct position that the idea of individual choice enjoys within the theoretical humanist ontology of the neoclassical tradition; to the extent that non-market institutions are impositions that individuals are compelled to adopt but do not deliberately choose, they entail a delimitation of choice.

5 Relaxation of the other two idealized conditions (i.e., "unbounded rationality" and "unique equilibrium") also makes it possible to insert "institutions" into the ontology of contracts. Consider, for instance, the status of "norms" and "habits" qua social institutions/devices in late neoclassical economics. Most late neoclassical economists would agree with the argument that human subjects are boundedly rational and would concede that human subjects need "norms" and "habits" to help them solve the complex economic problems with which they are confronted in exchanging commodities. Or, consider situations where there is no unique equilibrium. Faced with multiple equilibria with no clear reason to choose between possible equilibrium outcomes, rational agents find themselves dependent upon the so-called "focal points" and "conventions" that enable them to coordinate their independent choices without communicating. In this case, non-market social institutions (e.g., conventions, government directives) are treated, in a functionalist manner, as social devices that coordinate the selection of an equilibrium among multiple equally plausible ones. These two lines of inquiry will be pursued in chapters 8 and 9, respectively.

6 Coase mentions the following as some of the costs of using the price mechanism: the cost of "discovering what the relevant prices are" (search cost) and "the costs of negotiating and concluding a separate contract for each exchange transaction" (1937: 390–1). Writing half a century later, Steven Cheung offers a more comprehensive list: "[Transaction costs] include not only those of contracting and negotiating, but also those of measuring and policing property rights, of engaging in politics for power, of monitoring performances, and of organizing activities" (1992: 51).

7 In fact, as many others have noted, there is no clear statement of a "Coase theorem" in Coase's 1960 essay. Steven Medema (1994: 63), among others, notes that the first person to use the term "Coase theorem" was not Coase, but the eminent Chicago economist George Stigler (1965: 113).

8 The reader may note the elements of a Jevonsian (or Edgeworthian) understanding of the market as an exchange of commodities between two contracting agents.

9 For a deconstruction of the category of efficiency in mainstream economics and its associated framework of cost–benefit analysis, see Wolff (2006).

10 See also the various contributions to a recent volume edited by Claude Ménard (2000). Let us note, however, that today new institutional economics refers to a number of related yet distinct tendencies that build upon the contributions of the transaction costs approach but are not limited to it. Within this line of research, the works of Daron Acemoğlu, James Robinson, and Dani Rodrik are among the best known.

11 As noted in Chapter 4, the first generation of émigré economists (e.g., Oskar Lange, Jacob Marschak, Leonid Hurwicz) who were affiliated with the Cowles Commission were engaged parties in the socialist calculation debate, and they were implicated in Hayek's critique of the Walrasian assumptions pertaining to the epistemic status of knowledge. According to this critique, it was impossible for a Central Planning Board to gather the necessary information to calculate the equilibrium price, because this information was in fact "tacit knowledge" that emerges only during the competitive process and therefore cannot be revealed in the absence of actual competitive markets.

Given that they were implicated in this critique, they may have felt the need to theorize "knowledge." Nonetheless, the epistemic status of Hayek's concept of (tacit) knowledge was radically different from the epistemic status of the concept of "information" (Caldwell 2004). This, however, was not a concern for Walrasian economists, for they were more concerned by the economic policy implications (for it implied that "there are not enough markets") of Hayek's critique than its epistemological implications (Adaman and Devine 1996). Even though Hayek's concept of tacit knowledge was different from Stigler's concept of information qua commodity, since their policy conclusions were the same, they were indistinguishable in the eyes of post-Walrasian information economists.

12 Even though the absence of future markets was not an ontological absence, as in the post-Keynesian notion of "fundamental uncertainty" (Davidson 1991), but rather, an absence due to the prohibitive costs of gathering information, new information economists, perhaps because of their underlying normative commitment to corrective government intervention, identified themselves, on certain occasions, as *new Keynesian economists* (see also Rotheim 1998).

13 For a survey of the various criticisms of Stigler's search model, see Rothschild (1973). Peter A. Diamond (1971) argues that even when there are small search costs, the market equilibrium will result in monopoly price. For a discussion of the implications of Diamond's result for the role of competition under information problems, see Stiglitz (1994: 121–2).

14 While this point is not explicitly articulated in Coase's early writings, it is clearly articulated in the more recent new institutionalist writing. For instance, Cheung is very explicit on this point: "That transaction costs arise is no doubt partly attributable to our ignorance or lack of information. This applies not only in searching and negotiating, but also in knowing about the goods we purchase and consume. Ignorance, however, is only one factor. Another is the universality of maximizing behavior. Economists have long supported the proposition that individual maximization benefits society because it brings gain for all. *Yet it is the same maximizing behavior when we steal, cheat, lie, shirk, or break promises.* To be sure, if all of us were perfectly honest, the costs of transactions would be far lower. But this would amount to saying that we do not really maximize, in which case all other costs (including other types of transaction costs) would be far higher and the economy would collapse" (Cheung 1992: 52).

15 There is another theoretical humanist presupposition that the late neoclassical theories of the firm inherit from the neoclassical tradition: the assumption that labor is a *disutility* for the economic agent. In neoclassical models, this assumption provides the legitimizing microfoundations for conservative labor market policies, for it pins the responsibility for unemployment on the individual agent: as long as there are no rigidities in labor markets, then unemployment is an effect of the labor supply decision made by the economic agent. In the late neoclassical models discussed in this paragraph, labor continues to be represented as a source of disutility. The key difference between post-Walrasian models of the firm and the neoclassical theory of the firm was the insertion of the idea of asymmetric information.

16 This hypothetical notion of a market-clearing wage rate (or the Walrasian wage rate) is that little thing that sticks out and re-marks the (ghostly) presence of the Walrasian A-D model within this late neoclassical model of the labor market. If information asymmetries are endemic, how could we speak of a market-clearing wage rate even as a possibility?

17 Williamson explains the essential aspects of the new institutional analysis of the firm in the following manner: "The study of firms, markets, and mixed modes is approached as a unified subject in which *transaction cost economizing is central.* Organizational variety is explained by the fact that transactions differ in their attributes, on account of which their governance needs vary" (Williamson 1984: 196). On opportunism: "opportunism refers to the incomplete or distorted disclosure of information, especially to calculated efforts to mislead, disguise, obfuscate, or confuse" (Williamson 1984: 199).

18 But a "Good Old Chicago" economist such as D. N. McCloskey is less than impressed by the so-called radical implications of the "efficiency-wage" model as a theory of the firm that introduces the dimension of power for the first time to economic modeling of the labor contract:

> To use the natural metaphor, transaction costs put walls around institutions, the way transportation costs put walls around an island. [...] The cost of getting into and out of a job or a marriage or a country is like the cost of getting gold into and out of New York. At some differential between the price in Hong Kong and the price in New York the gold will flow from New York to Hong Kong; at the opposite differential it will flow in the opposite direction. The two differentials are of course the "gold points." At the gold points "the market works." That is, you won't find gold selling in New York for a price higher or lower than what it costs to bring some gold from Hong Kong. But inside the gold points the market doesn't "work." This means merely that strictly inside the range of prices set by the gold points a speculator would not find it worthwhile to send gold form one place to another. [...] Outside the gold points the prices are determined by international competition; inside the gold points they are determined by something else ... To repeat, within the gold points there is power.
>
> (McCloskey 1994: 157–9)

In other words, McCloskey claims that the transaction costs framework subsumes the information failures framework, and that the transaction costs approach has already incorporated the dimension of power into its analysis. "It is apparent from the analogy with gold points", McCloskey continues, "that whether or not the market 'works' depends on how closely one is examining it" (1994: 158). More on this below.

19 In an earlier article, Bowles (1985) claims that opportunism is not "simply a manifestation of human nature, but in part the result of the social institutions in which the production process takes place" (33). If, therefore, opportunism is an effect of one set of social institutions (e.g., "the capitalist firm"), then another set of institutions (e.g., "the democratic firm") may elicit cooperative behavior from the economic agents. Nevertheless, in their work, which argues for the superior efficiency of democratic firms, Bowles and Gintis deliberately refrain from making any assumptions about economic agents other than opportunism (Bowles and Gintis 1990). Indeed, for Bowles and Gintis, democratic firms may be more efficient precisely because they accommodate the underlying opportunism of economic agents better than hierarchical firms. We can see the same rhetorical trope in the writings of George Akerlof (1982), yet another prominent figure of the new information camp. In a series of papers, Akerlof developed a model of labor contracts as *partial gift exchanges* whereby the bosses pay above-the-market-clearing-level wages to workers and receive in return an extra amount of effort. In these models, the "institutional disciplinary devices" that secure the "effort" of otherwise opportunistic workers are replaced by the norms of "fair wage" that constrain the behavior of economic agents who are essentially opportunistic—otherwise there would not be any need for a "gift exchange." (There will be more on the debates on motivational diversity and the persisting primacy of opportunism at the level of preferences in Chapter 8.)

20 In their subsequent research, Bowles and Gintis (1996) explored how the unequal distribution of wealth in a given society may effect the risk-type of cash-poor worker-owners, and given their reliance on external finance, the growth of the democratic enterprise sector may indeed be inhibited. Needless to note, given the endemic information problems, a post-Walrasian economist would anticipate that the worker-owners would be on the short-side of the credit market, facing rationing.

8 Motivational diversity and cognitive limitations
Saving the human subject from its structuralist destitution

This chapter will trace the late neoclassical trajectories of the concept of the human subject as a centered, self-conscious, and autonomous unity. This notion of the human subject as the seat of economic rationality is one of the two constitutive presuppositions of neoclassical humanism. The other constitutive presupposition of neoclassical humanism, the concept of equilibrium, will be the topic of the next chapter. In terms of the concept of the human subject, the dominant tendency in neoclassical economics from the 1930s up to the 1970s was to assume as little as possible regarding the preferences that underpin the actual choices. In contrast to the ordinalist neoclassicisms of the mid-twentieth century, the distinguishing characteristic of the late neoclassical debates on economic rationality is the *reversal* of this positivist (or, as it was in the case of the Chicago School, pragmatist) tendency to assume as little as possible regarding the decision-making criteria (i.e., motivations) and decision-making processes (i.e., competence) of the economic agents. In this sense, these developments conform to *the response thesis* (from Chapter 6) that proposes to characterize *the late neoclassical condition as a patchwork of responses to the perceived crisis and limitations of Walrasian economics*. It is, therefore, possible to trace the genealogy of the late neoclassical debates on human rationality all the way back to the turn of the century, to the psychologism controversy that haunted the early neoclassicism (as discussed in Part 2).

Nevertheless, as will be demonstrated in this chapter, this reversal never entailed a departure from the theoretical problematic of neoclassical humanism. On the contrary, all the efforts discussed below, even when they revert (sometimes unwittingly and sometimes self-consciously) to a structuralist framework, remain within the theoretical humanist problematic of how to reconcile the interests (however defined) of autonomous and rational human subjects at the level of the social in a harmonious, growth-inducing, and "efficient" manner. Conforming to *the continuity thesis* (see Chapter 6), *the late neoclassical condition, far from representing a break from the neoclassical tradition, is squarely within it.*

Indeed, the late neoclassical departure from the mid-century (positivist or pragmatist) minimalist positions had a range of causes, and the departure manifested itself in diverse and contradictory ways. In order to understand the diversity of late neoclassical approaches, it is better to organize the literature around two central debates. Here, once more, the objective is to show not only *the differences among* but also *the presuppositions common to* diverse late neoclassical discourses. This will make it possible to substantiate *the conjunction of unity and dispersion thesis* articulated in Chapter 6 in this particular theoretical context. The first debate pertains to the nature and origins of human motivations. Some late neoclassical approaches, especially in the context of theorizing market failures and economic institutions, vigorously embraced and systematically applied the assumption of *opportunism* (the assumption of non-satiation augmented with narrowly defined self-interest seeking). In these models, while opportunism is theorized as the cause of market failures, social and economic institutions (including "pro-social norms" such as fairness, goodwill, and trust) are theorized as devices that would "correct" these market failures (Chapter 7). But this was not the only tendency that prevailed in late neoclassical economics. Others, rather than conceptualizing opportunism as the inherent motivational basis of human rationality, chose to devise economic models with agents that are *somehow* endowed with non-opportunistic motivational orientations (e.g., altruism, reciprocity). The qualifier "somehow" is rather deliberately used, because one of the two late neoclassical debates on the rationality postulate pertains to the theorization of the status and the nature of *motivational diversity* among human populations.

The other late neoclassical debate pertaining to the rationality assumption took place between, on the one hand, those late neoclassical writers who worked within the Nash refinements tradition of game theory and who continually augmented the already over-stretched standard neoclassical concept of rationality (discussed in Chapter 3) with additional cognitive powers verging on "hyper-rationality" and, on the other hand, those late neoclassical economists who, as a result of their interdisciplinary self-positioning in the intersections of economics, psychology, organizational studies, and cognitive sciences, chose to acknowledge the limitedness of the *cognitive competence* of the economic agents and, as a result, embraced concepts of bounded and procedural rationality.

To what extent, then, does the increasing volume of late neoclassical explorations of and debates on the aspects of the rationality assumption constitute a break from theoretical humanism, and to what extent are these developments manifestations of a wave of restoration and rehabilitation of theoretical humanism in mainstream microeconomics? In order to answer this question (and assess the validity of *the continuity thesis*), it is necessary to establish the general concept and architecture of economic rationality as it is produced, developed, and deployed by the proponents of the neoclassical tradition and to explain why it is a theoretical humanist construct. In what follows, I will begin by recovering some aspects of the earlier discussions on the ordinalist turn in the mid-century neoclassical economics. In doing so, the positivist and pragmatist versions of the neoclassical concept of the rational actor will be delineated, with the purpose of outlining the late neoclassical extensions to, reformulations of, and modifications to the concept of rationality. This general introductory discussion will be followed by two main sections of the chapter. First, the questions pertaining to *motivational diversity* in late neoclassical models of economic phenomena will be tackled, and a discussion of the late neoclassical debates on the origin and the nature of the preferences will be offered. Then, attention will be given to late neoclassical debates that pertain to the *cognitive competence* of rational actors. Both clusters of debates will provide insights pertaining to the restoration of theoretical humanism in late neoclassical economics.

8.1 Aspects of economic rationality: preferences, information, competence

The concept of rational choice, despite the significant amount of scrutiny it has received, continues to retain its central place within the late neoclassical literature. Philosopher Jon Elster defines rationality as a "normative" (as opposed to "descriptive") concept that "tells us what we ought to do in order to achieve our aims as well as possible" (1990: 20). Invoking David Hume's oft-quoted dictum "Reason is, and ought only to be the slave of the passions" (Hume 1960 [1739]: 415; cf. Elster 1990: 21), Elster claims that the standard rationality assumption does not "tell us what our aims ought to be" (1990: 20). In other words, according to Elster, the rational choice theory takes the aims ("passions") of the subject as given and "instructs" the subject on how to achieve those aims as well as possible. In other words, according to Elster's definition, rational choice theory is normative only in the sense that it instructs subjects on *how* to achieve their ends but not on *what* to achieve. With this formulation, Elster tries to push the questions of human motivation outside the domain of the rational choice theory.

Recall that the subject of theoretical humanism is defined early on (Chapter 2) as an autonomous, self-transparent, and rational self-consciousness who knows what his/her true preferences are and what improves his/her welfare; who can consistently translate these true and essentially transparent and consistent preferences into his/her choices; and who recognizes himself/herself (and is recognized by others) as an intentional and autonomous subject who is responsible for his/her choices (as is presupposed in the contract law). At some level, Elster's definition of the rational choice theory resonates with this theoretical humanist understanding of the human subject. The rational choice theory must be silent with respect to the causes of the preferences of the rational agent (her desires, passions, or aims), for only the agent (as a sovereign and self-transparent self-consciousness) can know what her ends are. Accordingly, for Elster, the role of the rational choice theory is to help the subject achieve her (exogenously determined) ends.

Nevertheless, it is open to debate whether or not rationality is intended as a normative (instructive) or a descriptive concept. On the one hand, some late neoclassical economists who embrace the augmented notion of (hyper-)rationality, when criticized by those who (logically or empirically) demonstrate the descriptive shortcomings of the assumption of rationality, claim that the concept is a normative one that describes not how people actually behave but how they ought to behave to achieve efficient outcomes. Yet, on the other hand, the neoliberal prescription for the privatization of publicly owned assets as well as the monetarist macroeconomic policy decisions are scientifically legitimized by models that assume *opportunism* (the rent-seeking behavior argument) and *hyper-rationality* (the rational expectations hypothesis) regarding the economic agents. Those who defend such marketization and economization policies or reforms regularly assert that these models of economic behavior have unambiguous descriptive claims.

Moreover, the concept of rationality, regardless of how it is intended, whether as a normative "toolbox" for decision-making or as a description of how actual agents behave, belongs squarely to the theoretical humanist problematic. When it comes to the formal attributes of the preferences (reflexivity, completeness, transitivity, etc.), it presupposes unity, self-transparency, and consistency on the part of the subject. The idea that there is a unique and "rational" way of attaining one's "predetermined ends" not only assumes self-knowledge on the part of the subject but also presumes the existence of a uniform index with which we can rank different methods of achieving our ends. Moreover, when combined with the other constitutive presupposition of theoretical humanism, namely, the economic concept of equilibrium as a desirable (e.g., Pareto efficient) state, rational choice theory posits that the preferred social state (or, bundle) is implied to be better for the subject than the one to which it is preferred.

In order to organize late neoclassical debates on rationality, it might be useful to begin by differentiating between the two distinct aspects of the neoclassical concept of rationality: the preferences (with their particular properties) that guide the decision-making process and the act of, or the process of, decision-making itself. To use a computer analogy, there is the *software*, the logical attributes of the preference orderings in general (including the motivational assumptions) and the particular information pertaining to the choice context under scrutiny, and then there is the *hardware*, the processor that calculates and processes the available information pertaining to the choice problem under consideration, given the preferences (see also Davis 2003).

The conceptual architecture of rational choice under *uncertainty* in the neoclassical tradition (early and late) builds upon three different classes of data: preferences, beliefs, and information (Hargreaves-Heap 1989; Elster 1990). *Preferences* refer to the desires, passions, or aims of the subject. *Beliefs*, on the other hand, refer to the subjective probabilities that the subject assigns to the states of nature based on the available *information*. Accordingly, in making a rational choice, the agent gathers the best available *information*, revises his/her *beliefs* according to the available information, and, based on his/her beliefs, takes the actions that will best satisfy his/her *preferences*. While the preferences, the information set, the subjective probabilities, and the rules of optimization pertain to the *software* aspect, the *acts* of preference formation, information gathering, belief formation, and optimization pertain to the *hardware* aspect of human rationality.

Not surprisingly, in the standard Arrow-Debreu (A-D) model, each of the abovementioned processes was assumed to function smoothly: the best available information was assumed to be readily available to the agent; the definition of the "contingent commodities" obviated the question of belief formation;[1] and the actors were assumed to be endowed with the cognitive capacity and competence to choose the consumption plans that would best serve their preferences and to devise the production plans that would maximize their profit. Moreover, even though the preferences are supposed to be a matter of "individual choice," they are assumed to be structured across the board by a very specific set of properties: completeness, reflexivity, transitivity, continuity, non-satiation, and convexity.

Let us take a closer look at the theoretical implications of the various axioms and presuppositions pertaining to the preference patterns, the informational requirements, and the cognitive competence of the rational economic agent in the A-D model. With regard to the axioms that structure the *preference* patterns: if the axioms of reflexivity, completeness, and transitivity hold, then the individual is considered to have a preference ordering (and hence, the individual is conceived as a unified and self-transparent self-consciousness); if, in addition, the axiom of continuity (the relative openness of all upper and lower contour sets) holds, the individual's preference ordering can be represented as a utility function; the axioms of non-satiation and convexity are necessary specifically for proving the *existence* of the equilibrium price vector (and hence, the existence of a harmonious and contradiction-free economic order is established); and finally, the implicit assumption that the individual's choices reflect what is best for his/her well-being given his/her initial endowments drives the welfare implications of the A-D model. In contrast to the axiomatic approach that undergirds the A-D model, the pragmatic Chicago understanding of the human rationality takes the utility function as its point of departure: "all human behaviour can be viewed as involving participants who maximize their utility from a stable set of preferences and accumulate an optimal amount of information and other inputs in a variety of markets" (Becker 1976: 14).

With regard to the assumptions pertaining to *information*: perhaps surprisingly for some, the amount of information that the economic agents in an A-D world need to know to make decisions is less than that needed by the Marshallian and the game theoretic agents. In an essay that compares the standard information assumptions made in these traditions, Michel De Vroey (2003) distinguishes between three different domains of knowledge: (1) physical domain (including the quality of goods and the states of the environment); (2) private economic data; (3) public economic data. An A-D agent, in addition to his/her own private economic data and preferences (self-transparency, self-consciousness), is assumed to have a perfect knowledge of only the first and the third domains of knowledge. "Due to the presence of the auctioneer," De Vroey argues, "economic agents do not need to know market excess demand functions (nor their underpinnings)" (2003: 467). The presence of the auctioneer obviates the need to have information regarding the private data of other agents in the economy, whereas in the Marshallian models of market exchange, agents are regularly assumed to possess complete knowledge pertaining to all the three domains listed above: Marshallian agents not only have information pertaining to the physical and public domains (as do the A-D agents), but also are assumed to know the market excess demand functions (which requires, in turn, that they know not only their own but also the other market agents' private economic data). Similarly, the defining assumption of game theoretic constructs (such as those underpinning the "efficiency-wage" models) is that the agent can, and in certain condition does, *possess* and effectively *process* complete economic knowledge pertaining to all three domains—particularly the private economic data of *other* agents. Let us take a closer look at this.

The difference between an A-D agent and a game theoretic agent can be best understood in terms of the amount of information that each is supposed to process through differentiating between *parametric* and *strategic* rationality. Under the assumption of parametric rationality, the agent treats others' choices as given; under the assumption of strategic rationality, the agent has to take into account others' choices in arriving at a decision. As noted above, the strategic rationality burdens the agents with additional informational requirements pertaining to the private economic data of other agents (e.g., "peeking into their mind")—informational requirements that are not needed under parametric choice situations. Christian Knudsen (1993a: 144–5), following Leif Johansen (1981), distinguishes among three kinds of *interaction*: (1) unconscious, indirect, and parametric; (2) indirect and functional; and (3) direct. The first category of interaction is what one finds in the context of the A-D-type perfect competition models, where the agents make choices without taking into account others' choices (unconscious and parametric) and where there is no room for communication or collusion among agents (indirect). (Let us also note in passing that the term *unconscious* is used not in its psychoanalytical sense, but in the cognitive sense to denote that an act is being done "automatically.") The second category of indirect and functional interactions captures the situations of imperfect competition, where agents have to take into account each other's "reactional patterns in the shape of functional relation" (Knudsen 1993a: 145). As an example of this case, consider the efficiency-wage models.[2] In such models, even though there could be no communication among agents (indirectness), the Boss (the Stackelberg leader) *knows* the utility function of the Worker (the Stackelberg follower) and maximizes his profit function by taking the latter into account (hence, functional). This particular additional informational requirement of the efficiency-wage models is a quite remarkable one, given the fact that the efficiency-wage models were intended to incorporate information failures into the analysis of the labor contract. The apparent contradiction is usually glossed over in the literature (De Vroey 2003). The third category of direct interactions refers to contexts where communication, collusion, and commitments are possible. In this sense, cooperative games are direct interactions. While parametric one-person rationality is sufficient for the first kind of interaction, the latter two require strategic rationality. The second type, however, can be singled out as the one that imposes the strongest informational requirements on the subject. We will see in the next chapter how the Nash equilibrium solution imposes the second type of informational requirements, namely, indirect and functional.

And finally, with respect to the *cognitive competence* of the economic agents: in the A-D model, the questions of how the best available information is gathered, how beliefs are formed and revised, and what concrete and material practices are entailed in taking the right courses of action, i.e., the "hardware" questions, are not taken into consideration. It is assumed that these cognitive processes can be effortlessly undertaken by economic agents. It should be emphasized, however, that the implied computer-like cognitive competence of rational agents did not fit easily with the theoretical humanist program of neoclassical economics. Accordingly, far from leading to a break with the theoretical humanist problematic, the questioning of the assumption of unlimited cognitive capabilities on the side of the economic agent actually entails a return to and a rehabilitation of theoretical humanism.

Much of the late neoclassical literature on rational choice inherits this architecture and proceeds to unpack its various aspects: the nature and the origin of the preferences of the subject, the process of information gathering and belief formation, and the scope of the cognitive capacities of the subject. Nevertheless, this unpacking never entails a departure from the theoretical problematic of neoclassical humanism. Since the various treatments of "information" in late neoclassical economics have already been discussed in Chapter 7, here the questions of information will be referred to only to the extent that they pertain to the supposed cognitive prowess of the human subject; the chapter will concentrate instead on the late neoclassical debates on questions pertaining to *the nature and the origins of preferences* (motivational diversity) and *the scope of the cognitive capacities* (bounded rationality) of human subjects.

8.2 Questions of motivational diversity

With the ordinalist turn, the neoclassical tradition claimed to have abandoned the project of peeking into the psyche of the economic agent. While the empiricist project of Samuelson aimed at testing the axioms of rationality from the actual observed choices of agents,[3] the rationalist project of Arrovian social choice theory insisted on remaining silent regarding the motivations of the subjects. Similarly, whereas Debreu's formalist program aimed at deducing the existence, efficiency, uniqueness, and global stability of general equilibrium from the minimum number of axioms necessary, the Chicago neoclassicals went so far as to declare the assumption of self-interest-optimizing behavior dispensable—even though they continued to use it as a good enough approximation or a convenient shorthand. Overall, the defining tendency of the period was to assume as little as possible about the preferences of the economic agent.

This tendency is reversed in late neoclassical economics. The developments in the various branches of game theory and experimental economics, in behavioral economics, and in social choice theory began to explore what is behind the act of "choice." Late neoclassical economists may have been compelled to explain what is behind the actual behavior (or choices) of the individual agent for a number of reasons. One important reason may be the growing concern with the reductionism of the assumption of opportunism (the assumption of self-interested non-satiation). The previous chapter has established the importance of the assumption of opportunism for the Coasean and post-Walrasian theories of market failures and economic organizations. The frankness with which these late neoclassical economists deployed the assumption of opportunism in their models of market failures, labor contracts, credit rationing, and rent-seeking reversed the dominant tendency to remain silent about what motivates the preferences. Ironically, the reversal itself made it possible to question the ubiquity of the assumption of opportunism.[4]

The questioning of the ubiquity of the assumption of opportunism took three forms. First, there was a perceived need to theorize the non-market and non-governmental ("third sphere") activities—such as gift-giving, voluntary contributions to charities, unpaid household labor—that are not easily modeled through the standard neoclassical models premised upon rational individuals with selfish preferences (e.g., Titmuss 1971; Arrow 1972; Becker 1981; Sugden 1984; Coate and Ravallion 1993; for a critical survey, see Adaman and Madra 2002).[5] Second, a significant accumulation of experimental "evidence" suggested that the economic subjects do not behave as predicted by the standard *homo economicus* models. Among a large repertoire of motivational dispositions, economists list altruisms (liberal and paternalist), fairness, and reciprocity (e.g., Rabin 1993; Ledyard 1995; Fehr and Gächter 1998a; 1998b; 2000). And third, there was a growing number of methodological/philosophical critiques (from within mainstream economics as well as from without) of the narrowness of the *homo economicus* assumption (e.g. Sen 1977; Collard 1978; for a range of feminist views, see the various contributions to Ferber and Nelson 1993).

These three factors in combination instigated the late neoclassical debates on the nature of preferences. The debates centered around two related questions: is there a motivational diversity? And if there is a diversity, how does one theorize the dynamics of this diversity? Addressing these questions in this order, this section will trace the vicissitudes of theoretical humanism in late neoclassical economics.

8.2.1 Is there a motivational diversity? (Opportunism, altruism, reciprocity)

The immediate late neoclassical response to the increased questioning of the presumed ubiquity of opportunism was to remain committed to the standard assumption that human beings are, *by nature*, selfish, opportunist, etc. In order to explain behaviors that do not conform to the predictions of the standard *homo economicus* assumption (e.g., gift-giving, reciprocity, behavior confirming with norms of fairness), these economists devised models in which the agent, even though s/he is selfish by nature, may be compelled to act (behave) *as if* s/he had non-selfish preferences when constrained by social norms or ethical concerns (e.g., Sugden 1984).[6] For these late neoclassical economists, the problem of "seemingly" non-selfish behavior became the portal through which *institutions* qua *constraints on actions* entered into economic models. In short, these late neoclassical economists tried to accommodate the non-standard economic behavior without changing the standard *homo economicus* assumption, but by supplementing it with external constraints on actions (social norms, rules of conduct, etc.).

Nonetheless, not all late neoclassical economists were willing to accept that human beings are selfish by nature. Following in the footsteps of Samuelsonian empiricism, a significant number of experimental economists began to argue that individuals "systematically" behave in non-selfish, "pro-social" ways (e.g., altruistically, reciprocally) and that it may be incorrect to assume that this is only due to the effects of external constraints on the optimizing acts of agents who are essentially selfish (e.g., Rabin 1993; Ledyard 1995; Fehr and Gächter 1998a; 1998b; 2000; Charness and Rabin 2002). Consider, for instance, *the ultimatum game*, in which the first subject divides up the pie as he wishes and offers a slice to the second subject, and the second subject either declines or accepts the offer (Güth et al. 1982). If the latter declines the offer, neither gets to eat the pie. The standard models predict that the second subject should prefer the thinnest of slices to no slice at all. Nevertheless, experiments have shown that, unless the first subject makes a "fair" (50–50) offer, the second subject tends to reject the offer. This result, of course, violates the "non-satiation" assumption.

Nevertheless, one has to be careful in assessing the theoretical implications of these experiments. As is always the case, the empiricism of experimental economics is not a "pure" empiricism, for the very design of the experiments themselves contributes to the results of the experiments (Hargreaves-Heap and Varoufakis 1995). From an ontological perspective that takes overdetermination seriously, the regularities that are "discovered" in well-delineated and designed experimental contexts are not universal truths regarding the true essence of human subjectivity— they are simply regularities (or "truths") that pertain to those experiments. The sheer fact that certain regularities and patterns emerge in experimental contexts does not warrant our interpretation of those regularities as the truth of human subjectivity. Precisely for this reason, it is quite possible to find experimental evidence that supports the assumption of universal opportunism as well as the assumption of motivational heterogeneity.

For instance, it would be quite useful to juxtapose the abovementioned experimental results, which give credence to the construction of analytical models premised upon agents with non-selfish or other-regarding preferences, with the experiments and simulations conducted by the likes of Vernon Smith (1991; 1994), Charles R. Plott (1990), and Dhananjay K. Gode and Shyam Sunder (1993; 1997). This group distinguishes between rationality as a concept that describes *individual behavior* and rationality as a concept that describes *market outcomes*, and argue that the concept of rationality is best understood as a description of the "average" economic agent. Echoing the Chicago-style selectionist "structuralism" discussed above, these economists argue that while the individuals may behave irrationally, if the "trading rules" are specified appropriately, the market outcomes will be consistent with the predictions of the standard neoclassical model. In fact, Gode and Sunder (1993; 1997) went so far as to simulate experiments with "zero-intelligent traders" (a computer algorithm that "behaves" randomly and does not "learn" from past experience) instead of human traders. For this group of researchers, as long as the appropriate "trading rules" are in place, it does not matter whether the individual actors act selfishly or not: "[W]hen embodied in market mechanism such as a double auction, [the invisible hand] may generate aggregate rationality not only from individual rationality but also from individual irrationality" (Gode and Sunder 1993: 136). Not surprisingly, in this literature, the main reference is to Gary Becker's 1962 article, "Irrational Behaviour and Economic Theory," where this prominent Chicago School economist argued that it does not matter whether individuals behave rationally or not—given the changes in opportunity sets, the behavior of the "average consumer" will be in line with the predictions of the standard theory (i.e., the law of demand).[7]

Nevertheless, even though experimental economists such as Smith and Plott and simulation economists such as Gode and Sunder try to generalize the allocative efficiency results that they gather from their "double-auction" experiments (where both sellers and buyers submit bids that are ranked from highest to lowest to generate demand and supply schedules) to give substance to Adam Smith's "invisible hand scenario" and his imputed ideas about human nature (in particular, the "propensity to truck, barter and exchange" (Smith 1991 [1776]: 19)) their results are much more limited in scope and application. If, as Smith, Plott, and Gode and Sunder seem to imply and even acknowledge, what makes markets work are the "trading rules" qua "social algorithms," then maybe there is something in these results that is contingent upon the particular market algorithm that is being used (Mirowski 2002: 560). It is somewhat telling that while the typical markets in contemporary economies predominantly take the form of posted-offer markets, Gode and Sunder's claim for the aggregate rationality of markets is based on more structured trading rules, such as double-auction markets, that require interaction from agents.[8] To put it differently, the claim that such experiments and simulations prove and validate the invisible hand scenario and the notions of human nature underlying it needs to be taken with a grain of salt. On the contrary, if anything, they give credence to the importance of institutions (i.e., the rules of the experiments, the algorithms of the simulations) in shaping social outcomes (see also Guala 2007: 138–43). In the end, given the importance of the institutions (rules and algorithms) in their design, experiments and simulations, far from discovering the "true" nature of human preferences and conclusively establishing whether human beings are, by nature, opportunistic or altruistic, have led to an endless back and forth between the two opposing positions.[9]

Despite the continuing opposition to the idea that there exists a meaningful diversity of motivations, and despite the ongoing insistence on the predictive relevance of the assumption of opportunistic behavior, the late neoclassical period differs from the earlier periods of neoclassical economics in that there is a concerted effort to theorize motivational diversity. But to what extent does this late neoclassical effort signal a break from the neoclassical problematic? To the extent that a particular motivational orientation (whether it is opportunism, altruism, or reciprocity) is seen to be an inherent attribute of human nature, to the extent that the human subject of the late neoclassical condition, regardless of his/her motivational orientation, continues to be a rational, unified, and autonomous self-consciousness, the late neoclassical approaches remain within the theoretical humanist problematic. Nevertheless, the second important set of questions that is being debated among the late neoclassical circles opens room for an oscillation into structuralism: if there is a motivational diversity, is it caused by evolutionary dynamics or by deliberate and ethical human choice?

8.2.2 How to theorize the origins of motivational diversity?

Indeed, the concern with the origins and causes of this motivational diversity is a distinctively late neoclassical concern. Nonetheless, the late neoclassical debate on this matter is far from settled. There are at least two radically opposed ways of theorizing the cause of motivational diversity: the "structuralist" way of evolutionary game theory and the "individualist" way of social choice theory. A discussion of these two starkly opposed ways of handling the causes of motivational diversity should suffice to give the reader a sense of the theoretical horizon of this particular debate.

The evolutionary game theorists explain the origin of preferences (and the origins of the motivational diversity, if they believe in its existence) by reverting to a structuralist language according to which the agency resides not on the side of the individuals but rather, on the side of the selection mechanism. Two quotations from important proponents of this line of modeling should be sufficient to make the point:

> We will explore the evolutionary dynamics of populations in which individuals are "programmed," perhaps genetically or perhaps by cultural experience, to play either cooperate or defect in a game.
>
> (Bergström 2002: 70)

> Notice a rough learning rule underlying differential replication has replaced the role usually assigned to conscious optimization. We do not specify why traits are copied. The previous paragraph leaves this issue open. Rather, we simply posit that successful traits are more likely to be copied.
>
> (Bowles and Gintis 1998: 214)

While Bergström is ready to make the assumption that individuals are "programmed," Bowles and Gintis are more careful. While they replace "conscious optimization" with "a rough learning rule," they bracket the question of why traits are copied. Yet at the end of the day, in both cases, the individuals are treated as bearers (*träger*)—as opposed to the conscious and deliberate choosers—of preference types ("traits").

Deploying models of "group selection" that they borrowed from the biological literature, evolutionary game theorists[10] began to argue that, if the individuals with non-selfish preferences stuck together and behaved as a group, they could survive against their selfish opponents (Cohen and Eshel 1976; Maynard Smith 1982). In other words, while being engaged in the hallmark project of theoretical humanism, namely, the identification of the essence of human subjectivity, evolutionary game theorists revert to a form of structuralism.[11] Nonetheless, the fact that the evolutionary game theory provides a structuralist explanation of the origins of the diversity of preferences (or lack thereof, for that matter) should not deflect us from the fact that this structuralist moment is ultimately in the service of a theoretical humanist project of unveiling human nature. Moreover, let me also note that the concept of structure in the evolutionary game theory is decisively an anthropomorphized concept:

> Nature will be shamelessly *anthropomorphized* here, for the sake of vividness and conciseness. Thus, when we say that "Nature wishes" the individual to maximize biological fitness, this is shorthand for claiming that individuals who maximize fitness will ultimately dominate the population. That is, biological fitness is closely linked to the number of offspring.
>
> (Robson 2002: 91; emphasis added)

It is, indeed, a matter of debate whether or not this anthropomorphization is only a "rhetorical" device deployed "for the sake of vividness and conciseness," or to what extent this language inadvertently reveals the teleological construct that undergirds the evolutionary game theoretic models. But, if we agree with D. N. McCloskey's (1994) call for taking rhetoric seriously, we should also take this anthropomorphization seriously. In fact, in a final turn of the screw, don't we find behind this anthropomorphization of the structure the humanist concept of *anthropos* with a given (human) propensity to survive, to reproduce its existence? Indeed, it is this theoretical humanist presupposition that underpins the structuralist machine of evolutionary game theory.[12]

But there is yet another way in which these evolutionary game theoretical models, despite their structuralist armature, rely upon a theoretical humanist presupposition. In models based on group selection, selected groups do get selected because they have found a solution to a prisoners' dilemma problem that functions as the state of nature scenario. Unlike selfish agents who choose to defect to pursue their narrowly defined self-interests (and fail to act as a collective), non-selfish and cooperating agents that abide by the pro-social norms have a better chance of cooperating with each other and thereby increasing their group fitness. One should ask, however, for what problem this group selection scenario is offered as a solution. The underlying scenario of this evolutionary game theoretical model is a very basic variant of the theoretical problematic of neoclassical humanism, and it serves as the silent humanist presupposition of its structural armature: how might we harmoniously and efficiently reconcile the diverse interests of autonomous economic agents? Yet what makes this a problem is the fact that, in the last instance, the evolutionary game theoretical models presuppose that human beings pursue their narrow self-interests—not unlike the concept of the human subject that informs all the standard neoclassical models!

In contrast to the anthropomorphized selection mechanism of evolutionary game theory, social choice theory handles the question of motivational diversity at the level of *anthropos* proper and without apologies. Amartya Sen, in his Nobel Prize-winning work on the theory of social choice, developed a philosophically sophisticated and thoroughly individualist theory of preference diversity. According to

Sen (2002: 5), *rationality*, defined as "reasoned scrutiny," means nothing without *freedom*. Sen's notion of freedom, however, is not simply the freedom of choosing among commodity bundles (as celebrated by the proponents of market society), but rather, the freedom to choose the criteria by which to choose. Sen claims that "part of the freedom an individual enjoys is to entertain different preference rankings" (2002: 615). Sen handles this with his concept of *meta-ranking* (preference over preferences). The subject, through "reasoned scrutiny," forms a ranking among the various criteria by which s/he can form preference orderings. This, for Sen, is true freedom. "Indeed", Sen argues, the "plurality of preferences can relate closely to the issue of the autonomy of a person" (2002: 617).

From its inception in the 1950s, the research agenda of social choice theory has been to devise rules for the aggregation of individual preference "orderings" (reflexivity, transitivity, and completeness) into a collective choice that mirrored as much as possible the rationality of the individual at the aggregate level (Arrow 1963; Sen 1970). The "multiple-self" literature extended this research program to an analysis of the individual with multiple sub-individuals.[13] In this literature, the question of how to handle multiple selves is formally equivalent to the problem of aggregating individual preferences at the social level. Sen's formulation of meta-ranking of rankings is, formally speaking, also a member of this family of multiple-self models.

Despite the similarity to the multiple-self models, Sen's formulation does introduce a very subtle philosophical twist by conceiving motivational diversity as a condition of the *freedom* of the subject. (This position should be contrasted with the aspects of the multiple-self literature that pathologizes the agent with multiple selves.) It is, indeed, a worthwhile project to incorporate into the neoclassical framework the idea that the human subject can reconsider, alter, modify, or change his/her preferences. (In fact, as a clinical practice, psychology is premised upon this basic working assumption.) At first blush, the idea of "ranking of rankings" seems to open up the concept of rationality to interesting possibilities. First and foremost, the analytical framework of "ranking of rankings" makes it possible to think of a human subject capable of switching between different preference patterns. Second, the idea that preference can be submitted to scrutiny implies self-reflexivity on the part of the human subject—an idea that has never been articulated within the neoclassical tradition.

Nevertheless, when rationality is defined as reasoned scrutiny and autonomy is defined as the "volitional possibility of changing one's preferences," the subject is once more conceptualized as the master of his own house.[14] In other words, the preference patterns can indeed change in Sen's framework; but there is still an author, a chooser who chooses between the different preference patterns. In other words, Sen re-centers the question of diversity of preferences around the reasoned scrutiny of "truly" rational subjects. Therefore, in social choice theory, we find, once again, the central construct of neoclassical humanism: the human subject as a centered (albeit with a multiplicity of preferences) and autonomous self-reflexive self-consciousness.

*　*　*

To recapitulate the discussion so far, late neoclassical debates on human motivations represent a significant widening and deepening of the research field, especially in contrast to the neoclassical silence on the matter. This is in stark contrast to the predominant tendency within the neoclassical tradition, which was to assume as little as possible about the human mind and to evade falling into psychologism: Samuelson's revealed preference approach, Arrow's "value-neutral" reformulation of preference orderings, and even the various versions of the Marshallian "selectionist" arguments should be read as various moments of this process of "impoverishment" of the concept of the human subject. The two most significant characteristics of the late neoclassical treatments of the human subject have been their frankness regarding the assumptions that they make about the motivations of the economic agents (recall the emphasis on the "opportunism" of the economic agent in both transaction costs and new information economics) and their concerted effort to peek into the mind of the human subject (recall various efforts in experimental economics) in order to offer a "richer" understanding of the motivations of the human subject (either as the survivor of an evolutionary process millions of years long or as a rational and autonomous self-consciousness). In this particular sense, late neoclassical debates on the motivational basis of human action constitute a restoration, rehabilitation, and deepening of theoretical humanism in the mainstream economics. It is even possible to consider this late neoclassical interest in a richer (but no less humanist) concept of the human subject as a return to Adam Smith's *The Theory of Moral Sentiments*.[15] In this volume, in contrast to the *Wealth of Nations*, Smith constructed a knowledge of the human subject who is capable of seeing things from someone else's point of view, and argued that *sympathy* and *the desire for social approval* will make it possible for human beings to coexist. Even though the sufficiency of sympathy and the innate desire for social approval for the reproduction of social cohesion and harmony is questioned in the *Wealth of Nations* (and ultimately denounced by the subsequent neoclassical appropriations of Smith's writings), Smith considered both volumes as parts of a broader inquiry into social science (Backhouse 2002: 121). It is, in fact, possible to read late neoclassical inquiries into the motivational basis of human rationality as a "nostalgia for the *true* humanist beginnings of modern economics" (Ruccio and Amariglio 2003: 109). The point not to be missed here is that both the modernist and impoverished neoclassical agent of the 1950s and 1960s and the nostalgic and enriched late neoclassical agents of the 1980s and 1990s are squarely within the theoretical humanist problematic, for both versions subscribe to a notion of the human subject that presumes autonomy, unity, self-transparency, and intentionality. In the next section, we will turn to another late neoclassical attempt to "humanize" the concept of the human subject, to the concept of bounded rationality and its uses in the late neoclassical context.

8.3 Questions of cognitive competence

In contrast to the debates on the motivational basis of human action, debates on the cognitive competence of human agents were centered on a single concept introduced to economics by Herbert Simon (1976; 1978a): bounded rationality. Given the complexity of most "real-life" problem situations, Simon argued, human cognitive capacities are bound to fail in all three levels of optimization: in gathering all the relevant information, in forming consistent and rational beliefs, and in choosing the action that would best serve the subject's interests. The enormity of the informational requirements of neoclassical models and the toll that they put on the computational capacities of the agents was too obvious not to be acknowledged (Radner 1970). Similarly, a number of "paradoxes" that emerged in an earlier generation of experimental economics (the Allais paradox demonstrating that decisions are not immune to framing effects, the Elsberg paradox revealing ambiguity aversion as a prominent trait, the phenomenon of preference reversal, etc.) demonstrated that rational choice under uncertainty is limited by perceptions, passions, and judgment (for surveys, see Elster 1990; Tversky and Kahneman 1990; Sugden 1991; 2005).

Nevertheless, it is important to appreciate the diversity of the theoretical context within which Simon's concept of bounded rationality was introduced. During the 1960s and 1970s, a number of developing and active research programs were not receptive to the late neoclassical proposition that the human subject has cognitive limitations. These developments were (and in many cases continue to be) so accentuated that it is quite possible to make the case for a strong tendency towards *hyper-rationality*. To begin with, within the tradition of game theory that focuses on the refinement of the Nash equilibrium concept (which will be further discussed in the next chapter), the assumption of *common knowledge rationality* (CKR) is the entry point of the research program, and this entry point axiomatically postulates that each player knows all the relevant information regarding the game, that each player knows that each player knows (ad infinitum), and that all players maximize their own expected utility functions (Sugden 1991). In addition to this assumption, classical game theorists assume that beliefs are also consistently aligned (the Harsanyi–Aumann doctrine); that is, the agents who are given the same information will draw the same inferences and will arrive at the same conclusions (for a critical discussion, see Hargreaves-Heap and Varoufakis 1995: 25–7). In fact, when game theorists wanted to incorporate "bounded rationality," they did so by trying to fold it into a meta-optimization framework (e.g., Rubenstein 1998).[16] In the field of macroeconomics, the rational-expectation hypothesis, gaining significant prominence in the 1970s and 1980s, assumed that economic agents "efficiently digest all available information, and adopt the predictions of the 'relevant' economic theory as their subjective expectations" (Bausor 1983: 1). Much less acknowledged is the expansion of the scope of rationality in the "efficiency-wage" models that were supposed to incorporate information failures (Shapiro and Stiglitz 1984; Bowles and Gintis 1993). Given their game theoretic setup, in these models, the amount of information that economic agents are supposed to process included the additional private economic data concerning their counterparts (De Vroey 2003).

In an attempt to differentiate his position from that of the hyper-rationalist tendency outlined above, Herbert Simon uses the distinction between *substantive* and *procedural* rationality. Substantive rationality is the notion of rationality that "is appropriate to the achievement of given goals within the limits imposed by given conditions and constraints" (Simon 1976: 130). As such, substantive, or *outcomes*, rationality is only concerned with the attainment of given goals (utility or profit maximization) and not with the process of reasoning.[17] To put it differently, for those economic analyses that are based on substantive rationality, the process of achieving given goals, the process of reasoning, is a black box: once substantial rationality is assumed, "economic analysis (descriptive or normative) could usually be carried out using such standard tools as differential calculus, linear programming, or dynamic programming" (Simon 1976: 131). Accordingly, substantive rationality implies that there is no need to theorize the particular *decision process* through which a given goal is achieved. In contrast, the concept of procedural rationality focuses on the decision-making process itself.

8.3.1 The infinite regress of unbounded (substantive) rationality

Simon's critique of the concept of substantive rationality, and *the optimization framework* that it is premised upon, can be summed up in the following manner: the informational assumptions of the A-D model regarding what the individual economic agents need to know are in fact limited compared with the amount of information that the economic agents in imperfect market models are supposed to possess. As noted earlier, an A-D agent faces a *parametric* environment: as long as s/he has perfect knowledge of all the commodities, all the possible states of nature (under uncertainty) into the future, and the complete price vector, s/he does not need to know anything about the others (namely, their private information regarding their preferences, wealth constraints, and technology). In two important theoretical contexts, under *non-parametric strategic* (i.e., game theoretic) contexts *and* when the optimization procedure turns back onto itself in order to optimize on the costs of the very act of optimization, the situation changes, and the problem of the infinite regress of unbounded rationality emerges.

Consider first, for instance, the game theoretic context, in which the strategy choice of each agent depends on the decisions of the other agent(s). In such *strategic* contexts, the choice-decision of the first agent is contingent upon the choice-decision of his opponent, and vice versa. Since "none can choose without making assumptions about how others will choose" (Simon 1976: 140), it is impossible to arrive at a decision without falling into an infinite regress of assuming that the other player makes a particular choice that is based on an assumption about your play, which in turn must be based on an assumption about the strategy choice of the other player and so on ....[18] Hence, the infinite regress of choice in the Nash theoretic settings.

Let us now consider the curious case of "optimum level of optimization." If optimization were understood as an actual set of procedures, it would be easy to see how optimization/substantive rationality will collapse into an infinite regress: given the costs of computational resources, trying *to optimize on the act of optimization* may indeed be the most rational course of action (Baumol and Quandt 1964). But once the agent begins to optimize on optimizing, then s/he should also consider optimizing on optimizing on optimizing. Or, to put it slightly differently, what would be the optimum amount of time and energy spent to find the optimum amount of time and energy to be spent on the act of optimization? When the concept of "bounded rationality" is domesticated and subsumed under the optimization framework in this manner, we find ourselves entangled in such infinite regress situations.[19] Unless, of course, the agent (arbitrarily) decides that the measures taken are sufficient and abruptly ceases to optimize (Simon 1959: 262–4; see also Laville 2000). Simon calls this "satisficing behavior."

Simon, therefore, intended his concept of "bounded rationality" and the concept of "satisficing" as a critique of the idealized vision of the optimizing agent with unheard-of computational skills. But his critique shared something in common with the object of its critique, with what Simon calls "the optimization paradigm." Without doubt, Simon's research program was intended to be critical of the optimization paradigm in/of economics, and those who try to subsume the concept of bounded rationality into the optimization paradigm are doing him an injustice. Yet at the same time, precisely because the foundational premise of Simon's research program was the analogy between the computer and the human mind, epistemologically (and, I would argue, ontologically) speaking, Simon's cognitive economics shares a common ground with the mainstream understanding of human rationality. In the next section, we will turn our attention to this matter.

8.3.2 Theoretical humanist presuppositions of cognitive economics

Simon is very clear about the central importance of the analogy between the human and the computer for his research program of cognitive economics:

> Complexity is deep in the nature of things, and discovering tolerable approximation procedures and heuristics that permit huge spaces to be searched very selectively lies at the heart of intelligence, *whether human or artificial.*
>
> (Simon 1978a: 12; emphasis added)

Indeed, this analogy informs much of the post-war mainstream *representations* of the human subject. The representation of the economic agent found in the A-D model, in the rational expectations model, or in the various game theoretic models mentioned earlier was essentially a "cyborg" hard-wired with "calculators" or, better yet, with "statistical software"![20] The analogy between the human and the computer that underpinned these variants of the optimization paradigm within the neoclassical tradition was based on the assumption of *substantive* rationality. In contrast, Simon's project of simulating "rule driven problem-solving strategies in complex contexts" (Davis 2003: 97) relied upon a different type of analogy between the human and the computer. Unlike the lightning cal-culators of the optimization paradigm, Simon's simulations were self-contained problem-solving algorithms that were supposed to capture the *procedural* aspect of rationality.

> The [...] field of cognitive simulation (or "cognitive science" as it is more and more being called) is concerned with programming computers to do the clever things that people do, but to do them by using the same information processes that people use.
>
> (Simon 1978b: 496–7)

Simon's cognitive (behavioral) economics is indeed different from the pseudo-cyborg neoclassical economics. Nevertheless, despite the fact that it concedes that human cognition has its limitations, cognitive economics remains a theoretical humanist project: the very project of simulating algorithms assumes that "there really does exist a well-defined optimization problem out there, and the solution to that problem is ultimately the benchmark of rationality" (Langlois 1986: 227). In this sense, Simon, despite being critical of the optimization paradigm, remains within the limits imposed by a Cartesian epistemology "that sees reason as conscious, logical deduction from explicit premises" (Ibid.: 226). Langlois contrasts Simon's framework with that of Shackle (1972), according to which, under conditions of "structural" (as opposed to "parametric") uncertainty, epistemological conditions of optimization cannot be obtained. In other words, at a very fundamental level, Simon continues to subscribe to an ontology of optimization. His research program does not question optimization as a benchmark; rather, he aims to study how human societies devise tools and methods to deal with the complexity of the problem.

On the other hand, it really does not matter how Simon intended to use the concept. The concept of bounded rationality soon became a valuable addition to the conceptual artillery of the late neoclassical field and was subsumed into a (softened) optimization paradigm. For instance, Kenneth Arrow, the founder of new information economics, argues that "the individual's very limited capacity for acquiring and using information is a fixed factor in information processing, and one may expect a sort of diminishing returns to increases in other information resources" (Arrow 1974: 39).[21] The idea that the "sensory perception abilities of human beings" are limited, therefore, is cited as yet another reason why markets may fail to perform in the way that the standard model predicts that they will perform, and as yet another functionalist explanation of non-market institutional arrangements as supplements to or substitutes for markets.

In this vein, consider a new institutionalist economic historian, Douglass North, who argues that institutions exist to reduce uncertainties, and uncertainties "arise as a consequence of both the complexity of the problems to be solved and the problem-solving software (to use computer analogy) possessed by the individual" (1990: 25). Once again, the "limits" of rationality and the "complexity" of the environment make it necessary to supplement human interactions with institutions. North argues that institutions "evolve to simplify the process. The consequent institutional framework, by structuring human interaction, limits the choice set of the actors" (1990: 25).

Even though North is quick to add that "[t]here is nothing in the above statement that implies that the institutions are efficient" (1990: 25), this does not change the fact that North and other late neoclassical economists implicitly refer to the efficiency paradigm of the standard neoclassical model. For these late neoclassical approaches, "bounded rationality" (just like "transaction costs") is just another factor that frustrates the achievement of the level of efficiency promised by the perfectly competitive model as embodied either in the Marshallian selection framework or in the Walrasian auctioneer framework, depending on the particular affiliation of the late neoclassical economist under consideration. For Arrow, bounded rationality is another reason why, if a society wants to economize on information costs, "incentive compatible" non-market institutions (i.e., authorities) will necessarily be "needed." For Williamson (1984), in a similar fashion, "hierarchies" emerge in order to make up for the fact that human beings are boundedly rational. For North, "the central puzzle is the persistence of inefficient institutions" (Vira 1997: 767). Without doubt, the relevant question here is the following: inefficient with respect to what criteria? The hidden standard in all these formulations is a variant of the standard model of perfect competition.

8.4 Saving the human subject from its structuralist destitution

Even though a number of assumptions of the architecture of rational choice were opened up for debate and some of the assumptions were significantly relaxed (albeit in a piecemeal fashion) within the late neoclassical context, none of these reformulations of the concept of rationality broke with the theoretical problematic of neoclassical humanism. When discussing the status of *information*, even though "information failures" were invoked, late neoclassical formulations of these failures were always articulated in reference to the assumption of perfect information, and continued to presume opportunism on behalf of the economic agents. When discussing the *nature of preferences* and the motivational basis of human action, even when the idea of motivational diversity was entertained (and the assumption of opportunism was weakened), it was handled as a matter of "choice" among different types—the chooser being either the individual (as it was for social choice theory) or an anthropomorphized Nature (as it was for evolutionary game theory)! And finally, when discussing the *limitations on the cognitive capabilities* of the individual agent, even when late neoclassical economists did not evade the issue by subsuming it more deeply into a version of substantive rationality (as in certain game theoretic formulations of the concept), they still presumed that the agent is rational, i.e., centered, self-conscious, and autonomous, albeit limitedly so.

In conclusion, let us return to the three theses on late neoclassical economics proposed in Chapter 6 (i.e., the conjunction of unity and dispersion, the continuity, and the response theses) and offer an assessment of the late neoclassical debates on rationality. Late neoclassical discussions of the various aspects of the concept of rationality betray a significant amount of dispersion (with a wide range of positions, frameworks, and research methodologies) yet continue to be structured around two key debates: is there a motivational diversity? How does one incorporate a concept of the process of decision-making into models of human rationality? To the extent that these debates are explorations within the broader theoretical problematic of neoclassical humanism, the late neoclassical condition does not constitute a radical departure from the neoclassical tradition. Rather, the late neoclassical condition displays a deepening and widening of a tradition that continues to be structured and centered around the problem of how to reconcile the interests (however defined) of autonomous and self-transparent human subjects at the level of the social in a harmonious, growth-inducing, "efficient" manner. And finally, the late neoclassical turn to a richer and more nuanced concept of the human subject that incorporates bounded rationality and motivational self-reflexivity is a response to the impoverished concept of the human subject that was expounded by the post-war neoclassical economists.

Notes

1 The ontological premise of the A-D model under uncertainty is that each economic agent has a complete description of all the possible states of nature, but does not know which state will actualize. In order to incorporate the dimension of uncertainty (as it is defined in the A-D universe), contracts are re-interpreted as *conditional contracts* and commodities as *contingent commodities*: For every commodity, agents will write conditional contracts in which the actualization of the transaction is made contingent upon the realization of a specified state. To put it differently, a contract can be written in such a way that it will not only specify its physical, temporal, and spatial coordinates but also the state of nature of its realization. Consequently, without needing to assign (subjective or objective) probabilities, the agent can define his/her consumption plan over these contingent commodities. Insurance policies are usually offered as a concrete manifestation of a contingent commodity. Nevertheless, "the range of contingencies for which conditional contracts are available is much more limited than would be ideally desirable in theory" (Arrow 1974: 34).
2 See also Chapter 7.
3 Paul Samuelson's desire to clean economic science of any assumptions regarding human psyche (i.e., "passions") was itself a corollary of another desire of neoclassical economists: the desire to separate the descriptive (or predictive), and hence, according to them, the scientific, aspect of economics from its normative and ideological aspects.
4 On this note, it is equally important to acknowledge an unexpected role played by the "value-neutral" treatment of preferences in Arrovian social choice theory. By refraining from assuming anything regarding the motivations that animate the preferences, Arrow inadvertently set the necessary conditions for imagining the possibility that the preferences can be animated by a diversity of motivations: "It is simply assumed that the individual orders all social states by whatever standards he deems relevant" (Arrow 1963: 17).
5 Consider, for instance, the case of "gift-giving." According to the standard models, gifting is an inefficient practice, for the giver spends money on something without knowing the true preferences of the receiver. Since the probability that the giver will give a gift that fulfills the receiver's needs will most probably be less than 1, giving the money that the giver would be willing to spend anyway directly to the receiver would be

a Pareto improving arrangement. The widely perceived crassness of gift checks attests to the problematic (if not "anomalous") nature of this standard neoclassical version of "gift-giving."

6 The question of the origins of "social norms" and "ethical concerns" (Where do they come from?) that function as constraints on the self-interest-optimizing behavior of the agents remains unanswered within the framework of methodological individualism (Schotter 1981; Elster 1989; Greif 1993). If one is serious about methodological individualism, institutions (i.e., social norms) should also be explained by referring to the behavior of the individual with selfish preferences. But weren't the social norms invoked in the first place to explain the non-selfish behavior of individuals with selfish preferences?

7 For a survey of simulations with "zero-intelligence robots" in the context of double-auction markets, see Brewer (2008).

8 According to experimental data, in posted-offer markets, "the prices tend to be higher and efficiency lower" compared with double-auction markets (Ketcham et al. 1984: 613). This is because the posted-offer format "allows much less interaction between buyers and sellers than is the case for the double auction" (Davis and Holt 1993: 217). The reduced interaction means less room for negotiation between the parties and poorer performance in arriving at competitive predictions.

9 Francesco Guala (2007) distinguishes between "testers," whose main objective is to test the standard theories of neoclassical orthodoxy, and "builders," who are more interested in "doing things with experiments" (i.e., setting up the rules that govern behavior through incentives, punishments, enforcement mechanisms; in short, the institutional context making people behave in ways that are predicted by the standard models). While this is a useful taxonomy to highlight the role of performativity in experimental economics, it needs to be problematized in two directions. First, the commitment to opportunism displayed by builders is in need of being justified theoretically, and its normative nature must be acknowledged. Second, there is no reason why testers whose research has opened room for non-opportunistic behavioral traits do not build economic machines that take "pro-social" traits as their point of departure. In particular, the mechanism design literature on the crowding-out effects of economic incentives on pro-social preferences attests to the fact that testers who are skeptical about the ubiquity of opportunism can also be builders (Bowles and Hwang 2008).

10 I insist on using "evolutionary game theory" rather than "evolutionary economics," as the latter term refers to the approach of the likes of Richard Nelson, Sidney Winter, and Geoffrey Hodgson, whose writings and research do not belong to the late neoclassical field.

11 There are sophisticated models of *differential replication* that take into account, alongside environmental *adoption*, individual *adaptation* (through learning, mimicking, etc.) (e.g., Bowles and Gintis 1998), as well as those that distinguish between *random* and *assortive* group formation (e.g., Bergström 2002).

12 This was also the gist of Paul Hirst's (1985: 29–42) criticism of G. A. Cohen's (1978) famous defense of historical materialism. For Cohen, what pushes history to move forward is the development of forces of production. In turn, what propels the development of forces of production is the "historical" condition of scarcity in the face of the wants and needs of "men" and the capacity of men to recognize their interests and take action to achieve their ends (rationality) (1978: 152). In a way, at the heart of the structuralist machinery of mode of production and forces of production, Cohen locates a humanist notion of "men."

13 See, for instance, the various contributions to Elster (1986) and Kara (1996). Ahmet Kara (1996) formally demonstrates that the problems of voting cycles arise when there are more than two selves!

14 Whereas, for instance, in psychology as well as in psychoanalysis, change requires substantial clinical "work" and working through in an analytical setting, and neither

its achievement nor its permanence once achieved can be guaranteed. Unconscious patterns formed through lifetime interactions within a developmental trajectory are difficult to alter and can never be fully transparent to the subject.

15 Fikret Adaman of Boğaziçi University brought this aspect of the late neoclassical rehabilitation of the theoretical humanism to my attention. An important early instance of this attempt to recover the true Smith from the modernist and impoverished representations of the human subject in post-war neoclassical models (Walrasian or Marshallian) can be found in Amartya Sen's *Ethics and Economics* (1987). A more recent and rather thoroughgoing effort is Deirdre N. McCloskey's *The Bourgeois Virtues: Ethics for an Age of Commerce* (2006).

16 In his critical assessment of such endeavors, Mirowski asks the obvious question: "[W]hy isn't the metaoptimization also bounded in some manner?" (2002: 478).

17 The term "outcomes rationality" is suggested by Uskali Mäki (1993: 16). Others have tried to explain substantive rationality by referring to Noam Chomsky's differentiation between *theories of competence* and *theories of performance* (Laville 2000: 125–6). While a theory of competence involves the study of the abstract knowledge of language that an idealized speaker is supposed to have, a theory of performance studies how language is deployed in actual practice. Laville suggests that optimization theory (or substantive rationality) is a theory of decision competence.

18 It is usually argued that the Nash equilibrium solution concept (a strategy combination in which each strategy is a best reply to the other) was developed in order to circumvent this problem of circularity and infinite regress; but it resolved the problem only by burying the agent under even more demanding informational requirements, such as the capability to peek into the opponents' mind ("Common Knowledge Rationality" and "Consistent Alignment of Beliefs"). More on this below.

19 Without doubt, none of these logical problems "exist" from the perspective of *substantive* rationality, for that framework does not concern itself with the *procedure* of decision-making and assumes that optimization happens instantaneously.

20 In his *Machine Dreams: Economics Becomes a Cyborg Science* (2002), Philip Mirowski tells a "noir" story of post-war neoclassicism, the collaborations of its proponents with the cyborg sciences, and the attempts of the neoclassical and late neoclassical economists to domesticate the radical implications of the cyborg sciences. A similar narrative can be found in John B. Davis's *The Theory of Individual in Economics* (2003). Both authors argue that the cyborg ontology of agency is only allowed in if its complicated human–machine interface (e.g., human using statistical software to produce) can be forced into the neoclassical category of the individual. Nevertheless, they rightly claim, this new cyborg ontology of agency is neither simply on the side of the machine nor on the side of the human but in between, in the moment of articulation of machine with human as an enabling prosthetic device.

21 Despite this conceptualization of bounded rationality, new information economics that Arrow inaugurated proceeds to construct agency-theoretic models in which the principal knows the agent's "best response functions" (Shapiro and Stiglitz 1984; Bowles and Gintis 1990).

9 Equilibrium and efficiency

Searching for social reconciliation in game theoretic contexts

This chapter will trace the late neoclassical trajectory of the concept of equilibrium as the harmonious reconciliation of the diverse interests of rational, autonomous, and self-transparent agents. The concept of equilibrium as the concept of harmonious reconciliation in economic theory is one of the two constitutive presuppositions of neoclassical humanism. Within late neoclassical economics, a particular subfield, the field of game theory, stands out as a particularly relevant context for exploring the trajectory of the concept of equilibrium. In the post-war era, the field of game theory gave birth to two new concepts of equilibrium (not to mention their various refinements): starting in the 1950s, the concept of Nash equilibrium associated with classical game theory and starting in the 1970s, the concept of evolutionary stability associated with evolutionary game theory. This chapter offers an analysis of the transition from classical to evolutionary game theory within late neoclassical economics as the result of a search for a more "robust" concept of equilibrium, and, in doing so, traces the different roles that the concept of the "institution" has played in this search.

In this chapter, these developments in the field of game theory will be assessed, once more, in light of the three theses on late neoclassical economics proposed in Chapter 6: the characterization of the late neoclassical condition as one of *dispersion and unity*, the *continuity* of late neoclassical approaches with neoclassical economics, and the status of late neoclassical economics as a *response* to a perceived crisis of Walrasian neoclassicism. Accordingly, the three questions will be posed: to what extent does the game theoretic concern with specifying and refining the notion of equilibrium conform to *the unity and dispersion thesis*? To what extent do the late neoclassical treatments of the concept of equilibrium represent a *break* from the neoclassical tradition and its concepts of equilibrium (e.g., Edgeworthian, Marshallian, and Walrasian concepts of equilibrium)? And finally, to what extent does the rise to predominance of game theoretic discourses represent a *response* to the purported crisis of Walrasian dominance during the post-war period?

The structure of the chapter is as follows. The next section recapitulates the basic history of the concepts of equilibrium that circulated within the neoclassical tradition and situates the game theoretical debates within this historico-genealogical context. The remainder of the chapter is divided into two main sections. Focusing on classical game theory and the concept of Nash equilibrium, Section 9.2 elucidates the theoretical humanist presuppositions of the Nash equilibrium concept and offers a critical evaluation of the philosophical implications of the classical game theoretic research program: even though the type of rationality assumed by the Nash program in game theory is bordering on hyper-rationality, the concept of Nash equilibrium failed to deliver unique and efficient equilibrium outcomes in a large class of games. In those cases, not unlike the new institutionalist and post-Walrasian economists discussed in Chapter 7, the game theoretic literature chose to supplement the individual rationality with a structure (i.e., a norm, a social convention, an algorithm, an institution). In discussing the ways in which "institutions" are introduced to facilitate equilibrium solutions, I distinguish between the left liberal and the pro-market positions within the game theoretic literature. Section 9.3 offers a discussion of the theoretical humanist presuppositions of the evolutionary game theory and critically evaluates the concept of spontaneous order. The latter concept serves as a response to the left liberal focus on the non-coincidence of efficiency and equilibrium (as illustrated in the "prisoners' dilemma" game). The concluding section asks whether or not the game theoretic language is necessarily a theoretical humanist construct and revisits the three questions posed above.

9.1 Concepts of equilibrium in the neoclassical tradition

Throughout the history of the neoclassical tradition, the concept of equilibrium has been formulated in a number of, not always complementary, ways. In the nineteenth century, the Jevonsian concept of exchange, in which two centered, rational, autonomous, and opportunistically motivated agents enter into a mutually beneficial transaction, articulated a very basic and foundational notion of equilibrium—a state that neither party has a reason to move away from. This notion of equilibrium, which could be visualized as two merchants shaking hands, is significantly different from the vision of equilibrium that informed the other, Walrasian, variant of early neoclassicism. According to this contemporaneous version of the concept of equilibrium, the economy is envisioned as a system of markets—as opposed to an exchange between two agents. In contrast to the Jevonsian vision of exchange equilibrium (which will, later on, be canonized in the Edgeworth Box), the Walrasian concept of equilibrium is an economy-wide equilibrium in which all markets (each with multiple buyers and sellers) simultaneously clear.

In addition to these two concepts of equilibrium, in the subsequent Marshallian consolidation of textbook neoclassicism, it is possible to identify a third concept of equilibrium. In contrast to the general equilibrium concept that informs the Walrasian vision, the Marshallian vision focuses on particular markets and deploys a concept of partial equilibrium. Moreover, in contrast to the Walrasian vision, where a fictional auctioneer adjusts the price vector until the economy-wide equilibrium is reached, the Marshallian vision relies on the biological metaphor of a selection mechanism, whereby the process towards equilibrium entails adjustments in the quantities supplied and demanded. In the Walrasian vision of price adjustment, when the markets close at the end of the day, all the buyers and sellers remain in the market; in the Marshallian-inspired vision of market adjustment, it is quite plausible that some agents may be forced to leave the market (and not simply scale down production) as a consequence of the adjustment process—for instance, those firms whose average variable cost is above the market price.[1] In fact, in the Marshallian vision, the market price fluctuates and arrives at an equilibrium in response to shifts in the demand and supply schedules (i.e., in response to the adjustments in quantity).

In the post-war period, as the émigré mathematical economists began to develop and refine the various aspects of the Arrow-Debreu (A-D) general competitive analysis, under the institutional support of the Cowles Commission and the RAND Corporation, the Walrasian vision of general equilibrium swiftly gained disciplinary currency and attained dominance within the neoclassical tradition, perhaps overshadowing other concepts of equilibrium. Nevertheless, as discussed in Chapter 4, by the end of the 1960s and throughout the 1970s, ironically as a result of the meticulous efforts of the adherents of the A-D model, the neoclassical tradition was confronted with an unpleasant predicament: if it wished to develop the idea of general equilibrium (i.e., harmonious and contradiction-free economic order) as a spontaneous and unintended outcome of the rational actions of individual economic agents, it seemed that it would have to give up the idea that each individual is unique, distinct, and autonomous. According to the Sonnenschein–Mantel–Debreu results, unless further restrictions are imposed on the types of preference that consumers can have in an A-D economy, it was impossible to establish the conditions necessary for the *uniqueness* and *global stability* of general equilibrium. This predicament meant for many neoclassical economists (but not all) the loss of the intended generality of a thoroughly individualist general equilibrium model. Accompanying the matters that pertain to the uniqueness and global stability of the general equilibrium, there was the problem of how to conceptualize the process of *price adjustment* (price determination). The auctioneer metaphor, invoked in order to motivate the *tâtonnement* process through which the suppliers and the buyers modify their plans (in relation to everyone else's plans) outside real time until equilibrium is finally reached, was far from convincing. Moreover, historically, the auctioneer metaphor was used by the left-leaning Walrasian economists (e.g., Abba Lerner, Oskar Lange) and (correctly) interpreted by neoclassical economists with pro-market leanings (e.g., George Stigler, Milton Friedman) as a euphemism for a central planning agency that the former camp would like to see guide the economy. As the predominance of the post-war left Keynesianism came to a close with the oil shocks of the early 1970s and with the rise of neoliberalism in the 1980s, the Walrasian skein of neoclassical economics, with its now politically anachronistic vision of general equilibrium that required government intervention to undertake the most basic function of markets, namely, the determination of the equilibrium price vector, was no longer an attractive proposition.[2]

Nevertheless, even though the Walrasian concept of general equilibrium had lost its magic, the characteristically neoclassical search for a *unique, stable,* and *Pareto optimal* equilibrium has not lost its hold over late neoclassical economics. Chapter 5 has already introduced the Marshallian-inspired Chicago alternative to the Walrasian auctioneer metaphor: for the proponents of the pro-market Chicago School, the metaphor of a selection mechanism (as opposed to the auctioneer metaphor) proved to be a convincing enough model of the process of market adjustment. The proponents of the ascendant Coasean new institutional economics also embraced the metaphor of a selection mechanism as the engine of institutional change and economic growth. Even though the left-leaning post-Walrasian economists (e.g., Akerlof, Stiglitz, Bowles) tried to soften the social Darwinian overtones of the new institutional literature through concepts such as "path dependency," the evolutionary metaphors quickly became a part of the late neoclassical discourse. Nevertheless, the full-on entry of the mathematical models of evolutionary change and stability into late neoclassical economics happened within the adjacent field of game theory and in the form of evolutionary game theory. In order to make its entrance, however, evolutionary game theory had to wait for the classical game theoretic path to be exhausted.

Indeed, the transition in the field of game theory from *classical* game theory to *evolutionary* game theory is parallel to the aforementioned transition from the disciplinary hegemony of the Walrasian auctioneer-led general equilibrium concept to that of the Marshallian selection-led partial equilibrium concept. The former transition is particularly important for the discussion of the persistence of theoretical humanism in late neoclassical economics because it is also a transition from one concept of equilibrium (Nash) to another (evolutionary stability).

Let us recall, if only in broad brush strokes, the basic contours of the history of game theory. Even though Cournot's model of imperfect competition is usually referred to as the earliest formulation of game theory in economics, the first systematic treatment of the game theoretic methodology is found in John von Neumann and Oskar Morgenstern's *Theory of Games and Economic Behavior* (1953), the first edition of which was published in 1944. The equilibrium concept that underpins the subsequent research in classical game theory, however, was formulated by John Nash (1950; 1951). The Nash program in game theory (i.e., classical game theory) is the study of equilibrium solutions for non-cooperative games, in which perfectly rational individual agents do not communicate or cooperate, and pursue all the necessary means to achieve their welfare-maximizing goals (Myerson 1999). Evolutionary game theory, on the other hand, "studies the population dynamics of a repeated game" in which "the number and types of players are allowed to change over time" (Sandler 1997: 173). Evolutionary game theory developed in the 1980s and 1990s as the enthusiasm over the Nash program in game theory began to wane (Samuelson 2002).[3] As a result of this undoubtedly incomplete transition, the late neoclassical tradition incorporated into its conceptual artillery the concept of "spontaneous order" (Sugden 1989)—a concept that is critically evaluated below from a Marxian surplus perspective.

The temptation is to map this transition in the field of game theory on to the difference between the Walrasian understanding of the auctioneer-led iterative process of price adjustment, which corresponds to the ontology of rational agent choice that underpins classical game theory, and the Marshallian understanding of the selection-led process of market adjustment, which corresponds to the social Darwinian ontology of survival of the fittest (or, in more careful formulations, "fitter") that underpins evolutionary game theory. For instance, Larry Samuelson welcomes evolutionary game theory because "it brings game theory closer to economics by viewing equilibrium as the outcome of an adjustment process rather than something that simply springs into being" (2002: 48). This analogy is, indeed, accurate to a certain extent. Nevertheless, accounting for the philosophical underpinnings of this transition in the field of game theory will require us to explore the concept of "spontaneous order" as it was formulated by the proponents of the Austrian tradition (Hayek 1988). With the evolutionary game theoretic formalization of the concept of "spontaneous order," a game theoretic school of thought inspired by the insights of the Austrian School became an interlocutor in the late neoclassical conversation. This is a particularly important point, which needs to be appreciated, for it means that there are three different formulations of the neoclassical problematic: the post-Walrasian "prisoners' dilemma" position, the selectionist Chicago "invisible hand" position, and the Austrian "spontaneous order" position.

In this theoretical context, it is perhaps appropriate to ask whether or not evolutionary game theory, to the extent that it veers towards the Austrian School, breaks from the neoclassical tradition. Or, to ask the same question from the other side, does evolutionary game theory serve to pull the Austrian perspective into the gravitational center of the neoclassical tradition, to be deployed by the latter as yet another reformulation of the theoretical humanist problematic of how to socially reconcile the interests of autonomous, self-conscious, and self-transparent human subjects?[4]

Interestingly enough, at the core of this transition, I locate, once again, the theoretical humanist problematic of neoclassical humanism, namely, the commitment to theorize the reconciliation of individual and collective rationality and the desire to establish the conditions of existence of a harmonious reconciliation (i.e., a Pareto efficient equilibrium) of individual interests. Evolutionary game theory contributed to the rehabilitation of the theoretical humanist presuppositions of this theoretical problematic on two accounts. First, as I discussed at some length in Chapter 8, evolutionary game theory provided a theoretical framework for understanding the origins and causes of human motivations and economic behavior (see, for instance, Robson 2002). Second, its core concept of *evolutionary stability*[5] gained currency within economics mainly because it has successfully narrowed down the set of plausible Nash equilibria. In other words, evolutionary game theory gained currency within the late neoclassical context because it contributed to the theoretical humanist project of neoclassical economics by reinforcing its behavioral foundations and by providing a new concept of equilibrium—one that addresses the problem of non-coincidence of Pareto efficiency and equilibrium.

In what follows, by focusing on the developments within the subfield of classical game theory, the central role that the Nash equilibrium concept has played in late neoclassical economics and its various theories of institutions will be discussed. Then, the chapter will proceed to show how the concept of evolutionary stability ("spontaneous order") is offered as an alternative to the concept of Nash equilibrium by evolutionary game theorists. In this context, the implications of this new concept of equilibrium for late neoclassical discussions on the origins and the evolution of economic institutions and their (comparative) efficiency will be explored. It is important to note that the transition from classical game theory to evolutionary game theory will not be investigated in terms of a transition from one set of mathematical apparatus to another one. The types of games chosen in each program, as well as the interpretation of these games and their solutions, have philosophical underpinnings and political implications. The chapter will concentrate on the philosophical and political dimensions of these late neoclassical research programs and not on the details and niceties of the mathematical innovations therein.

9.2 From general equilibrium to Nash equilibrium

It is now well established that the early mathematical formalizations of the A-D general equilibrium model were, in part, inspired by the generalization of the *n*-person equilibrium idea of Nash (Weintraub 1985: 90). Also, as I noted in the previous chapter, the notion of Nash equilibrium, even though it burdened the concept of rationality with further assumptions, was welcomed by the profession as a solution to the problems of circularity (and infinite regress) introduced by the interdependence of choices (Myerson 1999). Recall that in two-person non-cooperative games, when each agent has a *dominant strategy* that could be chosen regardless of the other agent's choice, there is no need to know anything about the other's choice, and hence there is no interdependence of choices (only an interdependence of outcomes).

Consider, for instance, the game of invisible hand, where the dominant strategy for both agents is to follow self-interest (Table 9.1). While *the outcome* of the game is dependent on what each agent chooses, the strategy choice of each agent is not interdependent: each agent, in making his/her choices, doesn't need to take into account the other's choice.

Unfortunately, games such as these (the A-D general equilibrium being an *n*-person version) constitute only a subset of the universe of games. For instance, when there is no dominant strategy but only a number of "rationalizable strategies"[6] (where the reasoning goes "since the Agent 1 is not going to play this way ...") without any "justifiable reason" to choose among them, the Nash equilibrium

Table 9.1 The invisible hand game

		Agent 2	
		Follow self-interest	Be altruistic
Agent 1	Follow self-interest	4, 4	2, 0
	Be altruistic	0, 2	0, 0

solution saves the day—by enabling the game theorist (and the gamers, for that matter) to narrow down the set of "plausible" strategies!

9.2.1 The underlying assumptions of the Nash equilibrium concept

Let us introduce the concept of Nash equilibrium by gradually building up its assumptions: the common knowledge rationality and the consistent alignment of beliefs. Within the classical game theoretic literature, in the absence of dominant strategies, when not only *the outcome* but also *the choice of strategy* becomes a matter of interdependence, it becomes necessary to impose the assumption of *common knowledge rationality* (CKR): If a proposition is "common knowledge," then "each player knows it to be true, each knows that the other knows it to be true, and so on" (Sugden 1991: 764). According to CKR, each gaming agent is assumed to make choices like a rational-expected-utility-maximizing-game-theorist who knows not only the mathematical structure of the game and all the possible theorems to find a solution, but also that all the other gamers are like himself. The assumption of CKR enables a rational agent to attribute an identical rationality to her opponent. As a result, it becomes possible for an agent to rule out the dominated strategies of her opponent and reduce her own "rationalizable" set of strategies, preferably to a unique one. For instance, if an agent does not have a dominant strategy, the first thing she does is to assume the CKR and ask whether her opponent has a dominant strategy. If the opponent has one, the agent "rationalizes" and narrows down her own set of strategies (see the first two questions on the right side of Figure 9.1).

Nevertheless, when there are "multiple" rationalizable strategies, the CKR is not enough to arrive at an equilibrium. It is at this stage that the Nash equilibrium solution comes to the rescue and makes one more assumption by requiring that everybody's beliefs should be consistently aligned. The notion of *consistent alignment of beliefs* (CAB) is based on the assumption that "when two individuals have the same information, they must draw the same inferences and come, independently, to the same conclusion" (Hargreaves Heap and Varoufakis 1995: 25). Accordingly, when an individual's and his opponent's views are consistently aligned, neither will need to change his or her plans when they learn about the other's plans.

> A set of rationalisable strategies (one for each player) are [sic] in a Nash equilibrium if their implementation confirms the expectations of each player about the other's choice. Put differently, Nash strategies are the only rationalisable ones which, if implemented, confirm the expectations on which they were based. This is why they are often referred to as self-confirming strategies or why it can be said that this equilibrium concept requires that players' beliefs are consistently aligned.
>
> (Hargreaves Heap and Varoufakis, 1995: 53)

Even this "hyper-rationality" may fail to deliver a unique equilibrium. There may be cases where there is no Nash equilibrium in pure strategies (the disorder game).[7] Or, there may be cases when there are "multiple" Nash equilibria with no

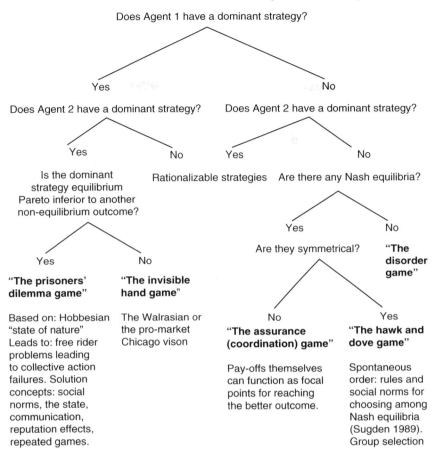

Figure 9.1 A taxonomic outline.

This chart enables us to elucidate the conceptual structure of the chapter. We begin by looking for *dominant strategies*. If both agents have a dominant strategy, we ask whether or not the *dominant strategy outcome* is Pareto optimal. If one has a dominant strategy and the other does not, we are in the realm of *rationalizable strategies*. (In these cases, CKR has to be assumed.) And if there are no dominant strategies, we ask whether there are any Nash equilibria. (In these cases, both CKR and CAB have to be assumed.)

clear reason to choose one of them (i.e., where none of them is Pareto superior to the rest) (the hawk and dove game). Or, even though there is a unique Nash equilibrium, it may be Pareto dominated by another non-equilibrium outcome (the prisoners' dilemma game). In such cases of multiple Nash equilibria or unique but Pareto dominated Nash equilibrium, the game theoretic literature is forced to supplement the individual rationality with a structure (a norm, a social convention, an algorithm, or an institution). In the next section, we will turn our attention to the role that this concept of institutions (qua supplementary "solution" devices) plays in the context of classical game theory.

9.2.2   *Theoretical humanism of the Nash equilibrium concept and the role of institutions*

How do institutions figure in the context of the game theoretic formulations of equilibrium and efficiency? We will consider two cases: the case when there are multiple Nash equilibria with no "justifiable reason" to choose between them (pure coordination games) and the case when there is a unique Nash equilibrium but it is Pareto dominated by another outcome (prisoners' dilemma games). The curious case of the non-existence of a Nash equilibrium in pure games will be considered in the conclusion of Section 9. 3. 2 (Table 9.2).

Let us begin with *pure coordination games*. When there are multiple equilibria, we further ask whether the Nash equilibria are identical or not. If the multiple Nash equilibria are not identical, as in the case of Table 9.2, it may be possible to settle for the Pareto superior of the outcomes. In the following scenario, the agents are workers in an open-shop workplace, where there is no obligation to go on strike. This is a "coordination" problem in which the agents benefit from coordinating their actions, for if one agent strikes and the other does not, the one who strikes loses her job, and vice versa. It is a game of "assurance": there are no dominant strategies, but two Nash equilibria—either no one should strike or all should strike simultaneously.

However, given its pay-off structure, where the strike–strike outcome Pareto dominates the not-strike–not-strike outcome, this game does not pose a serious problem.[8] In fact, pure coordination games where the outcomes are identical provide a more fundamental challenge. In such cases, the problem is the simple task of coordinating the choices of the agents. Yet, the standard CKR assumptions fail to provide a reason to choose between strategies. In order to generate a unique and stable equilibrium, game theorists introduced the concept of social institutions as an equilibrium selection device: the concept of "salience" (or "focal points") is developed to describe the role played by those institutions that coordinate the agents' decisions in unrepeated games without communication (Schelling 1960). The concept of "focal points" is extended to include conventions, social norms, and institutional arrangements that serve agents as prosthetic devices, to coordinate their actions to settle on one of the equally attractive or identical Nash equilibria. Put differently, in a world populated with rational agents, institutions exist in order to coordinate equilibrium outcomes. In this sense, the game of assurance (pure coordination) stages a version of the constitutive theoretical problematic of neoclassical humanism: how to establish the conditions of existence of

Table 9.2 The assurance game

		Worker B	
		Not strike	Strike
Worker A	*Not strike*	2, 2	2, 0
	Strike	0, 2	4, 4

equilibrium (i.e., harmonious reconciliation) in a world populated with centered, autonomous, and rational beings.

Let us now turn our attention to the ubiquitous *prisoners' dilemma game* (Table 9.3). In this game, the dominant strategy Nash equilibrium (Defect, Defect) happens to be Pareto inferior to the outcome that would result if both agents were to cooperate. The problem in this case is that without the presence of communication, trust, or credible threat between the agents, the standard CKR assumptions of rationality are not enough for "justifying" the Pareto superior outcome of cooperation. The prisoners' dilemma game has all the elements for staging the liberal version of the neoclassical problematic: the possibility of harmonious reconciliation of interests (i.e., Cooperate, Cooperate), the impediment (the absence of trust, the presence of narrowly self-interested behavior, etc.), and the policy conclusion (since the decentralized markets fail to deliver the sought-out social harmony, other institutional arrangements will be necessary to make this possible). This game formalizes "the state of nature scenario" of the liberal late neoclassical position (and retroactively, the liberal neoclassical position) that argues that "markets are not enough." According to this scenario, the existence of institutions is usually explained through the trope of "social devices"[9] that enable agents to reach the Pareto superior outcome.

Within the history of economic thought, there are a number of theoretical orientations whose position resembles this game, the Keynesian tradition being a prominent one. A very influential demonstration of the non-coincidence of equilibrium and efficiency is found in Keynes' demonstration of how capitalist macroeconomic equilibrium can be, and usually is, non-coincident with full employment. Keynesian tradition posits that a full employment economy is more efficient than an economy with less than full employment. In the context of post-war North American academia, these Keynesian ideas, in the form of macroeconomic general equilibrium models, found a home at the Cowles Commission. In other words, Keynesian insights (to Joan Robinson's chagrin) were quickly subsumed ("bastardized") into the general equilibrium framework of Walrasian neoclassicism. Within the late neoclassical context, post-Walrasian and new Keynesian economists, with their analysis of information imperfections in the factor markets (labor and capital markets), also correspond to this position (see Chapter 7). When read from the perspective of this left post-market genealogy, the "prisoners' dilemma" game gains an emblematic status as the privileged "state of the nature" game of the liberal wing of the neoclassical tradition. Since it is impossible to arrive at a Pareto optimal state of equilibrium as a result of the decentralized choices

Table 9.3 The prisoners' dilemma game

		Agent 2	
		Defect	Cooperate
		---	---
Agent 1	Defect	1, 1	3, 0
	Cooperate	0, 3	2, 2

of rational actors, it is necessary to supplement the individual rationality with a coordinating institution (e.g., the government, social norms).

The treatment of non-market institutions in the "prisoners' dilemma" game is quite different from their treatment in the "invisible hand" game (where the dominant strategy equilibrium is the Pareto optimal outcome). "Invisible hand" games (see Table 9.1) formalize the "state of nature" scenario embraced by the conservative wing of the neoclassical tradition, according to which "there aren't enough markets." The paradigmatic case of this research agenda (D. McCloskey calls it the "Nouvelle" Chicago approach) is exemplified in the work of Gary Becker—even though he is not a game theorist himself. In his work, all social phenomena (including institutions) are explained through the lenses of shadow prices and implicit markets:

> The economic approach is clearly not restricted to material goods and wants, nor even the market sector. Prices, be they the money prices of the market sector or the "shadow" imputed prices of the nonmarket sector, measure the opportunity cost of using scarce resources, and the economic approach predicts the same kind of response to shadow prices as to market prices.
>
> (Becker 1976: 7)

> When an apparently profitable opportunity to a firm, worker, or household is not exploited, the economic approach does not take refuge in assertions about irrationality, contentment with wealth already acquired, or convenient ad hoc shifts in values (i.e., preferences). Rather it postulates the existence of costs, monetary or psychic, of taking advantage of these opportunities that eliminate their profitability—costs that may not be easily "seen" by outside observers.
>
> (Becker 1976: 7)

Accordingly, in contrast to the liberal "prisoners' dilemma" late neoclassicism, which understands the institutions as supplements that fill in the holes within the commodity space (or as that which makes up for the market failures), the conservative "invisible hand" late neoclassicism understands the institutions as the outcomes of the optimizing choices of individual agents (or equivalently, the survivors of the selection mechanism that optimizes). In short, even though the particular ways in which they explain the institutions are different, they are two different versions of the same theoretical humanist problematic. And, of course, this is not necessarily a weakness of late neoclassical economics; on the contrary, the neoclassical tradition develops and unfolds around this internal conflict, this intrinsic antagonism, which is constitutive of its central theoretical problematic. Put differently, as much as this internal struggle causes problems for the neoclassical tradition, it also gives it vitality and energy and imparts an image of the neoclassical idiom as the mother-tongue of the discipline of economics—even though it is only one language among many that inhabit the terrain.

9.3 From Nash equilibrium to evolutionary stability

Developments in non-cooperative game theory and the abovementioned limitations of the Nash equilibrium solution in zeroing onto a unique outcome has led the game theorists either to introduce institutions, social norms, or conventions as solution concepts that will narrow down the multiple "rationalizable" equilibria to a unique one (Schotter 1981; Elster 1989; for a critical assessment Mirowski 1988) or to turn towards evolutionary game theory (Maynard Smith 1982; Sugden 1989; Samuelson 2002; Bowles 2004).

The equilibrium concept of evolutionary game theory, the concept of *evolutionary stability*, gained currency within the late neoclassical context, contributing to the theoretical humanist project of neoclassical economics by narrowing the set of plausible Nash equilibria. As always, this is not simply a matter of finding a mathematical solution to a given game—the games themselves, as well as the interpretation of their solutions, have philosophical underpinnings and political implications. In this case, the introduction of evolutionary game theory meant the introduction of a novel, Austrian formulation of the theoretical problematic of neoclassical humanism—one that is a rival to the previous formulations (i.e., to the "invisible hand" and the "prisoners' dilemma" versions). This is particularly remarkable, as it is important to underscore the resistance of the Austrian tradition to being subsumed into the neoclassical rubric, especially given its distinct ontological (process against equilibrium), methodological (critical of the use of mathematics), and epistemological (the role of "tacit" knowledge in the entrepreneurial discovery process) orientations (Caldwell 2004; Madra and Adaman 2014). In this manner, some of the insights of the Austrian School are also imported and subsumed into the idiom of game theory—rendering the latter a meta-language.

9.3.1 Evolutionary game theory and the concept of "spontaneous order"

In his later works, Friedrich von Hayek (1967; 1973; 1988) began to conceive of the markets as institutions that evolved spontaneously (neither deliberately nor naturally, but culturally). Hayek argued that certain *rules of conduct* have evolved because those groups that have adopted them were more successful. More importantly, he argued that the "*transmission* of rules of conduct takes place *from individual to individual*, the natural *selection* of rules will operate on the basis of the greater or less efficiency of the resulting *order of the group*" (Hayek 1967: 67).

It is Robert Sugden (1989), perhaps, who has given one of the most sophisticated late neoclassical elaborations of the Hayekian underpinnings of the evolutionary game theory. Rather than using the prisoners' dilemma, the invisible hand, or the assurance game, Sugden uses the hawk and dove game (Table 9.4), borrowed from mathematical biology, in which the agents have to make a choice between playing the Hawk and the Dove. If both choose to be Hawks, they spoil the proverbial pie; if both choose to be Doves, they share the pie. Again, there are no dominant

Table 9.4 The hawk and dove game

		Agent 2	
		Hawk	*Dove*
Agent 1	*Hawk*	0, 0	3, 1
	Dove	1, 3	2, 2

strategies, but in pure strategies there are two Nash equilibria (and, of course, there is the mixed strategy equilibrium), located in the other two cells where the agents play differently. In these cases, the one who plays Hawk gets the lion's share (three quarters of the pie) and the one who plays Dove gets the small portion.

How, then, will the choices of the agents be coordinated? Put differently, which of the two Nash equilibria will be the outcome of the game? Sugden argues that the only way to arrive at an equilibrium outcome is through "conventions" (a concept that resembles, but is richer than, Schelling's concept of "salience"). The examples that he provides include the norm of "first come first serve" and the institutions of a market economy, such as the institution of property rights.

There are two important implications of this game. First, it foregrounds the possibility of failing to reach an equilibrium outcome by relying only on the standard CKR assumption. Nevertheless, in this role, this game is no different from the other games discussed earlier. It is, however, different from the assurance game in the sense that the two pure strategy Nash equilibria present a *conflictual* setup. And, it is different from the prisoners' dilemma game in the sense that there is no *unique* Pareto superior outcome. For Sugden, these two games demonstrate that the program of classical game theory, which was inaugurated in 1944 by von Neumann and Morgenstern (1953) and consolidated by Nash (1950; 1951), is a "blind alley" (Nash 1989: 89).[10] Instead of trying to theorize equilibrium as an outcome of the hyper-rational choices of individual agents in an unrepeated non-cooperative game, Sugden pushes for a view that concedes that the equilibrium requires something other than human rationality, and that this something other is the concept of "conventions." And, conventions, Sugden (1989: 91) further argues, are "products of evolutionary processes". Once again, the evolutionary models come to the rescue of the neoclassical tradition to deliver the much sought-after equilibrium. Sugden is not alone in interpreting the evolutionary turn in game theory as a response to the "blind alley" of classical game theory. Larry Samuelson, in an essay that surveys the developments in the field, narrates the emergence of the field in a very similar way:

> In the 1990s, however, emphasis has shifted away from rationality-based to evolutionary models. One reason for this shift was frustration with the limitations of rationality-based models. These models readily motivated one of the requirements of Nash equilibrium, that players choose best responses to their beliefs about others' behavior, but less readily provided the second

requirement, that these beliefs be correct. Simultaneously, rationality-based criteria for choosing among Nash equilibria produced alternative "equilibrium refinements"—strengthenings [sic] of the Nash equilibrium concept designed to exclude implausible Nash equilibria—with sufficient abandon as to prompt despair at the thought of choosing one as the "right" concept.

(Samuelson 2002: 47)

Evolutionary game theory, as a burgeoning new field, refers to a wide variety of models with the common theme of "a dynamic process describing how players adapt their behavior over the course of repeated plays of a game" (Samuelson 2002: 48). In translating the biological metaphors into economics, Sugden proposes to "substitute *utility* for fitness and *learning* for natural selection" (1989: 91; emphasis added). Conventions let the agents arrive at an equilibrium, the agents learn to obey conventions, and once the conventions are established, they self-enforce themselves. The theoretical underpinning for this self-enforcing (stable) equilibrium is provided by the concept of *evolutionary stability*.

An *evolutionary stable strategy* (or ESS) is a pattern of behavior such that, if it is generally followed in the population, any small number of people who deviate from it will do less well than the others.

(Sugden 1989: 91)

Accordingly, once either of the two possible conventions that would coordinate the choices of agents (enabling them to play differently) is established, it becomes an ESS.[11] To put it in more concrete terms, the evolutionary model provides a mathematical formalization of the Hayekian thesis that the institutions of the market economy evolved spontaneously.

Order in human affairs, I have argued, can arise spontaneously, in the form of conventions. These patterns of behavior that are self-perpetuating—that can replicate themselves. In particular, rules of property—the essential preconditions for markets to work—can evolve in this way. These rules are not the result of any process of collective choice. Nor do they result from the kind of abstract rational analysis employed in classical game theory, in which individuals are modeled as having unlimited powers of deductive reasoning but no imagination and no common human experience. In this sense, at least, conventions are not the product of our reason.

(Sugden 1989: 97)

It is important to note that Sugden concedes not only that conventions may not necessarily be efficient (hence the absence of a unique Pareto superior outcome), but also that they may not be beneficial for everyone (hence the element of conflict in the pay-off structures of the two Nash equilibria). In other words, it is possible that (Pareto) inefficient conventions or conventions "that favor some people at the expense of others" (96) can prevail simply because they have been "more successful at replicating themselves than other patterns" (97). Sugden goes as far as to argue that

> if [conventions] can be said to have any purpose or function, it is simply replication. They do not serve any overarching social purpose; they cannot, in general, be justified in terms of any system of morality that sees society as having an overall objective or welfare function.
>
> (Sugden 1989: 97)

The notion of spontaneous order, the idea that the rules of property, the institutions of the market, are not the result of any process of rational or collective choice, betrays the Hayekian underpinnings of this evolutionary game theoretic model—though not necessarily the entire evolutionary game theory. In Sugden's account of spontaneous order, at the end of the day, the only thing that remains is the idea of equilibrium (defined, now, as evolutionary stability): even though the notion of efficiency is surgically removed from the notion of spontaneous order, the study of the conditions of existence of equilibrium remains a central concern.

9.3.2 Theoretical humanist presuppositions of evolutionary game theory

The notion of spontaneous order and its framing of the relation between the individual and the social is yet another formulation of the theoretical problematic of neoclassical humanism. Conventions become the lynchpin that delivers the much sought-after equilibrium among rational, centered, utility-maximizing subjects. Nevertheless, even though no efficiency claims underpin Sugden's concept of spontaneous order, this does not mean that the concept is a neutral one. On the contrary, the very theoretical humanist presuppositions of the concept of spontaneous order betray its partisanship.

Let us take a closer look at this. Sugden distinguishes between conventions and norms. The former are "nothing more than an established pattern of behavior" (1989: 95) that coordinates the choices of the rational agents in the hawk and dove game. Conventions achieve the status of norms when people "come to believe that they *ought* to act in ways that maintain these patterns" (1989: 95). But how do conventions transform into norms?

> The mechanism that can transform conventions into norms is the human desire for the approval of others. Although this desire is rarely considered by modern economists, introspection surely tells us that it is at least as fundamental as the desire for most consumption goods. That we desire approval should not be surprising: we are, after all, social animals, biologically fitted to live in groups. For most of us, being the focus of another person's ill-will, resentment or anger is a source of unease—something we prefer to avoid. This is a psychological externality: one person's *state*

of mind, as interpreted by another person, can affect that other person's happiness or utility.

(Sugden 1989: 95)

Therefore, underlying the social norms such as "the rules of property" is a "human desire" to evade the "psychological externality" caused by the disapproval of other human beings—note the echoes of a Smithian notion of human desire for approbation (Smith 1976 [1759–90]). People do not breach conventions, and even attribute moral value to them, because they do not want to be "the focus of another person's ill-will, resentment or anger" (Sugden 1989: 95). If the theoretical humanist problematic of the neoclassical tradition is to establish the conditions of existence of the reconciliation of the demands of the individual agents at the level of the social, the story of spontaneous order does precisely that: "conventions" solve the equilibrium selection problem of human societies without needing to revert to a "conflict" (Hawk and Hawk) and thereby spoiling the proverbial "pie." Humans follow conventions, and even turn them into norms, because of their psychological "desire for the approval of others" (95). Put differently, spontaneous order emerges because it accommodates the human desire for equilibrium, and it self-perpetuates into a regime of norms because it accommodates the innate human aversion to "being the focus of another person's ill-will, resentment or anger" (1989: 95).

There is something missing in this explanation of the emergence and reproduction of social institutions. What does it mean to argue that institutions emerge to solve games with multiple equilibria and once they emerge, perpetuate because there are psychological costs for breaking rules? Where is force, where is consent, where is revolution in this analysis of institutions? In motivating the "spontaneous" nature of "the institutions of a market economy," Sugden, in a paragraph that reveals his presuppositions, refers to informal and illegal markets as a proof of the spontaneous order argument:

> Although markets may work more smoothly when property rights are defined by formal laws and enforced by the state, they can come into existence and persist without any such external support. Think of how markets in foreign currency, gambling, prostitution, alcohol and narcotics can continue despite the attempts of governments to suppress them. Such markets can continue only because the participants recognize *de facto* property rights that the state does not. This raises the possibility that the institution of property itself may ultimately be a form of spontaneous order.
>
> (Sugden 1989: 86)

The first question that comes to mind when reading these sentences is why Sugden does not entertain the idea that participants in these criminal markets recognize *de facto* property rights because they are *also* enforced, granted not by the state, but by other, criminal, agencies? In this particular sense, Sugden's analysis is blind to the role that "brute" force plays in the constitutions of institutions.

In order to show the political implications of this blindness, I will interpret Sugden's "hawk and dove" game, given his explicit reference to "the rules of property," as a representation of the problem of sharing the social surplus. On the one hand, Sugden argues that conventions "cannot, in general, be justified in term of any system of morality that sees society as having an overall objective or welfare function" (Sugden 1989: 97). This is similar to the way anti-essentialist Marxian economics sees particular class structures qua concrete institutions that regulate the division of social surplus: no set of particular institutions can be justified according to universal criteria of efficiency, simply because no such universal criteria exist (Özselçuk and Madra 2005). Nonetheless, despite this interesting twist, Sugden's formulation is a conservative version of the neoclassical problematic.[12]

Because the eternal quest of neoclassical economics for equilibrium remains unquestioned, because the equilibrium and its stability are grounded in a particular psychological propensity of human agents, and finally, because the problem of the social division of surplus (i.e., the division of the pie) is formulated as a problem that needs to be solved through a stable equilibrium, the evolutionary game theory of Sugden offers a conservative version of the neoclassical problematic. Since all forms of struggles and negotiations over the division and distribution of surplus are coded as "social costs" (e.g., the spoiled pie when both actors play Hawk), even without the efficiency and welfare claims, equilibrium is still seen as an intrinsic "good," a virtue in itself. In this sense, the hawk and dove game, together with the concept of evolutionary stability, essentially constitutes a conservative state of nature scenario that sets up the problem of social division of surplus as something that needs to be regulated, ordered, and coordinated, where order (regardless of its distributional and welfare attributes) is privileged over disorder. Put differently, the hawk and dove game conceives the struggle over surplus as an intrinsic "bad"—even if it took the form of a vigorous and participatory democratic debate and negotiation over how to deal with the social surplus each time anew. In this sense, it is necessary not to lose sight of the partisan nature of concepts such as "conventions" or "equilibrium"; they reproduce a partisan and essentialist knowledge about the social that insists on privileging the reconciliation of individual and collective rationality, regardless of the justice, or even the efficiency, of this reconciliation.

The concept of "spontaneous order" and its circulation within the late neoclassical context is particularly relevant for an appreciation of a secular and anti-essentialist Marxian critique of the theoretical humanist problematic and its numerous versions within the neoclassical tradition. Underlying the left liberal and conservative versions of the neoclassical problematic (in their various versions from the early to the late neoclassical period) is an unquestioned belief in the existence of an absolute criterion of efficiency with which they compare and rank order the states of equilibrium. Common to all neoclassical concepts of equilibrium is the purported grounding of the efficiency of an equilibrium state in the rational and autonomous choices of self-transparent and self-conscious human subjects. In the late neoclassical period, the research, rather than questioning this foundational presupposition, moved on to investigate the conditions under which such reconciliation may be frustrated: transaction costs and information asymmetries (Chapter 7), non-selfish behavior and bounded rationality (Chapter 8), and multiplicity of equally plausible equilibria and coordination failures (this chapter). In all these theoretical developments, an overriding theme has been the desire to explain the non-coincidence of efficiency and equilibrium. Therefore, it is necessary to interpret the introduction of the concept of "spontaneous order" into the neoclassical corpus in this late neoclassical context, as a *response* to the purported crises of the Walrasian research program and its corollary in the field of game theory, the Nash program.

With the help of the concept of "spontaneous order," late neoclassical economics gains the capability to account for the non-coincidence of efficiency and equilibrium without giving up the normative force of the concept of equilibrium—even if it is not a Pareto optimal state, since it addresses the purportedly inherent human desire for equilibrium. By grounding equilibrium and order in the purportedly universal needs of human subjects, the concept of "spontaneous order" revitalizes the theoretical humanist project of the neoclassical tradition: establishing a social order that best accommodates the given interests of rational and autonomous human subjects. And in this precise sense, far from breaking with the neoclassical tradition, evolutionary game theory introduces the Austrian idea of "spontaneous order" to the conceptual artillery of the tradition.

In order to appreciate the normative import of the concept of equilibrium for the late neoclassical game theoretic literature (in both its classical and evolutionary variants), let's consider one more game. The disorder game depicted in Table 9.5 has no equilibrium in pure strategies. (A typical example of such games is the rock, scissors, and paper game.) Just like the rock, scissors, and paper game, the disorder game can perpetually continue, precisely because there is no equilibrium. In other words, because it lacks a pre-destined end point, it is the only "game" that deserves the name. Such games are relevant for our discussion of equilibrium precisely because they reveal the normative importance of the notion of equilibrium for economic theory. In this game, there is no rational reconciliation, there is no equilibrium, no *telos*.[13]

Without doubt, it has an equilibrium in mixed strategies. Nonetheless, even in this sense, it is an equilibrium contingent upon a randomized probability. In other words, the game of disorder permits no room for the guarantee of "necessity." And precisely for that reason, it does not have a place within the late neoclassical

Table 9.5 The disorder game

		Agent 2	
		Left	Right
Agent 1	Up	1, 0	0, 1
	Down	0, 1	1, 0

debate, which continues to uphold the quest for unique and stable "equilibrium" as its central economic problem.

9.4 Endless quest for social reconciliation

In the late neoclassical context, the use of game theory within mainstream economics has spread rather significantly. Today, almost all skeins of late neoclassical economics make use of game theory. In fact, I shall argue that the game theoretic representation of the strategic interdependency among autonomous and rational individual agents has become the dominant discourse of late neoclassical economics. Here, it is possible to identify a shift from the earlier, graphical representation of economic ideas (e.g., indifference map and budget constraint, supply and demand model, the IS-LM model) to the game theoretic representation of economic ideas (e.g., the oligopolistic competition game, the price-cutting game, the assurance game, the bank-run game, the battle of sexes game).

Nevertheless, it would be wrong to conclude that game theory is a box of tools and that there are various late neoclassical approaches that make use of these tools for their own partisan and ideological purposes. There is always an ideology inherent in tools. The (non-cooperative) game theoretic representations of economic scenarios, problems, or situations of strategic interdependence frame the insertion of the individual into the social as a matter of making *choices* according to pre-determined pay-off functions and in the absence of communication. When communication is introduced, it is not in order to change the underlying pay-off structures but to be able to coordinate the strategies played by the parties or to harmonize their "beliefs." Furthermore, game theoretic discourse has come to privilege "equilibrium" (with or without an associated absolute "efficiency" claim). In classical game theory, the "economic problem" in each game is to reach a unique Nash equilibrium and to assess the Pareto property of the equilibrium. In evolutionary game theory, the economic problem is to reach evolutionary stability. In this manner, game theoretic discourse reproduces the two key ideas of theoretical humanism: that the subjects have pre-determined interests and that the interests of the subjects can be reconciled.

In this chapter, I have discussed four different games (i.e., the invisible hand game, the assurance game, the prisoners' dilemma game, and the hawk and dove game) and argued that each game provides us with a version of the foundational theoretical problematic of neoclassical humanism. Initially, all the games discussed make the standard CKR assumptions of rationality about the human subject. They differ in the way each formulates and offers solutions to the problem of reconciliation of the individual and the collective rationality. For the invisible hand game, there is no interdependence of choices (only the interdependence of outcomes). In this sense, given the pay-off structure (with a unique dominant strategy equilibrium) and the assumptions about human rationality, there is not much of a problem here. The problems begin when the strategy choice of an agent is contingent upon the choice of other agent(s). But even in these cases, there are different ways to formulate the problem. For instance, the game of assurance abstracts from the aspect of conflict and reduces the problem of reconciliation into one of pure coordination. The game of prisoners' dilemma, on the other hand, provides a scenario in which the (Nash) equilibrium is a Pareto dominated outcome. This non-coincidence of efficiency and equilibrium is the central problem of the left/liberal wing of late neoclassical economics: institutions that facilitate conversation, trust, or third party enforcement (e.g., government) are theorized as solutions to this version of the problem of reconciliation. In contrast, the hawk and dove game (the privileged game of the evolutionary game theory) formulates a situation in which there is no universally efficient outcome and theorizes conventions such as "the rules of property" as solution concepts. Even though the concept of "spontaneous order" is stripped of absolute claims of efficiency, it continues to be grounded in human nature. In this sense, it constitutes a pro-market response to the left liberal concern with the non-coincidence of efficiency and equilibrium due to coordination failures of the decentralized market economies (as illustrated, for many, in the prisoners' dilemma type of games).

The important point is to recognize that all these games are different ways of formulating the same problem of reconciliation. In doing so, we should also recognize that there is no general theory of games, but a multiplicity of games, with each late neoclassical skein striving to redefine the problem of reconciliation in a manner that highlights its particular privileged and partisan concerns. Accordingly, the late neoclassical game theoretic literature, despite the fact it displays a significant amount of *heterogeneity* with respect to methodology, equilibrium concepts, privileged games, and political orientations, continues to be *unified* around the theoretical humanist problem of reconciliation. Again, despite the fact that the game theoretic turn within the mainstream economics, like other late neoclassical efforts, should be read as a *response* to the purported crisis of Walrasian neoclassicism, it fails to break from the constitutive theoretical problematic of neoclassical humanism. On the contrary, the late neoclassical developments within the field of game theory attest to the fact that the neoclassical research program and its theoretical humanist problematic are still alive and well.

Notes

1 This, of course, will lead to a change in the market supply and demand functions themselves. For somewhat divergent discussions of the difference between the Walrasian and the Marshallian adjustment rules, see Novshek and Sonnenschein (1987) and Katzner (2006: 333–8).

2 For recent Marxian accounts of neoliberalism that take history of economic thought into account, see David Harvey's *The New Imperialism* (2003) and Meghnad Desai's *Marx's Revenge* (2002). For a Foucauldian reading of neoliberalism as an intellectual tradition and a new form of governmentality, see Dardot and Laval (2013). For a history of neoliberal reason in economics that accounts for both its pro-market (i.e., Austrian and American (Chicago) neoliberals) and post-market (i.e., Ordo-liberal and post-Walrasian approaches) variants, see Madra and Adaman (2014).

3 Many commentators trace the origins of the entry of evolutionary metaphors into economics to Marshall's declaration that "the Mecca of economists lies in 'economic

biology'" (Vromen 1995: 1). In this lineage, it is also customary to reference a subset of the Marshallian structuralists (Alchian 1950; Friedman 1953; Becker 1962). But this lineage is shared by both evolutionary economics of the likes of Richard Nelson, Sidney Winter, and Geoffrey Hodgson and evolutionary game theory of the likes of Theodor Bergström, Larry Samuelson, and Robert Sugden. The latter tradition breaks off from evolutionary economics, as it directly adopts the biological models of the evolutionary game theory. An early text in this regard is none other than Gary Becker's analysis of altruism (Becker 1981)—the methodology deployed in this analysis of altruism is borrowed from mathematical biology and different from the Marshallian structuralism of the 1962 article (see Chapter 5). But the canonical reference is John Maynard Smith's *Evolution and the Theory of Games* (1982).

4 This question was posed to me by both Fikret Adaman of Boğaziçi University Istanbul and Irene van Staveren of the International Institute of Social Studies in The Hague (back then of Radboud University Nijmegen) during the "Whither Orthodoxy?" roundtable discussion at the *Rethinking Marxism 2006* Conference, October 26–28, University of Massachusetts Amherst.

5 For Richard Dawkins, an evolutionary theorist, the concept of evolutionary stability is "one of the most important advances in evolutionary theory since Darwin" (1989: 84).

6 Following Bernheim (1984), Hargreaves Heap and Varoufakis define *rationalizable strategies* as "those strategies that are left in a two-person game after the process of successive elimination of *dominated* strategies is completed" (1995: 48; emphasis added).

7 In mixed strategies, there is always a Nash equilibrium. How to interpret mixed strategy equilibrium remains, however, a central point of contention in game theory (Elster 1990: 25; Hargreaves Heap and Varoufakis 1995: 64–79). More on this below.

8 At least, this seems to be the consensus among the game theorists (Harsanyi and Selten 1988; Sugden 1995). But Andrew Colman convincingly argues that "the pay-off dominance principle, though intuitively compelling, is without a rational justification" (1997: 70). By "rational justification," Colman means that it is impossible to justify the Strike-Strike outcome without taking "radical departures from the standard rationality/ information assumptions of game theory or the rules of the game [namely the standard CKR assumptions of game theory]" (1997: 73), by assuming, for instance, repeated plays of the game (Taylor 1987), costless pre-play communication (Farrell 1987), or team rationality (Sugden 1995).

9 The following can be mentioned as examples of such social devices: institutions that impose the repeated game structure (e.g., the firms as long-term contracts); institutions that facilitate communication (e.g., clubs, unions, associations); institutions that impose credible threats (e.g., the government); institutions that facilitate trust (e.g., religious institutions).

10 Mirowski (2002) disagrees with this narrative. According to his interpretation, while the Nash program of non-cooperative games is indeed a blind alley, Von Neumann's project of an economics of finite automata is still waiting to be picked up. Needless to say, regardless of the opinions of these scholars, the Nash refinements program in game theory remains today alive and kicking.

11 This interpretation of the "dynamic" Hawk and Dove Game is slightly different from its conventional deployment. In the conventional model, the mixed strategy equilibrium, interpreted as a "population distribution," is the only solution. The value of the expected pay-off of Agent 1 when playing Hawk is

$$EV(H) = p(0) + (1 - p)3,$$

where p is the probability of Agent 2 playing Hawk. Similarly, the value of the expected pay-off of Agent 1 when playing Dove is

$$EV(D) = p(1) + (1 - p)2.$$

In mixed strategy solutions, expected pay-offs should be equal. Therefore, solving EV(H) = EV(D) for p,

$$p = 1/2.$$

Since the agents are identical, given the pay-off structure, each agent will play Hawk half the time. When translated into the population interpretation, this means that half of the population will play Hawk. In Sugden's model, with the introduction of the concept of convention, the mixed strategy equilibrium fails to be an ESS. Playing the pure strategy according to convention fares better than playing the mixed strategy. In this sense, the ESS is the convention-sanctioned pure strategy (e.g., ladies first, elders first, first come first serve).

12 It is important to differentiate Sugden's position from that of Hayek. Even though Hayek does not claim that the spontaneous order is necessarily Pareto optimum, he explicitly argues that it is dangerous to deliberately try to change the existing order (Nadeau 1998: 481–3). Sugden, in contrast, refrains from making this last point.

13 In other words, if there is a nihilist or ludic "postmodern moment" in game theory, one should begin looking for such a moment in games like Rock, Scissors, and Paper.

Part IV

Conclusion

10 Epilogue

The real divide in economics

This book argued that there is *no* clear *break* between neoclassical economics (up to the 1970s) and the contemporary mainstream economic approaches, including, inter alia, new institutional economics, new information economics, social choice theory, behavioral economics, evolutionary game theory, and experimental economics. Despite a significant degree of *heterogeneity* that characterizes the contemporary mainstream, the theoretical approaches and tendencies surveyed in this volume constitute a *unified* discursive formation articulated around the theoretical problematic of neoclassical humanism: the study of the conditions of existence of the reconciliation of the individual and collective rationality. Moreover, this late neoclassical condition and its particular character are explained, in part, as an outcome of a dialectical unfolding internal to the neoclassical tradition, as a *response* to its own mid-century drift towards structuralism (in both its Walrasian "the auctioneer" and Marshallian "selectionist" versions).

In this brief chapter, the first aim is to put the category of "crisis" in its place in light of the narrative provided in this volume. Emphasizing the dynamics of transformation in the neoclassical tradition, as it mutates in response to various crises and controversies, enables us to make a more realistic assessment of the effects of the 2008 Crash and the subsequent Great Recession on the direction that economics might take in the coming years. Second, an anti-essentialist Marxian surplus perspective is briefly sketched out as a non-theoretical humanist alternative to a prominent late neoclassical theory of power, the contested exchange theory, to demonstrate the real difference between the two approaches at a moment when they appear to be thematically closest to each other. And finally, a closing note is provided to mark the real divide in the discipline of economics.

10.1 "Crisis" as an engine of growth for the neoclassical tradition

Since the 1950s, neoclassical economics has evolved into a complex and diverse discursive social formation. In a sense, the tradition has matured and became more and more sophisticated. Given the amount of time, intellectual energy, and financial and institutional support that were and continue to be devoted to its development, this increasing sophistication should not come as a surprise. Yet, it would be wrong to interpret this growth, this branching out into applied fields, this diversification of the themes explored and the research methodologies deployed, this multiplication of the debates and controversies, as a break from the neoclassical tradition, from its constitutive theoretical problematic, and from the theoretical presuppositions that inform this constitutive theoretical problematic. On the contrary, this "flowering" of mainstream economics is the contemporary shape of neoclassical economics as a mature tradition. The "late" in the term "late neoclassical economics" should be read precisely in this sense.

The history of neoclassical tradition is not only a gradual accumulation of problems, contradictions, controversies, and disagreements pertaining to its foundational presuppositions, but also a series of elaborations on and reformulations of these foundational presuppositions of the neoclassical problematic. Is it possible to reconcile the conflict between the individual and the collective rationality? Is it possible to achieve an equilibrium that would reconcile the rational (consistent, self-transparent) and autonomous (freely chosen) demands of the individual economic agents? Is it possible to arrive at a unique equilibrium in non-cooperative games? What are the roles that the non-market institutions play? Are the non-market institutions outcomes of "shadow" prices? Or, are they solution devices that solve coordination and accountability problems? Or, are they social devices (i.e., conventions) that establish order? Are human beings hyper-rational or boundedly rational? Do economic agents need to second-guess their opponents? Which equilibrium concept is more appropriate to economic analysis: Walrasian general equilibrium, Marshallian market equilibrium, Nash equilibrium, or evolutionary stability? Or, is there any need for government involvement in the functioning of the markets? Why do markets fail? Do they fail because there are missing markets? Or, do they fail because there are endemic problems? If markets fail to function "properly," should this be remedied through the introduction of new markets or through the design and implementation of "incentive compatible" institutions? The list can easily be extended—as long as we remain within a conceptual horizon delimited by the boundaries of the theoretical problematic of neoclassical humanism.

Indeed, the central contribution of this book has been the identification of the constitutive theoretical problematic of the neoclassical tradition and its two foundational presuppositions (i.e., the human subject qua self-transparent self-consciousness and the teleological notion of harmonious reconciliation qua equilibrium). Reading the tradition through the lenses of this theoretical problematic, the aim has been to demonstrate that the neoclassical tradition was never unified around an object of analysis (e.g., the market), or a core model (e.g., the Arrow–Debreu model), or even a research methodology (e.g., mathematical modeling), but rather, around a theoretical problematic. This point also helped to explain the heterogeneity of the tradition: to the extent that there is no unifying object of analysis, core model, or even common research methodology, the neoclassical tradition can accommodate a significant amount of internal diversity.

Second, reading through the theoretical problematic rendered visible the fact that the contemporary mainstream (i.e., late neoclassical economics), contrary to the claims otherwise, remains within the neoclassical tradition and continues to operate within the neoclassical problematic. Finally, situating the theoretical problematic at the center made it possible to provide a mapping of late neoclassical economics as a collection of *responses* (from within the neoclassical problematic) to the perceived failure of the general equilibrium theory to convincingly accommodate the neoclassical problematic.

An important implication of the arguments put forward in this volume is that it might be misleading to expect a radical change in mainstream economics as a result of the 2008 Crash and the subsequent Great Recession. There are a number of important reasons for this. First, the field has been in crisis for a long time, perhaps since its inception. In fact, it has been thriving and unfolding as a result of and in response to its theoretical controversies and debates. This volume could be read as a witness account to the fact that all the foundational crises and controversies of the inter-war years still remain with us. For instance, the "psychologism" controversy—precipitated by the "old" institutionalist critiques—today has taken the form of debates around motivational diversity and cognitive limitations (Chapter 8), and the developments and internal divisions in experimental and behavioral economics can be seen as a continuation of this constitutive theoretical controversy. One can even discern the structure of a *longue dureé* dynamic: if the "structuralist drift" (in both its Walrasian and Chicago variants) towards assuming as little as possible regarding the human subject was, in part, a response to the psychologism controversy, the behavioral turn in economics can be read as a reaction to the austere, shallow, and dismembered representations of the human subject in post-war neoclassicism.

Or consider the marginalism controversy. Would it be so implausible to claim that it still continues today in the form of the debates surrounding the theory of the firm? All this drive towards opening the black box and theorizing the internal organizational structure of the firm can be read as an attempt to produce a robust theory of the firm from within the neoclassical theoretical problematic. In fact, Chapter 7 proposed to trace the genealogy of this debate to an even earlier moment in the history of economics, to Dobb's division between the production and the exchange perspectives. In the next section, an anti-essentialist production perspective on the theory of the firm was sketched in order to highlight the fact that the horizon of theoretical perspectives is not limited to one structured around the exchange perspective of the neoclassical humanism and its theoretical problematic of the reconciliation of the individual and the collective rationality.

And finally, the socialist calculation controversy, despite the collapse of the so-called real socialisms (or state capitalisms—depending on one's perspective), still continues in the form of a debate between mechanism designers and market reformers (Chapter 9). On the one hand, post-Walrasian mechanism designers, who view the world as a series of prisoners' dilemma games, argue that "markets are never enough" and propose either to regulate the existing markets or to supplant them with incentive compatible non-market institutions. On the other hand, while pro-market Chicago economists, who argue that "there aren't enough markets," push indiscriminately for further marketization, the proponents of the idea of "spontaneous order" argue that all attempts at social engineering are bound to have disastrous effects. At the level of macroeconomics, the same actors, with slightly different monikers, continue to enact the (almost exactly same) contending positions that were staked out when Keynes first made his intervention during the midst of the Great Depression. This situation became even clearer when Keynesianism came into vogue once more after the 2008 Crash.

On that note, it should be underscored that, more often than not, rather than displace, crises provide opportunities to further fortify (with auxiliary assumptions and modifications) the foundational precepts of a tradition. It is indeed true that the economic crisis of 2008 did provide some ammunition to question the most radically neoliberal ("there are not enough markets") versions of late neoclassical approaches. Yet, this definitely did not entail a decisive displacement of the theoretical humanist problematic of the neoclassical tradition. On the contrary, it provided an opportunity for more liberal market-skeptic ("markets are not enough") versions of late neoclassicism to come forth and offer their policy frameworks as the only viable alternative (Madra and Adaman 2014). To put it differently, the late neoclassical field is much more resilient to crises—even when they are as deep as the 2008 Crash—not despite, but precisely because of, being made up of diverse and, on a number of axes, rival research programs and skeins.

To recapitulate: the tradition, because it has been struggling with and, in fact, thriving on its crises and controversies since its inception, has become much more immune to their destabilizing effects. Moreover, its internal heterogeneity and diversity, albeit truncated in scope and structured around the theoretical humanist problematic of neoclassicism, make late neoclassical economics much more resilient in the face of crises. This book has tried to give some substance to these two theses. In conclusion, let us state a third one. It is important to note that late neoclassical economics, or neoclassicism as a mature tradition, through universalizing calculative behavior (even when allowing for motivational diversity and cognitive limitations), through indiscriminately framing all social problems from within the strategic idiom of game theory, and through submitting all institutions to the efficiency requirements of meta-markets (whether they be incentive compatible mechanisms or actual markets brought to existence through privatization of the commons), has become much more than a mere intellectual tradition or theoretical orientation. It has become a design for living, a new mode of life, a new governmental rationality, a new model of subjectivity (Foucault 2008; Dardot and Laval 2013; Mirowski 2013). For this reason, to the extent that it has become entrenched within the fabric of the modern society, it would be rather naïve to expect late neoclassical economics to be dislodged from its hegemonic position within the discipline and the broader society by an economic crisis—again, even when it is as deep as the Great Recession that followed the 2008 Crash.

10.2 An alternative: the Marxian surplus perspective

Yet, there are alternatives to this truncated horizon. In this sense, the analysis of late neoclassical economics provided in this volume should also be considered as a groundwork towards a Marxian critique. While the post-Althusserian anti-humanist tendencies within the Marxian tradition have produced rather acute critiques of neoclassical, Keynesian, and radical variants of humanism that circulate within the field of economics (Wolff and Resnick 2012; Amariglio et al. 1989; 1990; Ruccio and Amariglio 2003; Wolff 2006), today, given the attempts discussed in Chapter 1 to reconfigure the heterodox/orthodox division within the discipline, and given the prominence of the "break" thesis (as documented in Chapter 6), it is necessary to revitalize the anti-essentialist Marxian critique of theoretical humanism in the face of the continuing persistence and restoration of humanism in late neoclassical economics.

The aim of the critique provided throughout the volume has not been to question the empirical veridicality or logical consistency of the theoretical humanist positions articulated in the neoclassical tradition. In this sense, the volume does not criticize (late) neoclassical economics for its failure to represent the truth of the human subject. Rather, it is written from a perspective that maintains the necessity of a two-pronged critique of (i) the essentialist concept of the human subject as a centered, rational, and autonomous chooser and (ii) the teleological construct of the ultimate and harmonious reconciliation of the interests of these self-transparent chooser-subjects at the level of the society. In other words, the volume is written from a perspective that affirms the notion that neither the subject nor the society can ever be self-transparent and fully reconciled.

The name of this perspective, which distinguishes itself from both left- and right-wing theoretical humanisms, is the anti-essentialist Marxian surplus perspective (Resnick and Wolff 1987; 2006; Gibson-Graham 1996; 2006). What distinguishes this perspective from others (be they traditional Marxian or non-Marxian) is its commitment to produce a knowledge of the social from a perspective that analyzes the different forms of performance, appropriation, and distribution of surplus labor in their irreducibly contradictory and overdetermined relations with each other and with the rest of the social totality. Theoretical humanism, whether it is neoclassical or late neoclassical (or for that matter non-neoclassical), is radically opposed to this anti-essentialist Marxian surplus perspective.

Let us try to illustrate what is at stake in highlighting this perspective as an alternative by juxtaposing it to the late neoclassical treatments of the firm outlined in Chapter 7. There I argued that, despite the fact that late neoclassical economists represent themselves as capable of taking the sphere of production into account, they do so only from an exchange perspective that elevates the centered, rational, and autonomous subject presupposed in the contractual fiction to the level of a universal ontological truth about all human beings. Ironically, those radical political economists who criticized neoclassical economics for failing to offer an analysis of "the internal social organization of the firm" (Bowles 1985: 16) ended up joining the ranks of late neoclassical economists in theorizing the firm as a "governance structure" or, more generally, as a social device that supplements or supplants markets when the latter fail to function in the way that the standard neoclassical models predict that they will function.

Consider, for instance, the idea of "contested exchange" proposed by radical political economists Bowles and Gintis (1990) as a "radicalized" version of the "efficiency-wage" model articulated by left liberal late neoclassical economics. This radical political economy perspective, while explicitly taking the sphere of production into account, could not be farther away from the Marxist surplus perspective outlined here. First, this radical political economics perspective articulates a theory of the sphere of production from the exchange perspective that presupposes "opportunistic behavior" on the part of the human agents. Second, the fact that the exchange is "contested" does not indicate that the notion of "harmonious reconciliation" is abandoned. On the contrary, the very notion of "contestedness" is defined *vis-à-vis* (in the "absent presence" of) the idealized benchmark case of clearing markets. Moreover, the injustice of the contested exchange is an injustice defined from within the bourgeois framework of commutative justice, which sanctifies the exchange of equivalents.[1]

The aim of the anti-essentialist Marxian surplus perspective, in contrast, is not simply to take production into account—much less to do so from the teleological perspective of exchange! Rather, the Marxian surplus perspective aims to produce a knowledge of the social by tracing the overdetermined trajectories of the socially necessary abstract labor time, the conditions under which the latter is performed, the forms of its appropriation, the destinations towards which it is distributed, and so on. In contrast to the teleological construct that undergirds the exchange perspective of neoclassical humanism, the Marxian surplus perspective does not presuppose a social order under which the abstract labor time performed by direct laborers will be harmoniously distributed towards pre-destined ends (Özselçuk and Madra 2005). The Marxian surplus perspective, given its theoretical commitment to the concepts of contradiction and overdetermination, abandons the idea of harmonious reconciliation.

The abandonment of this Enlightenment-based belief in the possibility of a harmonious reconciliation entails the abandonment of the project of discovering the true essence of human nature that would serve as the normative "microfoundations" of that harmonious social order. In Chapter 8 (but also in chapters 7 and 9, to a lesser degree), various late neoclassical debates on the nature of the human motivations are surveyed. All of these efforts, while pushing the boundaries of the standard neoclassical research program, continue to remain within a philosophical horizon bounded by the theoretical problematic of neoclassical humanism. The Marxian surplus perspective, while acknowledging the constitutive role of the political processes of subjection and the cultural process of subjectivation (discussed in more detail in Chapter 2) in the making and unmaking of the different forms of the social organization of surplus labor (Madra 2006), neither posits a particular form of subjectivity as the universal essence of human nature (as the various proponents of experimental and behavioral economics aim to do) nor seeks to microfound a particular social organization of surplus labor in the inherent attributes of human essence (as late neoclassical economists of different stripes strive to do).

10.3 Delineating the real divide

This volume is, in part, motivated by a desire to counter an emerging narrative of a "pluralist turn" within contemporary mainstream economics. In particular, it is motivated by a desire to invite and provoke the heterodox economists to develop a clear, rigorous, and consistent position with respect to the proliferating mainstream narratives of a break from neoclassical economics. This is an especially urgent task because these narratives and declarations perpetuate an insidious impression that there is no real difference between the mainstream and the heterodoxy. As late neoclassical economists reconfigure what constitutes a legitimate criticism of neoclassical economics, the heterodox approaches and their critiques of the mainstream end up being marginalized and pushed aside. In this spirit, this monograph offered a "heterodox" *demonstration* of how the seemingly disparate research agendas and approaches, not despite but precisely because of their undeniable diversity, continue to remain committed to the theoretical humanist presuppositions and the constitutive theoretical problematic of the neoclassical tradition.

Let me conclude this study with a cautionary remark. To assume that the blurring of the frontier that separates the mainstream from the heterodoxy is only due to a rhetorical reconfiguration of the coordinates of the imaginary topography of the discipline by late neoclassical economists would be extremely naïve, to say the least. The blurring may equally well be due to the fact that many heterodox approaches (e.g., the radical political economy approach discussed in Chapter 7 and above) share the same theoretical humanist presuppositions with the various skeins of late neoclassical economics. To the extent that a heterodox economic approach takes the question of the reconciliation of the individual and the collective as its central problematic, it will also be implicated in the Marxian critique of theoretical humanism that motivates the analysis of late neoclassical economics offered in this volume.

Note

1 For anti-essentialist Marxian surplus critiques of the interpretations of the injustice of class exploitation from within the bourgeois framework of commutative justice, see Özselçuk and Madra (2005) and Madra (2006).

Bibliography

Adaman, Fikret, and Pat Devine. "The Economic Calculation Debate: Lessons for Socialists." *Cambridge Journal of Economics* 20, No. 5 (September 1996): 523–537.

Adaman, Fikret, and Pat Devine. "On the Economic Theory of Socialism." *New Left Review* I, No. 221 (January–February 1997): 54–80.

Adaman, Fikret, and Yahya M. Madra. "Theorizing the 'Third Sphere': A Critique of the Persistence of the 'Economistic Fallacy.'" *Journal of Economic Issues* 36, No. 4 (December 2002): 1045–1078.

Adaman, Fikret and Yahya M. Madra. "Understanding Neoliberalism as Economization: The Case of the Environment." In *Global Economic Crisis and the Politics of Diversity*, edited by Yıldız Atasoy. New York: Palgrave Macmillan, 2014: 29–51.

Akbulut, Bengi, Fikret Adaman and Yahya M. Madra. "The Decimation and Displacement of Development Economics." *Development and Change* 46, No. 4 (2015): 733–761.

Akerlof, George A. "Labor Contracts as Partial Gift Exchange." *Quarterly Journal of Economics* 97, No. 4 (November 1982): 543–569.

Akerlof, George A. "Gift Exchange and Efficiency-Wage Theory: Four Views." *American Economic Review* 74, No. 2 (May 1984): 79–83.

Alchian, Armen A. "Uncertainty, Evolution, and Economic Theory." *Journal of Political Economy* 58, No. 3 (June 1950): 211–221.

Alchian, Armen A. and Harold Demsetz. "Production, Information Costs, and Economic Organization." *American Economic Review* 62, No. 5 (December 1972): 777–795.

Althusser, Louis. *For Marx*. London: Verso, 1969.

Althusser, Louis. *Lenin and Philosophy and Other Essays*. Translated by Ben Brewster. New York: Monthly Review Press, 1971.

Althusser, Louis. *Writings on Psychoanalysis: Freud and Lacan*. New York: Columbia University Press, 1996.

Althusser, Louis. *The Humanist Controversy and Other Writings (1966–67)*. Edited by François Matheron. Translated by G. M. Goshgarian. London and New York: Verso, 2003.

Althusser, Louis, and Étienne Balibar. *Reading Capital*. London: Verso, 1970 [1965].

Amariglio, Jack. "The Body, Economic Discourse, and Power: An Economist's Introduction to Foucault." *History of Political Economy* 20, No. 4 (1988): 583–613.

Amariglio, Jack, and Antonio Callari. "Marxian Value Theory and the Problem of the Subject: The Role of Commodity Fetishism." In *Fetishism as Cultural Discourse*, edited by E. Apter and W. Pietz. Ithaca: Cornell University Press, 1993: 186–216.

Amariglio, Jack, Antonio Callari, and Stephen Cullenberg. "Analytical Marxism: A Critical Overview." *Review of Social Economy* 47, No. 4 (Winter 1989): 415–432.

Amariglio, Jack, Stephen Resnick, and Richard Wolff. "Division and Difference in the 'Discipline' of Economics." *Critical Inquiry* 17 (1990): 108–137. Reprinted in *Knowledges: Historical and Critical Studies in Disciplinarity*, edited by Ellen Messer-Davidow, David R. Shumway, and David J. Slyvan. Charlottesville: University Press of Virginia, 1993.

Anderson, Elizabeth. *Value in Ethics and Economics*. Cambridge, MA: Harvard University Press, 1993.

Andreoni, James. "Privately Provided Public Goods in a Large Economy: The Limits of Altruism." *Journal of Public Economics* 35, No. 1 (February 1988): 57–73.

Andreoni, James. "Giving with Impure Altruism: Applications to Charity and Ricardian Equivalence." *Journal of Political Economy* 97, No. 6 (December 1989): 1447–1458.

Appadurai, Arjun, ed. *The Social Life of Things: Commodities in Cultural Perspective*. Cambridge: Cambridge University Press, 1988.

Arrow, Kenneth J. "Toward a Theory of Price Adjustment." In *The Allocation of Economic Resources*, edited by Moses Abramowitz. Stanford, CA: Stanford University Press, 1959, 41–51.

Arrow, Kenneth J. "Economic Welfare and the Allocation of Resources for Invention." In *The Rate and Direction of Inventive Activity*, edited by Richard R. Nelson. Princeton: Princeton University Press, 1962: 609–625.

Arrow, Kenneth J. *Social Choice and Individual Values*, Second Edition. New Haven and London: Yale University Press, 1963. First edition in 1951.

Arrow, Kenneth J. *The Limits of Organization*. New York: W. W. Norton, 1974.

Arrow, Kenneth J. "Gifts and Exchange." *Philosophy and Public Affairs* 1 (1972): 343–362. Reprinted in *Altruism, Morality, and Economic Theory*, edited by E. S. Phelps. New York: Russell Sage Foundation, 1975: 13–28.

Arrow, Kenneth J. "Rationality of Self and Others in an Economic System." In *Rational Choice*, edited by Robin Hogarth and Melvin Reder. Chicago: Chicago University Press, 1987: 201–216.

Arrow, Kenneth J. "Cowles in the History of Economic Thought." In *Cowles' Fiftieth Anniversary*, edited by Alvin K. Klevorick. New Haven: Cowles Foundation: 1991. Accessed on March 8, 2016 from http://cowles.yale.edu/50th-anniversary-celebration.

Arrow, Kenneth J., and Gérard Debreu. "Existence of an Equilibrium for a Competitive Economy." *Econometrica* 22, No. 3 (July 1954): 265–290.

Arrow, Kenneth J., and Frank Hahn. *General Competitive Analysis*. San Francisco: Holden Day, 1971.

Backhouse, Roger E. *The Ordinary Business of Life: A History of Economics from the Ancient World to the Twenty-First Century*. Princeton and Oxford: Princeton University Press, 2002.

Balibar, Etienne. "Subjection and Subjectivation." In *Supposing the Subject*, edited by Joan Copjec. New York and London: Verso, 1994: 1–15.

Balibar, Etienne. "Structuralism: A Destitution of the Subject?" *differences: A Journal of Feminist Cultural Studies* 14, No. 1 (2003): 1–21.

Baumol, William J., and Richard E. Quandt. "Rules of Thumb and Optimally Imperfect Decisions." *American Economic Review* 54, No. 2, Part 1 (March 1964): 23–46.

Bausor, Randall. "The Rational-Expectations Hypothesis and the Epistemics of Time." *Cambridge Journal of Economics* 7 (1983):1–10.

Becker, Gary S. "Irrational Behavior and Economic Theory." *Journal of Political Economy* 70, No. 1 (February 1962): 1–13.

Becker, Gary S. *The Economic Approach to Human Behavior.* Chicago and London: University of Chicago Press, 1976.

Becker, Gary S. "Altruism in the Family and Selfishness in the Market Place." *Economica* 48, No. 189 (February 1981): 1–15.

Bergström, Theodore. "Evolution of Social Behavior: Individual and Group Selection." *Journal of Economic Perspectives* 16, No. 2 (Spring 2002): 67–88.

Bernheim, B. Douglas. "Rationalizable Strategic Behavior." *Econometrica* 52, No. 4 (July 1984): 1007–1028.

Bernheim, B. Douglas, and Oded Stark. "Altruism within the Household Reconsidered: Do Nice Guys Finish Last?" *American Economic Review* 78, No. 5 (December 1988): 1034–1045.

Bernstein, Michael A. *A Perilous Progress: Economists and Public Purpose in Twentieth Century America.* Princeton: Princeton University Press, 2001.

Blaug, Mark. "Was There a Marginal Revolution?" *History of Political Economy* 4, No. 2 (Fall 1972): 269–280.

Blaug, Mark. *The Methodology of Economics: Or, How Economists Explain.* Cambridge: Cambridge University Press, 1980.

Blaug, Mark. *Economic Theory in Retrospect.* Fifth Edition. Cambridge: Cambridge University Press, 1997.

Blumenberg, Hans. *The Legitimacy of the Modern Age.* Translated by Robert M. Wallace. Cambridge, MA: MIT Press, 1983.

Bourbaki, Nicolas. "The Architecture of Mathematics." *The American Mathematical Monthly* 57, No. 4 (April 1950 [1948]): 221–232.

Bowles, Samuel. "The Production Process in a Competitive Economy: Walrasian, Neo-Hobbesian, and Marxian Models." *American Economic Review* 75, No. 1 (March 1985): 16–36.

Bowles, Samuel. "Endogenous Preferences: The Cultural Consequences of Markets and Other Economic Institutions." *Journal of Economic Literature* 36, No. 1 (March 1998): 75–111.

Bowles, Samuel. *Microeconomics: Behavior, Institutions, and Evolution.* Princeton: Princeton University Press, 2004.

Bowles, Samuel, and Herbert Gintis. "Contested Exchange: New Microfoundations for the Political Economy of Capitalism." *Politics and Society* 18, No. 2 (1990): 165–222.

Bowles, Samuel, and Herbert Gintis. "The Revenge of Homo Economicus: Contested Exchange and the Revival of Political Economy." *Journal of Economic Perspectives* 7, No. 1 (Winter 1993): 83–102.

Bowles, Samuel, and Herbert Gintis. "The Distribution of Wealth and the Viability of Democratic Firms." In *Democracy and Efficiency in the Economic Enterprise*, edited by U. Pagano and B. Rowthorn. London and New York: Routledge, 1996: 82–97.

Bowles, Samuel, and Herbert Gintis. "How Communities Govern: The Structural Basis of Prosocial Norms." In *Economics, Values, and Organization*, edited by A. Ben-Ner and L. Putterman. Cambridge: Cambridge University Press, 1998: 206–230.

Bowles, Samuel, and Herbert Gintis. "Walrasian Economics in Retrospect." *Quarterly Journal of Economics* 115, No. 4 (November 2000): 1411–1439.

Bowles, Samuel and S.-H. Hwang. "Social Preferences and Public Economics: Mechanism Design when Social Preferences Depend on Incentives." *Journal of Public Economics* 92, No. 8–9 (2008): 1811–1820.

Breit, William and Roger W. Spencer, eds. *Lives of the Laureates: Thirteen Nobel Economists.* Third Edition. Cambridge, MA and London: The MIT Press, 1995.

Brewer, Paul J. "Zero-Intelligence Robots and the Double Auction Market: A Graphical Tour." In *Handbook of Experimental Economics Results, Volume 1*, edited by C. R. Plott and V. L. Smith. Amsterdam and New York: North-Holland, 2008: 31–45.

Brown, Vivienne. *Adam Smith's Discourse: Canonicity, Commerce and Conscience*. London and New York: Routledge, 1994.

Burawoy, Michael. *Manufacturing Consent: Changes in the Labor Process under Monopoly Capitalism*. Chicago: University of Chicago Press, 1982.

Burawoy, Michael. *The Politics of Production: Factory Regimes under Capitalism and Socialism*. New York and London: Verso, 1985.

Burczak, Theodore A. "The Postmodern Moments of F. A. Hayek's Economics." *Economics and Philosophy* 10, No. 1 (1994): 31–58.

Burczak, Theodore A. *Socialism after Hayek*. Ann Arbor: University of Michigan Press, 2006.

Butler, Judith. "Conscience Doth Make Subjects of Us All." *Yale French Studies* No. 88 (1995): 6–26.

Caldwell, Bruce. "Hayek's Transformation." *History of Political Economy* 20, No. 4 (Winter 1988): 513–541.

Caldwell, Bruce. *Hayek's Challenge: An Intellectual Biography of F. A. Hayek*. Chicago: University of Chicago Press, 2004.

Callari, Antonio. *The Classical's Analysis of Capitalism*. PhD diss. University of Massachusetts at Amherst, 1981.

Callon, Michel, ed. *The Laws of the Markets*. Oxford: Blackwell, 1998.

Camerer, Colin. "Progress in Behavioral Game Theory." *Journal of Economic Perspectives* 11, No. 4 (Fall 1997): 167–188.

Cassel, Gustav. *The Theory of Social Economy*. New York: Harcourt, 1924 [1918].

Charness, Gary, and Matthew Rabin. "Understanding Social Preferences with Simple Tests." *Quarterly Journal of Economics* 117, No. 3 (August 2002): 817–869.

Charusheela, S. *Structuralism and Individualism in Economic Analysis: The "Contractionary Devaluation Debate" in Development Economics*. PhD diss. University of Massachusetts at Amherst, 1997.

Charusheela, S. *Structuralism and Individualism in Economic Analysis: The "Contractionary Devaluation Debate" in Development Economics*. London and New York: Routledge, 2004.

Cheung, Steven N. S. *Will China Go "Capitalist"? An Economic Analysis of Property Rights and Institutional Change*. London: Institute of Economic Affairs, 1982.

Cheung, Steven N. S. "On the New Institutional Economics." In *Contract Economics*, edited by Lars Werin and Hans Wijkander. Oxford, UK and Cambridge, USA: Blackwell, 1992: 48–65.

Coase, Ronald H. "The Nature of the Firm." *Economica* 4 (1937): 386–405.

Coase, Ronald H. "The Problem of Social Cost." *Journal of Law and Economics* 3, No. 4 (1960): 1–44.

Coase, Ronald H. "The New Institutional Economics." In *Institutions, Contracts, and Organizations: Perspectives from New Institutional Economics*, edited by Claude Ménard. Cheltenham, UK and Northampton, MA: Edward Elgar, 2000: 3–6.

Coate, Stephen, and Martin Ravallion. "Reciprocity without Commitment: Characterization and Performance of Informal Insurance Arrangements." *Journal of Development Economics* 40, No. 1 (February 1993): 1–24.

Coats, A. W. " Sociological Aspects of British Economic Thought (ca. 1880–1930)." *Journal of Political Economy* 75, No. 5 (October 1967): 706–729.

Cohen, D., and I. Eshel. "On the Founder Effect and the Evolution of Altruistic Traits." *Theoretical Population Biology* 10, No. 3 (December 1976): 276–302.

Cohen, G. A. *Karl Marx's Theory of History: A Defence*. Oxford: Oxford University Press, 1978.

Colander, David. "The Death of Neoclassical Economics." *Journal of the History of Economic Thought* 22, No. 2 (June 2000): 127–143.

Colander, David, Richard P. F. Holt, and J. Barkley Rosser Jr. "The Changing Face of Mainstream Economics." *Review of Political Economy* 16, No. 4 (October 2004): 485–499.

Collard, David. *Altruism and Economy: A Study in Non-Selfish Economics*. New York: Oxford University Press, 1978.

Colman, Andrew M. "Salience and Focusing in Pure Coordination Games." *Journal of Economic Methodology* 4, No. 1 (1997): 61–81.

Connolly, William. *Politics and Ambiguity*. Madison: University of Wisconsin Press, 1987.

Cooter, R., and Rappoport, P. "Were the Ordinalists Wrong about Welfare Economics?" *Journal of Economic Literature*, 22, No. 2 (1984): 507–530.

Copjec, Joan. *Read My Desire: Lacan against the Historicists*. Cambridge, MA: MIT Press, 1994.

Coward, Rosalind, and John Ellis. *Language and Materialism: Developments in Semiology and the Theory of Subject*. London: Routledge and Paul, 1977.

Cullenberg, Stephen. *The Falling Rate of Profit: Recasting the Marxian Debate*. London: Pluto Press, 1994.

Cullenberg, Stephen, and Indraneel Dasgupta. "From Myth to Metaphor: A Semiological Analysis of the Cambridge Capital Controversy." In *Postmodernism, Economics, and Knowledge*, edited by S. Cullenberg, J. Amariglio, and D. F. Ruccio. London and New York: Routledge, 2001: 337–353.

Dardot, Pierre and Christian Laval. *The New Way of the World: On Neo-Liberal Society*. Translated by Gregory Elliot. London and New York: Verso, 2013.

David, Paul. "Clio and the Econometrics of QWERTY." *American Economic Review* 75, No. 2 (May 1985): 332–337.

Davidson, Paul. "Is Probability Theory Relevant for Uncertainty? A Post Keynesian Perspective." *Journal of Economic Perspectives* 5, No. 1 (Winter 1991): 129–143.

Davis, Douglas D. and Charles A. Holt. *Experimental Economics*. Princeton, NJ: Princeton University Press, 1993.

Davis, John B. *The Theory of the Individual in Economics: Identity and Value*. London and New York: Routledge, 2003.

Davis, John B. "The Turn in Economics: Neoclassical Dominance to Mainstream Pluralism." *Journal of Institutional Economics* 2, No. 1, 2006: 1–20.

Davis, John B. "Heterodox Economics, the Fragmentation of the Mainstream, and Embedded Individual Analysis." In *Future Directions for Heterodox Economics*, edited by R. F. Garnett and J. T. Harvey. Ann Arbor: University of Michigan Press, 2008, 53–72.

Dawkins, Richard. *The Selfish Gene*. Oxford: Oxford University Press, 1989.

De Vroey, Michel. "The Marshallian Market and the Walrasian Market Economy: Two Incompatible Bedfellows." *Scottish Journal of Political Economy* 46, No. 3 (August 1999): 319–338.

De Vroey, Michel. "Perfect Information a la Walras versus Perfect Information a la Marshall." *Journal of Economic Methodology* 10, No. 4 (December 2003): 465–492.

De Vroey, Michel. "On the Right Side for the Wrong Reason: Friedman on the Marshall-Walras Divide." *IRES Discussion Paper* No. 2004015, Université catholique de Louvain, 2004.

Debreu, Gérard. *Theory of Value: An Axiomatic Analysis of Economic Equilibrium.* New Haven: Yale University Press, 1959.

Debreu, Gérard. "Excess Demand Functions." *Journal of Mathematical Economics* 1, No. 1 (March 1974): 15–21.

Demsetz, Harold. "Towards a Theory of Property Rights." *American Economic Review* 57, No. 2 (May 1967): 347–359.

Desai, Meghnad. *Marx's Revenge: The Resurgence of Capitalism and the Death of Statist Socialism.* London and New York: Verso, 2002.

Diamond, Peter A. "A Model of Price Adjustment." *Journal of Economic Theory* 3, No. 2 (June 1971): 156–168.

Dobb, Maurice. *Political Economy and Capitalism: Some Essays in Economic Tradition.* New York: International Publishers, 1945.

Edgeworth, Francis Ysidro. *Mathematical Physics: An Essay on the Application of Mathematics to the Moral Sciences.* London: London School of Economics, 1932 [1881].

Edwards, Richard. *Contested Terrain: The Transformation of the Workplace in the Twentieth Century.* New York: Basic Books, 1979.

Elster, Jon. (ed.) *Multiple Self.* Cambridge, UK: Cambridge University Press, 1986.

Elster, Jon. *The Cement of Society.* Cambridge: Cambridge University Press, 1989.

Elster, Jon. "When Rationality Fails." In *The Limits of Rationality*, edited by Karen Schweers Cook and Margaret Levi. Chicago: Chicago University Press, 1990: 19–51.

Emmett, Ross B. "'What is Truth in Capital Theory? Five Stories Relevant to the Evaluation of Frank H. Knight's Contributions to the Capital Controversy." In *New Economics and Its History*, edited by John B. Davis. Durham and London: Duke University Press, 1997: 231–250.

Evensky, Jerry. "'Chicago Smith' versus 'Kirkaldy Smith'." *History of Political Economy* 37, No. 2 (2005): 197–203.

Farrant, Andrew. "Frank Knight, Worst-Case Theorizing, and Economic Planning: Socialism as Monopoly Politics." *History of Political Economy* 36, No. 3 (2004): 497–504.

Farrell, Joseph. "Cheap Talk, Coordination, and Entry." *Rand Journal of Economics* 18 (1987): 34–39.

Fehr, Ernst, and Simon Gächter. "Reciprocity and Economics: The Economic Implications of Homo Reciprocans." *European Economic Review* 42 No. 3–5 (May 1998a): 845–859.

Fehr, Ernst, and Simon Gächter. "How Effective Are Trust- and Reciprocity-Based Incentives?" In *Economics, Values, and Organization*, edited by A. Ben-Ner and L. Putterman. Cambridge: Cambridge University Press, 1998b: 337–363.

Fehr, Ernst, and Simon Gächter. "Fairness and Retaliation: The Economics of Reciprocity." *Journal of Economic Perspectives* 14, No. 3 (Summer 2000): 159–181.

Ferber, Marianne A., and Julie A. Nelson, eds. *Beyond Economic Man: Feminist Economic Theory and Economics.* Chicago: University of Chicago Press, 1993.

Fischer, Irving. *Mathematical Investigations in the Theory of Value and Price.* New Haven: Yale University Press, 1925 [1892].

Foucault, Michel. *The Order of Things: An Archeology of the Human Sciences.* London: Vintage, 1973 [1966].

Foucault, Michel. "The Subject and Power." Afterword to *Michel Foucault: Beyond Structuralism and Hermeneutics*, by Hubert L. Dreyfus and Paul Rabinow. Chicago: University of Chicago Press, 1983: 208–226.

Foucault, Michel. *The Birth of Biopolitics. Lectures at the College de France, 1978–79*. Edited by M. Senellart. Translated by G. Burchell. Basingstoke: Palgrave Macmillan, 2008.

Freud, Sigmund. *The Interpretation of Dreams*. Translated from the German and edited by James Stachey. New York: Avon Books, 1965 [1900].

Friedman, Milton. "The Methodology of Positive Economics." In *Essays in Positive Economics*. Chicago and London: The University of Chicago Press, 1953: 3–43.

Fullbrook, E. "Real Science is Pluralist." *post-autistic economics newsletter* 5 (March 2001): article 5.

Garnett Jr, Robert F. "Whither Heterodoxy?" *post-autistic economics review* 34 (October 2005): 2–21.

Geanakoplos, John. "Arrow-Debreu Model of General Equilibrium." In *The New Palgrave: General Equilibrium*, edited by John Eatwell, Murray Milgate, and Peter Newman. London and Basingstoke: Macmillan, 1989: 43–61.

Gibson-Graham, J. K. *The End of Capitalism (As We Knew It): A Feminist Critique of Political Economy*. London: Blackwell, 1996.

Gibson-Graham, J. K. *A Post-Capitalist Politics*. Minneapolis: University of Minnesota Press, 2006.

Gintis, Herbert, Samuel Bowles, Robert T. Boyd, and Ernst Fehr, eds. *Moral Sentiments and Material Interests: The Foundations of Cooperation in Economic Life*. Cambridge MA: The MIT Press, 2005.

Gode, Dhananjay K., and Shyam Sunder. "Allocative Efficiency of Markets with Zero-Intelligence Traders: Markets as a Partial Substitute for Individual Rationality." *Journal of Political Economy* 101, No. 1 (February 1993): 119–137.

Gode, Dhananjay K., and Shyam Sunder. "What Makes Markets Allocationally Efficient?" *Quarterly Journal of Economics* 112, No. 2 (May 1997): 603–630.

Granovetter, Mark. "The Nature of Economic Relations." In *Understanding Economic Process*, edited by S. Ortiz and S. Lees. Lanham and London: University Press of America (for Society for Economic Anthropology), 1992: 21–37.

Greif, Avner. "Contract Enforceability and Economic Institutions in Early Trade: The Maghribi Traders' Coalition." *American Economic Review* 83, No. 3 (June 1993): 525–548.

Guala, Francesco. "How to Do Things with Experimental Economics." In *Do Economists Make Markets? On the Performativity of Economics*, edited by D. McKenzie, F. Muniesa, and L. Siu. Princeton: Princeton University Press, 2007: 128–162.

Güth, Werner, Rolf Schmittberger, and Bernd Schwarze. "An Experimental Analysis of Ultimatum Bargaining." *Journal of Economic Behavior and Organization* 3, No. 4 (December 1982): 367–388.

Hahn, Frank. "Stability." In *Handbook of Mathematical Economics, Vol. II*, edited by Kenneth J. Arrow and Michael D. Intriligator. Amsterdam, New York, Oxford: North-Holland, 1982: 745–794.

Hahn, Frank. *Equilibrium and Macroeconomics*. Cambridge, MA: The MIT Press, 1984.

Hahn, Frank. "In Praise of Economic Theory." *The 1984 Jevons Memorial Fund Lecture*. London: University College, 1985.

Hahn, Frank. "Auctioneer." In *The New Palgrave: General Equilibrium*, edited by John Eatwell, Murray Milgate, and Peter Newman. London and Basingstoke: Macmillan, 1989: 62–67.

Hall, R. L. and C. J. Hitch. "Price Theory and Business Behaviour." *Oxford Economic Papers* No. 2 (May 1939): 12–45.

Hands, Wade, and Philip Mirowski. "Harold Hotelling and the Neoclassical Dream." In *Economics and Methodology: Crossing Boundaries*, edited by R. Backhouse, D. Hausman, U. Mäki, and A. Salanti. London: Macmillan, 1998: 322–397.

Harcourt, Geoffrey C. *Some Cambridge Controversies in the Theory of Capital*. Cambridge: Cambridge University Press, 1972.

Hargreaves Heap, Shaun. *Rationality in Economics*. Oxford: Basil Blackwell, 1989.

Hargreaves Heap, Shaun. "Rationality." In *The Theory of Choice*, edited by S. Hargreaves Heap, M. Hollis, B. Lyons, R. Sugden, and A. Weale. Oxford: Blackwell, 1992.

Hargreaves Heap, Shaun, and Yanis Varoufakis. *Game Theory: A Critical Introduction*. London and New York: Routledge, 1995.

Harsanyi, John C. "Advances in Understanding Rational Behavior." In *Rational Choice*, edited by J. Elster. New York: NYU Press, 1986: 82–107.

Harsanyi, John C., and Richard Selten. *A General Theory of Equilibrium Selection in Games*. Cambridge, MA: MIT Press, 1988.

Harvey, David. *The New Imperialism*. Oxford: Oxford University Press, 2003.

Hausman, Daniel M. *The Inexact and Separate Science of Economics*. Cambridge: Cambridge University Press, 1992.

Hausman, Daniel M. "Revealed Preference, Belief, and Game Theory." *Economics and Philosophy* 16 (2000): 99–115.

Hayek, Friedrich A. "The Use of Knowledge in Society." *American Economic Review* 35, No. 4 (September 1945): 519–530. Reprinted in *Individualism and Economic Order*. Chicago: University of Chicago Press, 1948: 77–91.

Hayek, Friedrich A. *Studies in Philosophy, Politics and Economics*. Chicago: University of Chicago Press, 1967.

Hayek, Friedrich A. *Rules and Order*. Vol. 1 of *Law, Legislation, and Liberty*. Chicago: University of Chicago Press, 1973.

Hayek, Friedrich A. von. *The Fatal Conceit: The Errors of Socialism*. Edited by W. W. Bartley III. Chicago: University of Chicago Press, 1988.

Hayek, Friedrich A. *Hayek on Hayek*. Edited by S. Kresge and L. Wenar. Chicago: University of Chicago Press, 1994.

Heinrich, Joseph, Robert Boyd, Samuel Bowles, Colin Camerer, Ernst Fehr, and Herbert Gintis, eds. *Foundations of Human Sociality: Economic Experiments and Ethnographic Evidence from Fifteen Small-Scale Societies*. Oxford: Oxford University Press, 2004.

Hicks, John R. "The Foundations of Welfare Economics." *Economic Journal* 49, No. 196 (December 1939): 696–712.

Hicks, John R., and R. G. D. Allen. "A Reconsideration of the Theory of Value." *Economica* (Part 1) N.S. 1, No. 1 (February 1934): 52–76 and (Part 2) N.S. 1, No. 2 (May 1934): 196–219.

Hicks, John. *A Revision of Demand Theory*. Oxford: Clarendon Press, 1956.

Hindess, Barry. *Philosophy and Methodology in the Social Sciences*. Sussex: The Harvester Press, 1977.

Hirst, Paul Q. *Marxism and Historical Writing*. London: Routledge & Kegan Paul, 1985.

Hodgson, Geoffrey M. "Behind Methodological Individualism." *Cambridge Economic Journal* 10, No. 3 (September 1986): 211–224.

Hodgson, Geoffrey M. *Economics and Evolution: Bringing Life Back into Economics*. Ann Arbor: University of Michigan Press, 1993.

Hodgson, Geoffrey M. "The Approach of Institutional Economics." *Journal of Economic Literature* 36, No. 1 (March 1998a): 166–192.

Hodgson, Geoffrey M. "Institutional Economic Theory: The Old versus the New." In *Why Economists Disagree: An Introduction to Alternative Schools of Thought*, edited by D. Prychitko. Albany: State University of New York Press, 1998b: 155–177.

Hume, David. *A Treatise of Human Nature*. Edited by L. A. Selby-Bigge. Oxford: Oxford University Press, 1960 [1739].

Hunt, E. K. *History of Economic Thought: A Critical Perspective*. Second Edition. Armonk, NY: M.E. Sharpe, 2002.

Ingrao, Bruna, and Giorgio Israel. *The Invisible Hand: Economic Equilibrium in the History of Science*. Translated by Ian McGilvray. Cambridge, MA and London: The MIT Press, 1990.

Jaffé, William. "Menger, Jevons and Walras De-Homogenized." *Economic Inquiry* 14, No. 4 (December 1976): 511–524.

Janssen, Maarten C. W. *Microfoundations: A Critical Inquiry*. London: Routledge, 1993.

Jevons, W. Stanley. *The Theory of Political Economy*. Edited by R. D. C. Black. Harmondsworth: Penguin Books, 1970 [1871].

Johansen, Leif. "Interaction in Economic Theory." *Economie Appliquée* 3 (1981): 229–267.

Kara, Ahmet. *The Economic Self as a Multidimensional Complexity: Towards a Critique and Reconstruction of Economic Theory*. PhD diss. University of Massachusetts at Amherst, 1996.

Katzner, Donald. "Methodological Individualism and the Walrasian Tâtonnement." *Journal of Economic and Social Research* 1 (1999): 5–33.

Katzner, Donald. "The Current Non-Status of General Equilibrium Theory." Department of Economics, Working Paper 2004-10, University of Massachusetts Amherst, 2004.

Katzner, Donald. *An Introduction to the Economic Theory of Market Behavior*. Northampton, MA: Edward Elgar, 2006.

Ketcham, Jon, Vernon L. Smith, and Arlington W. Williams. "A Comparison of Posted-Offer and Double-Auction Pricing Institutions." *Review of Economic Studies* 51, No. 4 (October 1984): 595–614.

Kirman, Alan P. "Whom or What Does the Representative Individual Represent?" *Journal of Economic Perspectives* 6, No. 2 (Spring 1992): 117–136.

Kirzner, Israel M. "Rational Action and Economic Theory." *Journal of Political Economy* 70, No. 4 (August 1962): 380–385.

Knight, Frank H. "Some Fallacies in the Interpretation of Social Costs." *Quarterly Journal of Economics* 38, No. 7 (1924): 582–606.

Knudsen, Christian. "Equilibrium, Perfect Rationality and the Problem of Self-Reference in Economics." In *Rationality, Institutions and Economic Methodology*, edited by Uskali Mäki, Bo Gustafsson, and Christian Knudsen. London: Routledge, 1993a: 133–170.

Knudsen, Christian. "Modelling Rationality, Institutions and Processes in Economic Theory." In *Rationality, Institutions and Economic Methodology*, edited by Uskali Mäki, Bo Gustafsson, and Christian Knudsen. London: Routledge, 1993b: 265–299.

Koopmans, Tjalling C. *Three Essays on the State of Economic Science*. New York: McGraw-Hill, 1957.

Kozel, Philip M. *Market Sense: Towards a New Economics of Markets*. New York: Routledge, 2005.

Kristjanson-Gural, David. "Demand and the (Re)distribution of Value: A New Marxian Approach." *Rethinking Marxism* 15, No. 1 (January 2003): 117–140.

Krueger, Anne. "The Political Economy of Rent-Seeking Society." *American Economic Review* 64, No. 3 (June 1974): 291–303.

Lacan, Jacques. *On Feminine Sexuality, the Limits of Love and Knowledge: The Seminar of Jacques Lacan Book xx, Encore 1972–1973.* Edited by J. A. Miller. Translated (with notes) by B. Fink. New York and London: W. W. Norton & Company, 1998.

Laclau, Ernesto. *New Reflections on the Revolution of Our Time.* London: Verso, 1990.

Laclau, Ernesto, and Chantal Mouffe. *Hegemony and Socialist Strategy.* London: Verso, 1985.

Langlois, Richard. "Rationality, Institutions, and Explanation." In *Economics as a Process: Essays in the New Institutional Economics,* edited by Richard N. Langlois. Cambridge: Cambridge University Press, 1986: 225–255.

Laville, Frederic. "Foundations of Procedural Rationality: Cognitive Limits and Decision Processes." *Economics and Philosophy* 16 (2000): 117–138.

Lavoie, Don. "Hermeneutics, Subjectivity, and the Lester/Machlup Debate: Toward a More Anthropological Approach to Empirical Economics." In *Economics as Discourse,* edited by Warren Samuels. Boston, Dordrecht, London: Kluwer Academic Press, 1990: 167–184.

Lawson, Tony. *Economics and Reality.* London: Routledge, 1997.

Ledyard, John O. "Public Goods: A Survey of Experimental Research." In *A Handbook of Experimental Economics,* edited by A. Roth and J. Kagel. Princeton: Princeton University Press, 1995: 111–194.

Lee, Frederic. *Post-Keynesian Price Theory.* Cambridge and New York: Cambridge University Press, 1998.

Lester, Richard A. "Shortcomings of Marginal Analysis for Wage-Employment Problems." *American Economic Review* 36, No. 1 (March 1946): 63–82.

Lewin, Shira B. "Economics and Psychology: Lessons for Our Own Day from the Early Twentieth Century." *Journal of Economic Literature* 34 (September 1996): 1293–1323.

Little, I. M. D. "A Reformulation of the Theory of Consumer's Behaviour." *Oxford Economic Papers,* New Series, 1, No. 1 (January 1949): 90–99.

Loasby, Brian J. *Knowledge, Institutions and Evolution in Economics.* London and New York: Routledge, 1999.

Lyons, Bruce, and Judith Mehta. "Contracts, Opportunism and Trust: Self-Interest and Social Orientation." *Cambridge Journal of Economics* 21, No. 2 (March 1997): 239–257.

McCloskey, D. N. "The Consequences of Rhetoric." In *The Consequences of Economic Rhetoric,* edited by Arjo Klamer, D. N. McCloskey, and Robert M. Solow. Cambridge: Cambridge University Press, 1988: 280–294.

McCloskey, D. N. *Knowledge and Persuasion in Economics.* Cambridge: Cambridge University Press, 1994.

McCloskey, D. N. "The Good Old Coase Theorem and the Good Old Chicago School: A Comment on Zerbe and Medema." In *Coasean Economics: Law and Economics and the New Institutional Economics,* edited by Steven G. Medema. Boston, Dordrecht, London: Kluwer Academic Press, 1998: 239–248.

McCloskey, D. N. *The Bourgeois Virtues: Ethics for an Age of Commerce.* Chicago: University of Chicago Press, 2006.

Macherey, Pierre. *A Theory of Literary Production.* New York and London: Routledge, 1978.

Machlup, Fritz. "Marginal Analysis and Empirical Research." *American Economic Review* 36 (September 1946): 519–554.

Madra, Yahya M. "Questions of Communism: Ethics, Ontology, Subjectivity." *Rethinking Marxism* 18, No. 2 (April 2006): 205–224.

Madra, Yahya M., and Joseph T. Rebello. "The Crisis of Identity in Modern Economics." Unpublished mimeo, 2005. [Available from the authors upon request.]

Madra, Yahya M., and Fikret Adaman. "Public Economics after Neoliberalism: A Historical-Theoretical Perspective." *European Journal of the History of Economic Thought* 17, No. 4, (2010): 1079–1106.

Madra, Yahya M., and Fikret Adaman. "Neoliberal Reason and Its Forms: De-Politicization through Economization." *Antipode* 46, No. 3 (2014): 691–716.

Mäki, Uskali. "Economics with Institutions: Agenda for Methodological Enquiry." In *Rationality, Institutions and Economic Methodology*, edited by Uskali Mäki, Bo Gustafsson, and Christian Knudsen. London: Routledge, 1993: 3–44.

Mandler, Michael. *Dilemmas in Economic Theory: Persisting Foundational Problems of Microeconomics.* Oxford: Oxford University Press, 1999.

Marglin, Stephen. "What Do Bosses Do? Part 1." *Review of Radical Political Economy* 6, No. 2 (Summer 1974): 60–112.

Marglin, Stephen. "What Do Bosses Do? Part 2." *Review of Radical Political Economy* 7, No. 1 (Spring 1975): 20–37.

Margolis, Howard. *Selfishness, Altruism, and Rationality: A Theory of Social Choice.* Cambridge: Cambridge University Press, 1982.

Marshall, Alfred. *Principles of Economics.* Eighth Edition. London: Macmillan, 1920 [1890].

Marx, Karl. *Capital,* Vol. I. Translated by Ben Fowkes. Harmondsworth: Penguin/NLR, 1976 [1867].

Marx, Karl, and Friedrich Engels. *Werke, Band 23.* Berlin, DDR: Dietz Verlag, 1968.

Maynard Smith, John. *Evolution and the Theory of Games.* Cambridge: Cambridge University Press, 1982.

Medema, Steven. *Ronald H. Coase.* London: Macmillan, 1994.

Meier, Stephan. "A Survey of Economic Theories and Field Evidence on Pro-Social Behavior." In *Economics and Psychology: A Promising New Cross-Disciplinary Field*, edited by B. S. Frey and A. Stutzer. Cambridge, MA: MIT Press, 2007.

Ménard, Claude, ed. *Institutions, Contracts and Organizations: Perspectives from New Institutional Economics.* Cheltenham, UK and Northampton, MA, USA: Edward Elgar, 2000.

Menger, Carl. *Principles of Economics.* New York: New York University Press, 1981 [1871].

Mirowski, Philip. "Physics and the 'Marginalist Revolution.'" *Cambridge Journal of Economics* 8 (1984): 361–379.

Mirowski, Philip. *Against Mechanism.* Totawa, NJ: Rowman and Littlefield, 1988.

Mirowski, Philip. *More Heat Than Light: Economics as Social Physics, Physics as Nature's Economics.* Cambridge: Cambridge University Press, 1989.

Mirowski, Philip. *Machine Dreams: Economics Becomes a Cyborg Science.* Cambridge: Cambridge University Press, 2002.

Mirowski, Philip. *Never Let a Serious Crisis Go To Waste: How Neoliberalism Survived the Financial Meltdown.* London and New York: Verso, 2013.

Mirowski, Philip, and D. Wade Hands. "A Paradox of Budgets: The Postwar Stabilization of American Neoclassical Demand Theory." In *From Interwar Pluralism to Postwar Neoclassicism*, edited by Mary S. Morgan and Malcolm Rutherford. Durham and London: Duke University Press, 1998: 260–292.

Mirowski, Philip, and Dieter Plehwe, eds. *The Road from Mont Pelerin: The Making of the Neoliberal Thought Collective.* Cambridge, MA: Harvard University Press, 2009.

Mongin, Philippe. "The Marginalist Controversy." In *The Handbook of Economic Methodology*, edited by John B. Davis, D. Wade Hands, and Uskali Mäki. Cheltenham, UK and Northampton, MA: Edward Elgar, 1998: 558–562.

Mouffe, Chantal. *The Return of the Political.* London: Verso, 1992.

Mueller, Denis. *Public Choice II.* Cambridge: Cambridge University Press, 1989.

Myerson, Roger B. "Nash Equilibrium and the History of Economic Theory." *Journal of Economic Literature* 37, No. 3 (September 1999): 1067–1082.

Nadeau, Robert. "The Spontaneous Order." In *The Handbook of Economic Methodology*, edited by John B. Davis, D. Wade Hands, and Uskali Mäki. Cheltenham, UK and Northampton, MA: Edward Elgar, 1998: 477–483.

Nancy, Jean-Luc. "Introduction." In *Who Comes after the Subject?* edited by Eduardo Cadava, Peter Connor, and Jean-Luc Nancy. London: Routledge, 1991: 1–8.

Nash, John F. Jr. "Equilibrium Points in N-Person Games." *Proceedings of the National Academy of the Sciences of the United States of America* 36, No. 1 (January 1950): 48–49.

Nash, John F. Jr. "Non-Cooperative Games." *The Annals of Mathematics* 2nd Series, 54, No. 2 (September 1951): 286–295.

Nelson, Richard R., and Sidney Winter. *An Evolutionary Theory of Economic Change.* Cambridge: Cambridge University Press, 1982.

Nelson, Richard R. "Recent Evolutionary Theorizing about Economic Change." *Journal of Economic Literature* 33, No. 1 (March 1995): 48–90.

North, Douglass C. *Institutions, Institutional Change and Economic Performance.* Cambridge: Cambridge University Press, 1990.

North, Douglass C. "Institutions." *Journal of Economic Perspectives* 5, No. 1 (Winter 1991): 97–112.

North, Douglass C. "Understanding Institutions." In *Institutions, Contracts, and Organizations: Perspectives from New Institutional Economics*, edited by Claude Ménard. Cheltenham, UK and Northampton, MA: Edward Elgar, 2000: 7–10.

North, Douglass C. *Understanding the Process of Economic Change.* Princeton: Princeton University Press, 2005.

Novshek, William, and Hugo Sonnenschein. "General Equilibrium with Free Entry: A Synthetic Approach to the Theory of Perfect Competition." *Journal of Economic Literature* 25, No. 3 (September 1987): 1281–1306.

Özselçuk, Ceren, and Yahya M. Madra. "Psychoanalysis and Marxism: From Capitalist-All to Communist Non-All." *Psychoanalysis, Culture and Society.* 10, No. 1 (April 2005): 79–97.

Pareto, Vilfredo. *Manual of Political Economy.* Translated by A. S. Schwier. New York: A. M. Kelley, 1971 [1906].

Perelman, Michael. *The Invention of Capitalism: Classical Political Economy and the Secret History of Primitive Accumulation.* Durham & London: Duke University Press, 2000.

Piaget, Jean. *Structuralism.* Translated and edited by Chaninah Maschler. New York: Harper Torchbooks, 1970.

Plott, Charles R. "Rational Choice in Experimental Markets." In *The Limits of Rationality*, edited by Karen Schweers Cook and Margaret Levi. Chicago: Chicago University Press, 1990: 146–175.

Rabin, Matthew. "Incorporating Fairness into Game Theory and Economics." *American Economic Review* 83, No. 5 (December 1993): 1281–1302.

Radner, Roy. "Problems in the Theory of Markets under Uncertainty." *American Economic Review* 60, No. 2 (May 1970): 454–460.

Reder, M. W. "Chicago School." In *The New Palgrave Dictionary of Economics,* Vol. 1, edited by John Eatwell, Murray Milgate, and Peter Newman. London and Basingstoke: Macmillan, 1987: 413–418.

Resnick, Stephen A., and Richard D. Wolff. *Knowledge and Class: A Marxian Critique of Political Economy.* Chicago: University of Chicago Press, 1987.

Resnick, Stephen A., and Richard D. Wolff. "Radical Economics: A Tradition of Theoretical Differences." In *Radical Economics*, edited by Bruce Roberts and Susan Feiner. Norwell, MA and Dordrecht: Kluwer Academic, 1992: 15–43.

Resnick, Stephen A., and Richard D. Wolff. "Althusser's Liberation of Marxian Theory." In *The Althusserian Legacy*, edited by E. Ann Kaplan and Michael Sprinker. London and New York: Verso, 1993: 59–72.

Resnick, Stephen A., and Richard D. Wolff, eds. *New Departures in Marxian Theory*. New York and London: Routledge, 2006.

Resnick, Stephen A., and Richard D. Wolff. "Marxism." *Rethinking Marxism* 25, No. 2 (April 2013): 152–162.

Rizvi, S. Abu Turab. "The Microfoundations Project in General Equilibrium Theory." *Cambridge Journal of Economics* 18 (1994): 357–377.

Rizvi, S. Abu Turab. "Responses to Arbitrariness in Contemporary Economics." In *New Economics and Its History*, edited by John B. Davis. Durham and London: Duke University Press, 1997: 273–288.

Robbins, Lionel. *The Nature and Significance of Economic Science*. London: Macmillan, 1932.

Roberts, Bruce. "The Visible and the Measurable: Althusser and the Marxian Theory of Value." In *Postmodern Materialism and the Future of Marxist Theory*, edited by A. Callari and D. F. Ruccio. Hanover and London: Wesleyan University Press, 1996: 193–211.

Robson, Arthur. "Evolution and Human Nature." *Journal of Economic Perspectives* 16, No. 2 (April 2002): 89–106.

Roemer, John E. "An Anti-Hayekian Manifesto." *New Left Review* I, No. 211 (May/June 1995): 112–129.

Rotheim, Roy J., ed. *New Keynesian Economics/Post Keynesian Alternatives*. London and New York: Routledge, 1998.

Rothschild, Michael. "Models of Market Organization with Imperfect Information: A Survey." *Journal of Political Economy* 81, No. 6 (1973): 1283–1308.

Rubenstein, Ariel. *Models of Bounded Rationality*. Cambridge: The MIT Press, 1998.

Ruccio, David F., and Jack L. Amariglio. *Postmodern Moments in Modern Economics*. Princeton: Princeton University Press, 2003.

Rutherford, Malcolm. *Institutions in Economics: The Old and the New Institutionalism*. Cambridge: Cambridge University Press, 1994.

Safra, Zvi. "Contingent Commodities." In *The New Palgrave Dictionary of Economics*, Second Edition, edited by S. N. Durlauf and L. E. Blume. London and New York: Palgrave Macmillan, 2008. *The New Palgrave Dictionary of Economics Online*. Site imprint Palgrave Macmillan. October 25, 2015. http://www.dictionaryofeconomics.com/article?id=pde2008_C000329. doi:10.1057/9780230226203.0306

Samuelson, Larry. "Evolution and Game Theory." *Journal of Economic Perspectives*, 16, No. 2 (Spring 2002): 47–66.

Samuelson, Paul. "A Note on the Pure Theory of Consumer's Behaviour." *Economica* 5 (1938): 61–72.

Sandler, Todd. *Global Challenges: An Approach to Environmental, Political, and Economic Problems*. Cambridge: Cambridge University Press, 1997.

Schelling, Thomas C. *The Strategy of Conflict*. Cambridge: Cambridge University Press, 1960.

Schotter, Andrew. *Economic Theory of Social Institutions*. Cambridge: Cambridge University Press, 1981.

Screpanti, Ernesto. "The Postmodern Crisis in Economics and the Revival of Institutionalist Thought." *Rethinking Marxism* 12, No. 1 (Spring 2000): 87–111.

Screpanti, Ernesto, and Stefano Zamagni. *An Outline of the History of Economic Thought.* Oxford: Oxford University Press, 1993.

Sen, Amartya K. *Collective Choice and Social Welfare.* San Francisco: Holden Day, 1970.

Sen, Amartya K. "Rational Fools: A Critique of the Behavioral Foundations of Economic Theory." *Philosophy and Public Affairs* 6 (1977): 317–344.

Sen, Amartya K. "Behaviour and the Concept of Preference." *Economica* 40 (1973): 241–259. Reprinted in *Rational Choice*, edited by Jon Elster. New York: New York University Press, 1986: 60–81.

Sen, Amartya. *On Ethics and Economics.* Oxford and Cambridge, MA: Basil Blackwell, 1987.

Sen, Amartya K. "Internal Consistency of Choice." *Econometrica* 61, No. 3 (May 1993): 495–521.

Sen, Amartya K. *Rationality and Freedom.* Cambridge, MA and London: The Belknap Press of Harvard University Press, 2002.

Sent, Esther-Mirjam. "Engineering Dynamic Economics." In *New Economics and Its History*, edited by John B. Davis. Durham and London: Duke University Press, 1997: 41–62.

Sent, Esther-Mirjam. "Pleas for Pluralism." *post-autistic economics review* 18 (February 2003): article 1.

Sent, Esther-Mirjam. "Behavioral Economics: How Psychology Made Its (Limited) Way Back into Economics." *History of Political Economy* 36, No. 4 (2004): 735–760.

Sent, Esther-Mirjam. "Simplifying Herbert Simon." *History of Political Economy* 37, No. 2 (2005): 227–232.

Shackle, G. S. L. *Epistemics and Economics: A Critique of Economic Doctrines.* Piscataway, NJ: Transaction Publishers, 1972.

Shapiro, Carl and Joseph E. Stiglitz. "Equilibrium Unemployment as a Worker Discipline Device." *American Economic Review* 74 (June 1984): 433–444.

Simon, Herbert A. "Theories of Decision-Making in Economics and Behavioral Sciences." *American Economic Review* 49, No.1 (1959): 253–283.

Simon, Herbert A. *Administrative Behavior.* Second Edition. New York: Macmillan, 1961.

Simon, Herbert A. "From Substantive to Procedural Rationality." In *Method and Appraisal in Economics*, edited by S. J. Latsis. Cambridge: Cambridge University Press, 1976: 129–148.

Simon, Herbert A. "Rationality as Process and Product of Thought." *American Economic Review* 68, No. 2 (May 1978a): 1–16.

Simon, Herbert A. "On How to Decide What to Do." *Bell Journal of Economics, The RAND Corporation* 9, No. 2 (Autumn 1978b): 494–507.

Smith, Adam. *The Theory of Moral Sentiments.* Edited by D. D. Raphael and A. L. Macfie. Oxford: Clarendon Press, 1976 [1759–1790].

Smith, Adam. *An Inquiry into the Nature and Causes of the Wealth of Nations.* Amherst, NY: Prometheus, 1991 [1776], 9–28.

Smith, Vernon L. "Rational Choice: The Contrast between Economics and Psychology." *Journal of Political Economy* 99, No. 4 (August 1991): 877–897.

Smith, Vernon L. "Economics in the Laboratory." *Journal of Economic Perspectives* 8, No. 1 (Winter 1994): 113–131.

Stark, Oded. "Altruism and the Quality of Life." *American Economic Review, Papers and Proceedings* 79, No. 2 (May 1989): 86–90.

Stark, Oded. *Altruism and Beyond: An Economic Analysis of Transfers and Exchanges within Families and Groups.* Cambridge: Cambridge University Press, 1995.

Stavrakakis, Yannis. *Lacan and the Political.* New York: Routledge, 1999.

Stigler, George. "The Economics of Information." *Journal of Political Economy* 69 (June 1961): 213–225.

Stigler, George. *Essays in the History of Economics.* Chicago: Chicago University Press, 1965.

Stiglitz, Joseph E. "Post Walrasian and Post Marxian Economics." *Journal of Economic Perspectives* 7, No. 1 (Winter 1993): 109–114.

Stiglitz, Joseph E. *Whither Socialism?* Cambridge, MA and London: The MIT Press, 1994.

Stiglitz, Joseph E., and Carl Walsh. *Principles of Microeconomics.* Third Edition. New York and London: W.W. Norton & Co., 2002.

Streissler, Erich. "To What Extent Was the Austrian School Marginalist?" *History of Political Economy* 4, No. 2 (1972): 426–441.

Sugden, Robert. "Reciprocity: The Supply of Public Goods through Voluntary Contributions." *Economic Journal* 94, No. 376 (December 1984): 772–787.

Sugden, Robert. "Spontaneous Order." *Journal of Economic Perspectives* 3, No. 4 (Autumn 1989): 85–97.

Sugden, Robert. "Rational Choice: A Survey." *Economy Journal* 101 (July 1991): 751–785.

Sugden, Robert. "A Theory of Focal Points." *Economic Journal* 105 (May 1995): 533–550.

Sugden, Robert. "Experiments as Exhibits and Experiments as Tests." *Journal of Economic Methodology* 12, No. 2 (June 2005): 291–302.

Tabb, William K. *Reconstructing Political Economy: The Great Divide in Economic Thought.* New York and London: Routledge, 1999.

Taylor, Michael. *The Possibility of Cooperation.* Cambridge: Cambridge University Press, 1987.

Thompson, Grahame. "Where Goes Economics and the Economies?" *Economy and Society* 26, No. 4 (1997): 599–610.

Titmuss, Richard. *The Gift Relationship: From Human Blood to Social Policy.* London: George Allen and Unwin, 1971.

Tversky, Amos, and Daniel Kahneman. "Rational Choice and Framing of Decisions." In *The Limits of Rationality*, edited by Karen Schweers Cook and Margaret Levi. Chicago: Chicago University Press, 1990: 60–89.

Ullmann-Margalit, Edna. "Invisible-Hand Explanations." *Synthese* 39 (1978): 263–291.

Van Horn, Robert, Philip Mirowski, and Thomas A. Stapleford, eds. *Building Chicago Economics: New Perspectives on the History of America's Most Powerful Economics Program.* Cambridge and New York: Cambridge University Press, 2012.

Vanberg, Victor. *The Constitution of Markets: Essays in Political Economy.* London and New York: Routledge, 2001.

Vira, Bhaskar. "The Political Coase Theorem: Identifying Differences between Neoclassical and Critical Institutionalism." *Journal of Economic Issues* 31, No. 3 (September 1997): 761–779.

von Neumann, John. "Zur Theorie der Gesellshaftsspiele." *Mathematische Annalen*, 100 (1928): 295–320. Translated as "On the Theory of Games of Strategy" by Sonya Bargmann in *Contributions to the Theory of Games* 4, edited by A. Tucker and R. Luce. Princeton: Princeton University Press, 1959: 13–42.

von Neumann, John. "Uber ein Okonomischen Gleichungssystem." In *Ergebnisse eines Mathematischen Kolloquiums*, edited by Karl Menger, 8 (1937).

von Neumann, John, and Oskar Morgenstern. *Theory of Games and Economic Behavior.* Third Edition. Princeton: Princeton University Press, 1953.

Vromen, Jack J. *Economic Evolution: An Enquiry into the Foundation of New Institutional Economics.* London: Routledge, 1995.

Walker, Donald A. "Competitive Theories of Tatonnement." *Kyklos* 25 (1972): 345–363.

Walker, Donald A. *Walras's Market Models*. Cambridge and New York: Cambridge University Press, 1996.

Walras, Léon. *Elements of Pure Economics*. Edited by W. Jaffé. London: Allen & Unwin, 1954 [1874–77].

Weale, Albert. "Social Choice." In *The Theory of Choice*, edited by S. Hargreaves Heap, M. Hollis, B. Lyons, R. Sugden, and A. Weale. Oxford: Blackwell, 1992.

Weintraub, E. Roy. *General Equilibrium Analysis: Studies in Appraisal*. Cambridge, UK: Cambridge University Press, 1985.

Weintraub, E. Roy. *How Economics Became a Mathematical Science*. Durham and London, Duke University Press, 2002.

Weiss, Yoram. "The Formation and Dissolution of Families: Why Marry? Who Marries Whom? And What Happens upon Divorce?" In *Handbook of Population and Family Economics*, edited by M. R. Rosenzweig and O. Stark. Amsterdam: Elsevier, 1997: 81–123.

Williamson, Oliver E. *Markets and Hierarchies: Analysis and Antitrust Implications*. New York: Free Press, 1975.

Williamson, Oliver E. "The Economics of Governance: Framework and Implications." *Journal of Institutional and Theoretical Economics* 140 (1984): 195–223. Reprinted in *Economics as a Process: Essays in the New Institutional Economics*, edited by Richard N. Langlois. Cambridge: Cambridge University Press, 1986: 171–202.

Williamson, Oliver E. *The Economic Institutions of Capitalism: Firms, Markets, Relational Contracting*. New York: Free Press, 1985.

Williamson, Oliver E. "Contested Exchange versus the Governance of Contractual Relations." *Journal of Economic Perspectives* 7, No. 1 (Winter 1993): 103–108.

Wolff, Richard D. "Ideological State Apparatuses, Consumerism, and U.S. Capitalism: Lessons for the Left." *Rethinking Marxism* 17, No. 2 (April 2005): 223–235.

Wolff, Richard D. "'Efficiency': Whose Efficiency?" In *New Departures in Marxian Theory*, edited by Stephen A. Resnick and Richard D. Wolff. New York and London: Routledge, 2006: 303–305.

Wolff, Richard D., and Stephen A. Resnick. *Contending Economic Theories: Neoclassical, Keynesian, Marxian*. Cambridge, MA: The MIT Press, 2012.

Wolff, Richard D., Bruce Roberts, and Antonio Callari. "Marx's-Not Ricardo's- 'Transformation Problem': a Radical Reconceptualization." *History of Political Economy* 14, No. 4 (Winter 1982): 564–582.

Wolff, Richard D., Bruce Roberts, and Antonio Callari. "A Marxian Alternative to the Transformation Problem." *Review of Radical Political Economics* 16, No. 2 (Summer/ Fall 1984): 115–135.

Wong, S. *The Foundations of Paul Samuelson's Revealed Preference Theory*. Boston: Routledge and Kegan Paul, 1978.

Xenos, Nicholas. *Scarcity and Modernity*. London and New York: Routledge, 1989.

Zizek, Slavoj. *The Sublime Object of Ideology*. London and New York: Verso, 1989.

Zizek, Slavoj. *Looking Awry: An Introduction to Jacques Lacan through Popular Culture*. Cambridge, MA and London: MIT Press, 1991.

Zizek, Slavoj. "The Parallax View." *New Left Review* II, No. 25 (January/February 2004): 121–134.

Index

Printed in the United States
By Bookmasters